C000129964

Fully Boo

Fully Booked

The Stan Stennett Story

Enjoy

STAN STENNETT WITH TERRY GRANDIN

Stan Stennett M.B.E
2010.

VERTICAL EDITIONS

www.verticaleditions.com

First published in the United Kingdom in 2010 by Vertical Editions, Unit 4a, Snaygill Industrial Estate, Skipton, North Yorkshire BD23 2QR

www.verticaleditions.com

ISBN 978-1-904091-42-4

A CIP catalogue record for this book is available from the British Library

Cover design and typeset by HBA, York

Printed and bound by JF Print Limited, Somerset

CONTENTS

ACKNOWLEDGMENTS

I would like to thank my wife Betty for more than 60 years of happy married life. She has shared in all the decisions made throughout our time together and without her I know life would not have been the same.

I also want to thank our two boys, Roger and Ceri, who have supported me right from when they were old enough to take an interest in the theatre.

I have made many friends in show business and I am delighted that my dear old pal Eric Sykes has written a foreword for this book.

Finally, my appreciation goes to Terry Grandin who has patiently put my life story into words in a very special way that I am sure you will enjoy.

Stan

FOREWORD

It gives me great pleasure to write a foreword to *Fully Booked*. I now understand why it took Stan and Terry so long to write it . . . there are only 24 hours in a day and the book certainly does justice to the title!

What Stan has accomplished in his colourful and excitingly busy march through life is amazing. The book covers over 70 years of Stan's life on stage, in clubs, on TV, doing after dinner speaking and raising money for charity. Whilst all this would be enough for most people, Stan still found time to become an experienced qualified pilot. Not for him overnight train journeys—it was just a swing of the propeller and a few hours later Stan would be landing on the nearest airfield to the theatre he was appearing at. He even commercially flew cargo abroad! Yet in spite of his crowded log book, he still finds time to play golf . . . when does he find time to sleep? Or perhaps he doesn't!

Stan's hectic schedule is crammed into this wonderful book and it provides a glimpse back into a bygone age of variety acts, musical hall, TV soaps and more. I thoroughly recommend reading his story and I'm sure you'll enjoy it as much as Stan has enjoyed living it.

Eric Sykes
OBE, CBE

PROLOGUE

The sound of thunder rumbled across the black sky and flashes of lightning filled the air like a back-drop, while vivid red and yellow flames danced and crackled their way up through the roof. The flames were being fanned by a strong wind and thick white smoke began swirling around in front of us.

If you thought that was a scene from one of my many pantomimes and you are waiting for Billy and Bonzo to rush on stage and save the day, then sadly you are very much mistaken. After making people laugh for almost all my 70 years or so in show business, I was fully aware that what was happening in front of us was certainly no laughing matter. Our beautiful house was going up in smoke and flames right before our eyes and my dear wife Betty and I had been lucky to get out through the front door when we did.

The wind had been blowing and a storm had moved in from the west. It was gusting at about 60/70 miles an hour. We had only been in bed for a short time after arriving home late from the Lyric Theatre down west in Carmarthen. It was 5 January 1999 and it had been the last night of our pantomime, *Cinderella*. The season had gone well and we were in a happy, but tired, mood as we took the 90 minutes or so drive home down the M4 motorway. After a cup of tea we were off to bed.

Betty awoke with a start when she heard a dull thud at about 4.00am, and then she thought she could smell burning. She got up to have a look around while I was still flat out fast asleep, probably running over every scene of the pantomime in my dreams as usually happened straight after a show.

It was then that she saw some white smoke wafting up inside the house and quickly came back to the bedroom to wake me from my slumber. When the electricity was fitted to the property, the cables came in between the floor levels, and the smoke was drifting about around the utility room ceiling in that very area.

Just before going to bed we had suffered a power cut and the lights had gone off. The thud Betty heard was the power coming back on but it arrived with such a surge that the box connector had been burnt. That appeared to be the cause of the fire beneath the floorboards and ceiling. The area of wood in the floor and ceiling joists was of course very extensive, as it usually is in a chalet-bungalow style house. The property was over 40 years old as it was built in 1955 so everything in the roof space was like tinder and very dry. Betty had me out of bed and running around like a headless chicken while the floor in the corner of the bathroom was now well alight. We raced downstairs and out of the back door. I grabbed my hose pipe, connected up, and sprayed water on the area I thought was most in need of a dousing.

Our next door neighbours, Margaret and Roy Pike, had also woken up and on seeing the smoke and flames, telephoned the fire service requesting immediate attention.

Betty and I began removing as much as we could from the house and made a number of trips before I thought it became too dangerous for her to go back inside. I sent her to stay in the safety of the Pikes' residence while I hurried to clear the garage where I was storing three cars, one of them a Rolls Royce. I then carried on salvaging as much as possible from the burning house which by now was well alight.

While I was bringing out another box I heard a fire engine coming up the hill. The appliance stopped at the bottom of our driveway even though the flames were shooting up into the night sky right at the other end of the property. I found out later that they were looking for a hydrant to supplement their water supply.

While this was going on I ran from Roy's house, where I was stacking the boxes, to meet two firemen who were heading for the front of the house. Too late—it was like a scene straight out of the Keystone Cops. By the time I had reached them they had taken an axe to my lovely oak door. All they had to do was open it as I had already unlocked it while removing as many possessions as I could. The next thing they did after gaining entry was damage a precious oil painting that we had hanging on the wall just inside the front door.

The firemen eventually found a hydrant about 500 yards down the road close to the T junction with Pantmawr Road and they began connecting their hoses to bring the water up the hill to fight the fire. The force of water coming out of each hose was very low, apparently because of the distance it was being forced to travel, so the officer in charge requested a pump. They even ran out of water a number of times as they waited for the pressure to build back up. Another two or three fire engines arrived but they were all suffering from the same lack of pressure and the extra bodies did nothing to prevent further fire damage to our lovely home.

In between all these stoppages I went back into the house to collect as much of my memorabilia as possible but it was devastating seeing the flames shooting up in front of us with very little action coming from the fire service. I grabbed some boxes and packed into them as many of my scrapbooks, programmes, photograph albums and posters as I could. They would all have been a great loss had they been left in the house to burn.

I then contacted Ceri, my youngest son who lived about two miles away in Thornhill, and he was quickly on the scene to help me get as many articles to safety as we could. He had much of his own valuable and unique collection of Welsh football memorabilia stored with us and so we needed to get all his belongings to a safe place as soon as possible.

By now the roof had almost completely gone up in flames and the stone walls were blackened and unsafe. It was terrible standing there helpless while burning roof timbers fell inside the house with a sickening crash to help stoke up the flames.

Eventually they managed to gain control over the fire but it was a long job and there was a great deal of damage both to the structure and to all the remaining furnishings. We had concentrated on saving the memorabilia, leaving the furniture, fixtures and fittings to the ravages of the fire.

By the time they had dampened everything down, and there was as much water damage as there was fire damage, I was covered in soot, wet, and very annoyed at the half-hearted attempts to restrict the blaze.

To add insult to injury, the following day the firemen, I will never get used to calling them firefighters, located a hydrant only 100 yards away. This would have saved a lot of time had they found it on their arrival when we needed it most. If that had happened then I am sure not so much of our house would have been left in ruins.

I was very dubious about the wiring into the property as our neighbours had told us that under certain conditions 'arcing' could take place and that was obviously dangerous. The following day when the fire had been extinguished and everything dampened down, Electricity Board personnel came to inspect the damage and they took away the cables that brought the electricity into the house. When I enquired as to why they needed to do that they told me it was for safekeeping.

A few days later I asked my solicitor to look into some sort of claim as I was convinced that the surge in power was responsible for the fire. It was then that we found out that the Electricity Board had rather conveniently misplaced the offending cables. They were nowhere to be found.

Although we were covered by insurance for rebuilding I still believed the South Wales Electricity Board to be liable. I was also unhappy with the Fire Service when we discovered they could have used a far closer hydrant.

My insurances covered the house and contents and I also had a policy for storage and for renting another property while rebuilding took place. It turned out though that the storage money had to come from the allowances for the contents. The full cost of renting a place in Lisvane (£1,200 a month) had to come out of storage costs when I believed it should have been a separate issue.

Among the items I lost were four priceless guitars. Not financially so, but priceless to me as they were very special instruments. One was a Django Reinhardt Maccaferri and another was a Les Paul Special. I also had a trumpet damaged though I still use it and you can see the heat marks on it to this very day.

Betty and I loved that house. We had moved in during 1960 when Roger was 11 years old and Ceri was a baby of three months. It had been a little too expensive for us when we first looked at it but when I was signed up for the *Black and White Minstrels Show* the contract gave us the security we needed to make the move. Now it had been almost burned to the ground.

I couldn't leave the site for one moment during the following days as the thought of any strangers sifting through the ashes of what had been our home for the last 40 years was too much to bear. Eventually I moved a caravan on to the front of the property and I stayed there for almost 12 months until rebuilding works were completed, leaving Betty living in the rented accommodation in Lisvane.

As I looked at the smouldering ruins while sitting down on a pile of belongings stacked up and ready for storage, my mind continually drifted back to my days on the boards, a career that had started so many years ago. I thought about the many friends that I had made in the theatre such as Eric Morecambe and Ernie Wise, Billy Daniels, Lonnie Donegan, Max Wall, Max Miller, Eric Sykes, Norman Wisdom and many more. I recalled the theatres I had performed in including the famous London Palladium, the Glasgow Empire and the Finsbury Park and the memories all came flooding back as I sat in front of the blackened rubble.

1

OUT OF THE ASHES

'Families are like fudge, mostly sweet but with a few nuts.'

* * * * *

I was born on 30 July 1925 in Ty Robert, a whitewashed stone-built farmhouse belonging to my grandparents. It was situated deep in the countryside in a tiny village called Rhiwceiliog which was near Heol-y-Cyw, Bridgend.

It was quite a lonely place situated about a mile off the main road on the side of a hill, and our nearest neighbours were about half a mile away, a bit too far if you wanted to borrow a cup of sugar. If you travel along the M4 towards Swansea and look up to your right where the wind turbines are positioned on the hillside, that was about where the farmhouse was located.

My mother was a kennelmaid to Lady Blandy-Jenkins who was the landowner living nearby in Llanharan. Mother was unable to take care of me so my grandparents adopted me from almost the moment I came into the world.

I was christened Stanley Llewellyn Stennett.

You see, my mother Doris was only 18 when I was born and she wasn't married. In those days it was a terrible stigma to be born out of wedlock but, of course, in these modern times it doesn't seem to matter at all. I can honestly say it never affected me in any way, partly because I never broadcast the fact to anyone, and also because all the family rallied round to make sure I had a happy childhood, even if it did mean a fair bit of travelling later on.

My grandfather had been a staff furrier sergeant in the First World War and at the farm he had a small blacksmith's shop. He had a big bushy moustache and looked like one of those characters you see in those early silent films. Farmers from all around the surrounding area would bring their horses to him for shoeing as he was the only blacksmith for miles around.

He also kept a few sheep, a couple of cows, some pigs and a number of chickens so I reckon I was almost a farmer's boy. One of my favourite tasks was searching the field for the free range eggs which I collected in a bucket filled with straw. I then took them back very proudly to my Gran who could usually be found busying herself in the kitchen.

It was really more of a smallholding than a farm, yet it kept us all occupied as everyone mucked in to do the chores. It had stone floors, small windows and an outside toilet. The rooms were all tiny and yet it never appeared to be crowded. It seems quite primitive compared to dwellings nowadays but back then it was what everyone was used to living in.

We even had a scarecrow in one of the fields that was so ugly none of the local crows would touch the crop—a few of them even brought back the corn they had stolen in previous years. There was also a large kennels where my mother looked after the hounds for the master. That kept her busy because the hounds all had to be fit and ready especially when there was going to be a hunt.

My grandparents had 13 children of their own so there was family everywhere and it was a bit like a Whitsun Treat when they all came to call. Families are like fudge, mostly sweet but with a few nuts.

A cousin of mine called Jean Davies used to visit regularly and we would play together out in the fields as we were about the same age. On one occasion there was a pig running around in the road down by the Eagle in Brynna. We went a bit too close to the porker and it gave a snort and chased us all the way down the lane as far as the stile leading up to Ty Robert. At the time Jean was a bit faster at running than me and she reached the stile first.

But I was not so chivalrous in those days and I knocked her off so that I could get over the stile in front of her to escape the charging pig. We both ended up lying in the grass on the other side of the fence. The pig took one long soulful look at us, grunted, and slowly trundled off back to where he had come from.

I have returned to the area several times just to drive down and stop to look over the fields where I spent those early happy days. So much has changed that it is difficult to remember exactly where some things happened but the world was certainly a different place back in the Twenties.

I went to school as soon as I was old enough. I would have been four or five and can remember the earthenware plates and cups we used. When I played Fagin in *Oliver Twist* at the Sherman Theatre in Cardiff a few years ago it constantly reminded me of my early school days. Not that it was an austere place with uncaring teachers, far from it, as my early schooldays were very happy. I can recall my Gran giving me bread and jam sandwiches to take to school and having cocoa to drink while I was there.

Around Ty Robert there were a lot of coalmines and many of my uncles worked below the surface. It was amusing to know that when my adoption became official, all my uncles became my brothers, and my aunts were now my sisters. In the same way, all my cousins were now my nephews or nieces.

Dick Stennett, one of my 'new' brothers, was buried for five days after a fall at Wern Tarw Colliery. He eventually emigrated to Australia taking my younger brother Peter with him. Now

Peter really was my brother, but as I had been adopted, I became his uncle. Confusing isn't it? Edgar Stennett, another brother, but of course also originally an uncle, was awarded the Military Medal in the Second World War during the Desert campaign. A third brother, Cliff, used to like singing a song called 'I'm alone because I love you'. It was one of the top crooner songs of the day. He was a horse trainer and jockey for Lady Blandy-Jenkins but later moved away to work up in Yorkshire at Harewood House for Lord Harewood, the Queen's cousin. He went on to train horses for the Princess Royal while he was up there.

My grandparents were both God-fearing people and we were all brought up in the correct manner which included going to church. Mind you, going to church doesn't make you a Christian any more than standing in a garage makes you a car. Once a month I would be taken into Bridgend on a single-decker Western Welsh bus by my grandmother who would be going there to take provisions from the farm to sell in the market.

I was the only baby in the house and probably spoiled rotten because I remember only very happy days. If today's youngsters were given the same opportunities I'm sure the world would be a better place.

My first school was Brynna Infants and I loved every minute of my time there. Although I was only four or five years old I walked all the way through the country lanes on my own for about a mile to reach school. That is something you wouldn't dream of allowing your children to do these days. But then no one ever bothered me and local farmers used to pop their heads over fences and hedges just to say hello as I made my way along the lanes.

After another year or two had passed we moved from the smallholding to a little street in Ty Merchant on the eastern side of Pencoed close to the railway line. My grandfather had now retired from the furrier trade so we left the farm. I was the only one still living with my grandparents, but not long after making the move my grandfather, who had been unwell, passed away so it was just Gran and me.

I soon got to know my way around Pencoed and began helping 'Evans the Crossing'. Mr Evans operated a level crossing on the main Paddington-Swansea main line and he lived in a house next to the railway line directly opposite ours. He told me that he knew a man who cheated the railway company by buying a return ticket and not going back.

The local bobby, PC Sid Worgan, used to strike fear into all of us children but we still managed to do a bit of scrumping for apples and pears during the late summer without him finding out and chasing us.

Next door to us in Ty Merchant they kept three or four goats. The field behind our houses sloped up and there was a brick wall dividing it from the back gardens. We used to sit on the wall with our backs to the field and the goats would run down and butt us off the wall. Those were the days.

I regularly attended the Band of Hope Methodist Church and enjoyed joining in all the hymns. Best of all though was getting my card stamped for the Whitsun Treat which usually meant a marvellous trip to the seaside at Porthcawl.

I went to school at Pen Prysg and enjoyed it there as well. I was fairly good at arithmetic but my spelling was poor and hasn't improved much over the years. It helped being the teacher's pet—she kept me in a cage at the back of the class. I was always the joker, probably trying to attract attention, and although I didn't realise it at the time, I am sure that was the start of my interest in a show-biz career. I have kept in touch with the school ever since, and the children still come every year to our pantomime, as do the children from my other school in Brynna.

Bwllfa Harris Buses ran in Pencoed, another source I would later call on. I used the name for a character in *Welsh Rarebit* who was known as Bwllfa Jones. The church hall was near the school and on Thursdays you could watch silent films while on other days perhaps play snooker or billiards.

Then we were on the move again, but only for a short distance to The Green in Pencoed where Gran and I lived with my Uncle Dick and Aunty Olive. They had seven children, one of them was Jean, my pig-chasing cousin, and they treated me as if I was one of their own.

Dick was a larger than life character who had been badly gassed during the First World War. He liked nothing better than sitting in his chair telling us stories and singing daft little songs. He used to tease us that the Mari Llwyd would come and get us if we were naughty. I based a number of my characters in later years on dear old Uncle Dick.

I lived there with Gran for two years before packing the bags and going on the move once again. This time we travelled a lot further and ended up in Gorseinon with my Aunty Florrie and Uncle Jack. He was known locally as Jack Fish, no doubt because he had a fish round. He went cockle picking in Penclawdd and then fishing in the River Loughor and sold anything he caught. We went to Gorseinon by bus with just a couple of bags holding all our worldly possessions.

Aunty Florrie also had a lot of children but one had just joined the RAF and another was going to live in Belgium so there was room. I was now 10 years old. My new school was down by Bassett's Bus Station but in the evenings I worked in a local cinema, nowadays a billiard hall, selling ice cream. Selling ice cream meant that I could get into the cinema without having to pay, so in that way I never missed any of the films. The ice cream came from the Italian shop next door to the cinema which was known by all the local kids as the 'Bug-House'.

I was mainly fascinated by Western films starring the likes of Tom Mix, Buck Jones, Ken Maynard and of course the great Gene Autry. When I saw Gene playing his guitar and singing while galloping along on his horse it made me want to try to do the same as he made it look so easy. Thankfully, I decided to concentrate solely on the singing side and 'South of the Border', a Gene Autry favourite, would be the first song I ever learned to play.

My cousin Tommy Evans, the one who later went to Belgium, bought a Humber car with an open top and running boards. We used to drive up to Fairwood Common and try to catch some of the wild horses roaming there. We were told that if you were lucky enough to rope one you could keep it, but we never got close enough to any to find out if that was true. What we would have done with a horse if we had been successful I have no idea. I suppose I would have had to ride it home as Tommy would have been driving the car.

I hit on the idea of picking lumps of coke from the tip at the Gowerton Steelworks to make some extra money. I was industrious for a youngster but I had a good incentive. I had seen a second hand guitar in a local shop and I had set my heart on owning it.

If you wanted to earn a few pennies in those days the opportunities were there. You could get sixpence for a bag of coke. I would put a full bag on my bike and push it home before exchanging it for a piece of silver. There were no rubber tyres on my bike wheels. I rode it on the rims so that it would shower sparks in the night. Mind you, it was also because I couldn't afford the tyres.

Before long I had earned enough money and proudly went to the shop where I bought my first guitar. It was an acoustic jazz Radiotone and cost me about £4 which was quite a lot of money in those days. It saw me through a number of years but sadly I don't have it now. If I did it would be a collector's item worth about £5,000.

I was always the first to stand up and sing and I used to like dressing up. Very quickly I developed a little routine where I sang 'Sing a Song of Sixpence' in a variety of accents I had heard on the radio. There were loads of good programmes on the radio in those days including *Henry Hall's Guest Night* which was one of my favourites.

Soon though the wanderlust bit again and it was time for Gran and me to move once more. We headed east to Cardiff where we were to stay with yet more relations in Wheatley Road in Ely. It was 1936 and I was 11 years old.

Unlike the other homes we had lived in, this one was different because we wouldn't be living with an aunty and uncle. In Ely we would be living with my mother Doris and her husband and their three boys. My half-brothers were Reg, Alec and Peter and their surname was Neale.

Reg eventually married Margaret Thomas who represented Great Britain at the 1952 Olympic Games in Helsinki and also the Rome Olympics of 1960. She was a gymnast and Reg was a coach at her Cardiff Olympic club. He was one of the GB officials in Rome and used to tell us how he bumped into Cassius Clay who was then an unknown boxer.

All three boys were good footballers but Alec was the best and even had a trial with Arsenal before settling for life with Barry Town. He now lives in Carmarthen. Peter eventually emigrated to Australia with Dick Stennett who was really my uncle but became my brother. I am not starting all that again.

I never felt any special bond with my mother, after all I was now 11 and had never met her before, nor did I ever feel the need to. My Gran had looked after me and that was good enough. My real mother was genuinely just like an aunty would have been. We lived there for three years and I went to Windsor

Clive School to begin with before moving up to Gladstone School, but that was not until we had moved to Cathays to live with Aunty Ethel and Uncle Fred.

When I was still at Windsor Clive a group of us lads were caught being naughty and sent to the sportsmaster for six of the best. The parents of one of the boys then took the teacher to court because they reckoned the punishment handed out was too severe. The rest of the lads who were caned, me included, were treated to a trip to the Queen's Cinema to watch a Crazy Gang film and before that we all had tea at the Carlton. The trip was probably paid for by the school, or perhaps even by the teacher who had administered the punishment. After that outing of course, when it came to our turn to stand up in court, we all said that the cane hadn't hurt us. That was the end of that, the case was thrown out, and the teacher carried on as normal.

I soon chummed up with some of the local lads in Ely and was particularly friendly with Billy Highgate, Harry Grant and Dai Oxenham. Dai's father worked for Edwards Bakery. He had a harmonica so I saved up and bought one and we played together for a while. Later on we became part of the Ray Gibson Harmonica Band joining the 80 or 90 harmonica and accordion players already under his wing.

These instruments were very popular before the war and there were lots of accordion bands in and around Cardiff. Among them were Waldini and his Accordion Band who played at the Park Hall, while another popular act was Hilda Banwell's All Girl Accordion Band. It was about this time that you could find Tessie O'Shea (before she was 'Two Ton'). She would be playing her ukulele and singing in various halls while also doing shows at St David's Hospital. We played concerts throughout the year and had a big party at Christmas where 10 shillings (50p) was paid to everyone in the Harmonica Band. That may sound like a lot of money for those days but don't forget we had played for 12 months for that money—and I had chapped lips because of it. Nevertheless, it was my first experience of being paid for making music.

When we eventually moved to Cathays, it was to another big family as Aunty Ethel and Uncle Fred had five children, so once again I was adding to the numbers. Of course now it was war time and every house had an air raid shelter down the garden amongst the vegetable plots. One of the five children was Bob and he reckoned he could hear the German bombers taking off. He was always quick off the mark and first to make it to the shelter so perhaps he could.

2

LEARNING AND
PERFORMING

'. . . As Groucho Marx once said—military justice is to justice
what military music is to music.'

* * * * *

There was a dance teacher in Cardiff called Kitty Slocombe
and my cousin Barbara Neale was one of her dancers. I was
envious of Barbara because she was already up there on the
stage and by now I was convinced that was where I wanted
to be. She became my brother Reg's sister when he was
adopted by my Aunty. Still confusing isn't it?

Kitty was married to a band leader named Keith
Matthews. Now Keith worked the ballrooms at the City Hall
and Pavlova in Cardiff, the Marina and Paget Rooms in
Penarth and Bindles in Cold Knap—all the places in the area
for good entertainment. He also played at the Olympia
Cinema where the manager was called Mr Keyes.

Gran and I had now moved out to Tewkesbury Street in
Cathays and I rarely saw my old mate Dai, although he would
often ring me up in later years and pass comment on any
shows of mine that he had seen.

I then met up with Steve Gibson at a concert and we
clicked immediately. He was already a semi-pro with the
Modernaires, a singing group. He was a bus conductor on

the No. 39 Ely Bridge route and he would later marry Olive Guppy who had a dancing school and was also a fine pianist and accordion player. Steve played double bass and it was a comical sight seeing him going to gigs on his bike with the double bass slung over his shoulder. It was not long before I joined in with the vocal group and we did concerts all over South Wales, even playing on Sunday nights at the Olympia.

It is hard to imagine that although Steve was a bit older than me, I was still only 14. There was an American group called the Modernaires who used to sing with the Glenn Miller Band. They did comedy vocals and we based our act on them. In our group there were three boys, George Hodge had joined us on accordion, along with three girls. We worked hard and became very professional. George, who was in the RAF, was courting Olive's sister Dot. He was the only one among us to use a stage name and was known as Hal Norris on tour.

I left school just before my 15th birthday and went to work for the Maypole. I was given a bicycle with a basket on the front so that I could deliver groceries all round the area. I had spent all my life with my Gran travelling here, there and everywhere, and I desperately wanted to pay her back for everything she had done for me.

My weekly wage was 10 shillings and I was so looking forward to handing over my first pay packet to her on the Friday after my first week of deliveries. Sadly, I never had the chance because my dear Gran passed away the day before, on the Thursday. Many years later I was talking to Roy Hudd and he told me that he was also brought up by his grandmother. We had a good rapport after sharing that common upbringing and I still keep in touch with Roy.

I was working at the Maypole when I met my future wife, Betty. She had a job in the post office in Whitchurch Road and lived with her parents in Talygarn Street in Cathays. I used to go into the post office to buy stamps from her whether I wanted them or not. I would press my nose up against the counter window and sing like Dick Haymes, the American crooner. Betty had just left school and I was now 16.

After a while I began to get itchy feet as the travel bug bit me, so I left the Maypole and joined Pickfords—not humping furniture—but making general deliveries in a lorry. When I started with the company I was put in with a driver called Wilf Keenor. He was the brother of Fred Keenor the famous footballer who captained Cardiff City when they beat Arsenal to win the FA Cup at Wembley in 1927. Perhaps my interest in football began from there as we had plenty of time to talk about all things to do with the game.

Almost as soon as I started at Pickfords I was encouraged to get behind the wheel of the lorry to practise reversing or parking up. Of course I wasn't allowed on the roads but the depot in Tyndall Street was big enough to drive up and down. It was also a clever move on the management's part because if every van boy learned to drive, they would always have a good supply of drivers within the company.

Sometimes we started deliveries at 3.00am, perhaps taking the daily newspapers up the Valleys. If I was appearing with the Modernaires in the evening I would call home on the way back into Cardiff, put my stage clothes on under my overalls, and then be taken back to the yard.

We used to work all hours in those days but that is how we knew it had to be. If you wanted to make progress in the entertainment business then you had to put in the hours. The Modernaires received about £20 for a show. This was shared between all six of us so it certainly wasn't a fortune but it was a start. I knew by then that entertaining on stage was what I wanted to do for the rest of my life.

In no time at all we were doing shows as far afield as Gloucester, Swansea, Haverfordwest, even travelling down to London. We also worked most of the Valleys theatres. It was a good apprenticeship in the business, particularly for me, as don't forget I was still only a teenager.

As well as the Modernaires, I also worked with the Bert Miller Band who had residencies at the Marina and Bindles Ballrooms, and the Jack Evans Sextet who were based in the Capitol Ballroom. They had a trumpeter called Garfield Ireland who lived in Cathays Terrace. It was after listening to him that I started teaching myself the trumpet and then later I began playing the instrument with the Modernaires. This brought something fresh to the act so was useful on two fronts.

I also had a spell at the Savoy Ballroom in Barry, yet another billiard hall now, with the Stan Hopkins Sextet. Joe Thomas was the drummer and Reg Chick was the bass player. Reg was very professional, but you wouldn't want to meet him on a dark night as most of his front teeth were missing.

By now I was interested in anything musical and there used to be a music shop opposite the Castle run by Sid Clements. They had everything there and it was good just going in to have a browse around. I could spend hours in there just looking at all the instruments.

Cardiff and the surrounding area was now a little hotbed of music and particularly of guitar players. It all stemmed from the docks where there were probably more different nationalities than anywhere else in the country, and there were also lots of ballrooms and theatres employing resident bands.

The Eddie Graves Band played the Philharmonic Ballroom with Eddie's sister Molly Graves on the accordion. Molly later married Benny Lichfield who led one of the BBC's orchestras. Drummer Benny Romoff was another with his own band. Benny was also in the rag trade, while the

Henry Verrows Band could be found at the Central Hotel. The standard of musicianship at all these venues was high so I knew that if I wanted to succeed in the business I would have to work hard.

On the morning of my 17th birthday I had a driving test with Pickfords chief engineer, passed, and an hour later took a load of peas up to Treforest on my own.

A few months later I did an audition for the great Tommy Trinder at the New Theatre in Cardiff. I parked my Pickfords van outside the theatre and nipped inside to do my act. Tommy was happy with what I did for him but said I looked too much like him and could put him out of work, so he was unable to offer me anything. By now I was living in Tewkesbury Street with the Proctors and my cousin George received his call-up papers the same time as me. We both went into the army.

His brother Tommy was in the navy but another brother, Bob, didn't get called up as he had bronchial problems. All the Proctor boys had been good footballers playing for Fairoak in the local Cardiff league. My brother Reg was a useful goalkeeper and one day his side played against Fairoak and Tommy broke his jaw. He had to eat through a straw for ages. It was a good job they were cousins or Reg would have killed him. The Proctor boys had a sister called Nancy and she used to look after us all. She also made all my stage clothes which was a great help.

I had a big thrill one evening when I made my usual trip to play with the Henry Verrows Band at an American Servicemen's camp in Sully. When we arrived at the base we were told that we were not wanted that night as they had flown in some top class performers to entertain the troops stationed there.

It was a star-studded cast as Jerry Colonna, the singer

Marilyn Maxwell, and the now legendary Bob Hope all appeared. What a fantastic experience for me, and I would meet up with Bob Hope in different circumstances many years later. It must have been a bit of a homecoming for Bob as I understand his mother came from Barry.

While still driving the lorry for Pickfords as my regular job, I was now also doing three or four shows a week at venues like the Students Union in Park Place, Cardiff. I had a regular spot working with a little jazz quartet that was made up of local musicians who joined together to make the kind of music that was popular at the time. We modelled ourselves on the Benny Goodman sound. Betty would come to some of these gigs and we would walk home together after the shows had finished.

Another great spot to play was the Big Windsor down the Docks. I had hours of pleasure playing with, and listening to, the great Vic Parker—or Narker Parker as he was called. The Docks were a hotbed of music and many brilliant musicians were found down there every evening.

Albert and Les Ward from Severn Grove already had a good act about that time. They went on to become very popular and not many people know that Albert and Les backed Charlie Drake on his hit record 'My Boomerang Won't Come Back'. Les did all the strange vocals while Albert played the washboard.

Driving a Pickfords' lorry still meant an early start for me as I used to collect the morning papers from the General Station and take them up the valleys where they were distributed to all the newsagents. It was not unusual to find myself working 90 hours a week for the company as we were short-staffed due to the number of drivers that had been called up for army training.

My cousin George drove the Little Rhondda route and I

was assigned to Big Rhondda. We shared lots of things in those days but in particular a smart plaid jacket. George wore it when he took out any young ladies, and I wore it when I was playing at gigs. It was a strange coincidence that we received our call-up papers at the same time.

I knew exactly what it was when the brown envelope without the stamp finally arrived on my doorstep. Well, who else did I know that owned a Post Office? In no time at all I had taken my medical and was on the way to a camp in Chester. I was sent a pass for my train but George had to report to Catterick so we never met up in the army, only back home occasionally while on leave.

Once in Chester I was sent to one of the huts where about 20 or 30 lads were already settled in. The next day we were on the parade ground doing drill. They were a good bunch of boys and although it was a totally different life from the one I was used to, they made me feel at home in those early difficult days.

I was in Chester for only six weeks before being sent to Blackpool where I joined the Royal Artillery on a driving course. I did a lot of training on the front at Blackpool but just because I was on a driving course didn't mean that I drove a truck around all day—far from it. One of our drills was to run the whole way down the length of the North Pier, throw ropes over the side, and climb down them onto the sand. On one occasion, it was now 1943, something went wrong as I went down the rope and I fell off and broke my ankle. I used to recall that incident when I played at the North Pier in 1960 starring alongside Michael Holliday, Des O'Connor and two young lads known as the Allisons.

After the D-Day landings in June 1944 it wasn't long before the 49th Brigade, me included, were sent over to

Arromanches on the Normandy coast. The coastline seemed to be littered with wrecks and the Mulberry harbours were still in position for offloading supplies. It must have been a terrifying experience for the lads who were first to arrive on those beaches in Normandy, and that oily smell from the sunken ships and damaged transport scattered about must have taken months to disappear.

From Arromanches I was dispatched to Belgium and stationed just north of Antwerp. As a fully qualified driver my job was to transport troops on 24 hour passes from the Antwerp area and take them to Mechelen, near Brussels, which was a safe area. After dropping them off, I would then collect another lot to take back up north.

On one occasion my lorry was stolen. I had stopped at a NAAFI in Antwerp on my way and then went looking for a shop that I was told had musical equipment for sale. When I returned to the spot where I parked my lorry it had disappeared so I was forced to go to the Military Police and tell them I had lost it. Fortunately for me they had more important things to worry about and ordered me to contact base myself to give them the bad news. The end result was that I was charged with losing army property. I was very lucky that my commanding officer was a Welshman called Colonel John. He took pity on me at my court martial and let me off the hook, but it was a worrying experience. I was glad not to end up in a military prison. As Groucho Marx once said— military justice is to justice what military music is to music.

One of my musical mates about this time was a 6 foot 5 inch cockney called Jim Cobby. He was as tough as old boots and had hands like shovels. I would play guitar while he joined in on the fiddle. He was a bit of an opera buff and *Cavalleria Rusticana* was his favourite. I have seen him break down and cry while listening to the music. He had an accident on his bike and ripped his ankle open but that didn't stop him playing the fiddle. I often wonder what became of big Jim.

When the war ended it didn't mean that the job was over and everyone came home straight away, far from it. There was still a lot of work to be done and I was sent to a Unit in Bologna, Italy called 'Stars in Battledress'. I was to be the driver/performer for one of the groups based there.

There were a number of servicemen in the Unit who later became famous artists. Norman Vaughan, a sergeant, was in a show called *Ace High*. He produced it as well as doing a number of spots throughout the evening. *Ace High* was a successor to other services shows such as *Ridin' High* and *Sky High*. They were all put on by what was known as Combined Services Entertainment. In another show, Norman worked with a beautiful Italian girl who looked just like Sophia Loren.

Harry Secombe, Spike Milligan and Charlie Chester were also out there during my spell in Italy. Spike had undergone a difficult war having seen plenty of action and both he and Harry were in the Royal Artillery. Spike was born in India and though he lived most of his life in England he was declared stateless in 1960 and refused a passport. He took out Irish citizenship as his father was from Ireland but what a way to treat someone who fought for his country.

I never worked with them in any shows but that didn't stop us enjoying our time together when we were all at base camp. Harry did exactly the same comedy routine for which he would later became famous—singing and blowing raspberries—and he used to do the shaving act. He would sing 'Figaro' while shaving and cutting himself to pieces. He would end up with bits of cotton wool all over his face. Spike was crazy even then, in a funny sense, as he mixed zany humour with trumpet and guitar playing.

Another mad act out in Italy was Sid Millward and the Nitwits, while Reg Varney, later to be seen in *On the Buses*, worked with a young stooge named Benny Hill. It was so much better than doing guard duty in Aldershot, and for lots of army personnel it meant the first steps on the road to a life in the entertainment world.

In my post of army driver I was responsible for taking a complete show, performers as well, around the various camps in Italy and we even travelled into Austria to entertain the troops. Al Monte and a comedian called Stainless Stephen— he must have been from Sheffield—were amongst those I took around the country. There is no doubt though that I had the most enjoyment driving Ivy Benson's All Girl Band to places like Graz, Vienna and Trieste.

Ivy was very professional and her girls were all top class musicians. As well as driving, I was also stage manager and had the devil of a job making sure the troops didn't get too close to the girls while they were on stage. I met Ivy many times later on during our show-biz careers and we appeared on each other's *This is your Life*.

At this time my act consisted of playing guitar and trumpet and telling a few gags, while I was already polishing up some impressions. Driving and performing continued until well into 1947, almost five years after I first received that brown envelope. Just before demob I was sent back to the UK and stationed at Battersea Park. We were still an operational group and did shows all over the country—even as far afield as Ireland. Once I found my feet I quickly became involved with music and together with seven other lads we formed a group known as the Johnny Clay Band with Johnny on trumpet. Later I was sent to Newport Barracks to wait for my release back into Civvy Street.

While at the Barracks I entered a few talent contests and did very well. I was self-taught but felt that I had definitely improved over the time I had been in the army. I had more control of my act and was ambitious to follow a career in entertainment, so army life had turned out to be very good for me. After coming first in a show at Ynysyngharad Park in Pontypridd, I had the luck that everyone needs in this business when I entered the Royal Gwent Hospital talent show. I won—first prize was a week working with Vic Lewis and Jack Parnell at the Pavilion Theatre on Stow Hill. I also received the handsome sum of £20 which was quite a windfall in those days.

My week's stint at the Pavilion went so well that Vic offered me a full-time job working and touring with his band. I thought about it long and hard but decided to decline his offer because I had been away from home for five years. All I really wanted to do was spend more time with Betty.

Unknown to me, one of the adjudicators at that talent show had been Mai Jones who was a well-known light entertainment producer for BBC Wales. There was no one in Wales who did as much for light entertainment and new talent as she did and many an act had her to thank for their first break in the business. I carried on working locally and used to perform at Sunday evening concerts in the Olympia Cinema in Queen Street, Cardiff. The queues used to be long for every performance as people had been starved of good entertainment during the war years and there was very little to do straight after.

Bert Miller and his Dance Orchestra provided the music. The Modernaires were the headliners in one particular show in April 1947. They were now known as Radio's Ace Harmony Act having continued to perform during the war with a slight change of personnel. As well as back singing and performing with the Modernaires, I had my own spot doing impressions, telling gags, singing and playing guitar and trumpet.

Two months later at the same venue, the programme consisted of the Modernaires in the first half of the show, the Harmaniacs who opened the second half, while I had a solo spot just before the big finale. The Harmaniacs consisted of Steve Gibson on bass guitar, Hal Norris on accordion and I provided the comedy as well as guitar and trumpet. We mixed up music with comedy and began developing a good act. The future was beginning to fall into shape.

By the following month, the Sunday Evening Concerts were being billed as Bert Miller and his Dance Orchestra with the Modernaires and the Harmaniacs. Unfortunately, as the Modernaires became better known, they were told they had to change their name to avoid confusion with the American group. The three of us decided to concentrate solely on the Harmaniacs, while two of the girls continued their singing career elsewhere and the other decided to retire from show business. That meant the end of the singing group. That is how it continued that year with the Harmaniacs gaining popularity while I also continued with my own solo spot. Joining us on many of the bills was Olive Guppy with her accordion.

But unknown to me, Mai Jones had never forgotten seeing me in that talent contest and my life was about to change. Mai was a lovely person who was always on the lookout for new talent and I will forever be extremely grateful to her for giving me my first real opportunity in the business.

She made a special note of my name after the Royal Gwent talent show and when an opening came up on a popular radio programme called *Welsh Rarebit* she contacted me. That was a show coming live from the BBC studios in

Cardiff. There were no such things as recorded programmes in those days and I was signed up on a full 18 months contract. I received the princely sum of £3 per show because that was the set fee for a local artist. It took me a long time to work my way around this but later on, as my agent was based in London, I enrolled as a London-based comedian which enabled me to earn more money. For that £3, by the way, I also had to attend rehearsals for the weekly show even though I worked on my own.

To save money I wrote all my own scripts which had to be shown to the powers-that-be at the BBC before I was allowed to use them. That was the case for everyone, not just me. Scripts were no good after being aired on radio so I constantly needed new material. Everyone tuned in to *Welsh Rarebit* and in its heyday, it had a fantastic following. The show was made in front of an invited audience perhaps at the Drill Hall in Dumfries Place in Cardiff, or maybe around the corner in the Cory Hall which used to be opposite Queen Street Station. I was still driving for Pickfords but also managed spots on other shows for the BBC such as *Workers Playtime* and *Midday Music Hall*. I had to swap many a shift to make sure I was available at the right time for whatever programme I was appearing on.

Although my act was becoming more visual, I never had to change a great deal if I was doing a show for radio. I could still use my vocal impressions, sing a few songs, and play the guitar and trumpet.

It was on a *Midday Music Hall* programme that I first met Max Wall. He was at the top of the tree. In the Thirties he had worked in America and was probably the main person held up as being the epitome of all good comedy dancers. Most of those who came after him used part of his act. Max was a comedian's comedian. When he was in town most people in the business would see him—not to copy his act—but to appreciate a real professional doing the business. His piano routine alone was worth any entrance fee. It was superb. His Professor Wallofsky character when he dressed in black tights had to be seen to be believed.

Midday Music Hall went on the air from the Playhouse Theatre in Northumberland Street in London. That was a well-known venue and *Hancock's Half Hour*, *Jimmy Edwards* and *Educating Archie* were other shows to come from there at that time. Sometimes we used the Paris Cinema in Lower Bond Street and shows are still recorded from there to this day. I would travel up by train usually early in the morning, do the show, and travel back in the late afternoon.

I also did a programme from Manchester called *Make 'Em Laugh*. We had a live audience and were given items to talk about, totally unrehearsed. A young Les Dawson, Max Wall and a relatively unknown Bruce Forsyth were also on the show at various times. It was later, after watching Max Wall, that Bruce added bits of comedy to his own dance routines.

Back to *Welsh Rarebit* where I did my act in front of those huge mikes you sometimes see in old newsreels. They were so different from the sound equipment nowadays but at the time they were the best available. One of the stars of *Welsh Rarebit* was Eynon Evans who came from Caerphilly. He was one of the main scriptwriters and wrote the part of Tommy Trouble. He also played Willie. And who could ever forget Gladys Morgan. I can still hear that laugh now.

About an hour before the actual programme started I would go out to warm up the audience and get them in a good mood. The Lyrian Singers sang a few numbers and after about half an hour everything was checked and the live performance started, usually at 7.30pm. So I warmed up the audience, attended rehearsals and did my act—all for the princely sum of £3—what a deal. No wonder it didn't take me long to link up with an agent.

I needed a new script every week but soon learnt not to give away all my best material on radio, as once it had been used it was finished. It was different for singers but comedians had to learn quickly how to present gags in different forms so that they sounded fresh. That was important to any act. In the midst of all these shows I was booked for one of the most important days of my life.

On 29 March 1948 I married Betty at St Mary's Church in Whitchurch Road. We only had a small reception at the Church Hall in Monthermer Road as all I had saved was my £40 demob money. There was no chance of a honeymoon as the Harmaniacs needed work but it was still a great occasion and one that Betty and I will never forget.

We wrote around for auditions and did a Sunday Concert or two and as a result were signed up by Ernie Cash of the Metropolitan Vaudeville Agency. Ernie was well into his sixties when we first met up with him and he had been in the business for a long time. At first he took 10% but as time went on that increased to 15%. He had to work hard for that money though because unless he found us work he didn't get paid. Ernie's brother Joe was a tailor specialising in band uniforms. All the colliery bands, and there were dozens of them, needed uniforms so the Cash boys provided them. They also ran an Army and Navy Stores in Praed Street, Paddington opposite the Railway Hotel. Ernie handled the agency while Joe ran the store.

Ernie never had any big acts on his books, only bread and butter performers, but he would take an act and work hard to build up a good following. If your impression of agents is cashmere overcoats and black hombergs then you are not far off the mark. Ernie drove a huge Austin Sheerline, it was like a tank. He looked after us very well. If I had a sore throat he would be first with the cough mixture. After the Harmaniacs finished I became their 'boy' and I trusted the two of them completely.

Bernard Woolley was another agent typically always seen with a big cigar but he wore a stetson not a homberg. He had mainly novelty acts like Musical Marie. She would be in a small marquee somewhere in Blackpool attempting to beat the world record for non-stop piano playing. People would pay to watch while she played and tried not to fall asleep. Another act doing exactly the same thing was Syncopating Sandy. Between the Empire Theatre and Playhouse in Nottingham was a small piece of ground and it cost sixpence to go into a tent to see him play.

Bernard had something like Cinerama in a building in Blackpool. The screen was a circle all round and you had to get in through the roof to see the show. I worked for Mr Woolley when *Welsh Rarebit* went on tour round the country. George and Alfred Black, and Will Collins, father of screen goddess Joan, had important agencies around that time. Lou and Leslie Grade and Bernard Delfont (they were cousins) also started as agents. The Grades had been a dance act before they decided there was more money to be made behind the scenes.

I had plenty of opportunities throughout my career to leave Ernie and join up with other bigger agencies but I wanted to be as fair to him as he was to me and the other two lads. I stayed loyal to Ernie and wouldn't leave him. I was brought up like that and wanted to be able to sleep at night. But that didn't stop him hating me though because, after all, he reckoned I took 90% of his salary. I was now at a stage where I had to make some important decisions.

3

ON THE ROAD

'It was a real education watching a master like Max Miller working his audience. He earned himself a certain reputation for being near the knuckle . . . "They say you can't mix business with pleasure but I know a few girls in Brighton who are doing it."'

* * * * *

There was no way I could still drive for Pickfords as well as working the music halls as it was so exhausting. Something had to give and I didn't want it to be me. It was hard doing a day job and then appearing at theatres in the evenings as we had been doing throughout 1948.

I decided to see Pickfords' area manager, Mr Reid and ask him for some advice. Without too much hesitation he told me to go ahead with my dream of a life on stage, but only if that was what I really wanted. Betty and I then had long discussions as did Steve, Hal and their wives. Steve was now married to Olive Guppy. We came up with a plan that we should all travel together, the wives were good friends in any case, and so we eventually decided on that basis to take the plunge as full-time professionals in the entertainment industry.

Ernie Cash was off the mark in no time and one of our first bookings was at the Winter Gardens in Margate where we appeared in early November 1948. Also on the bill was Jon Pertwee, who became a very good friend of mine, while the star of the show was none other than Sam Costa. The Harmaniacs were listed in the programme, for the very first time, as 'Certified Insanely Funny'. That was known as our bill matter.

Jon Pertwee went on to have a long career in show business, also appearing in star roles in *Dr Who* and *Worzel Gummidge* on BBC television. At that time his catch phrase as the postman from a radio programme called *Waterlogged Spa* was *'Tear 'Em Up'*. Sam Costa was a famous radio comedian of the time in programmes such as *Much Binding in the Marsh* with Kenneth Horne and his catchphrase was *'Good morning sir, was there something?'*

We spent Christmas back in our own homes and I never thought for one moment that it would be my last quiet Christmas at home for many years without any pantomimes or seasonal shows. In January 1949 we had a big break when Ernie managed to book us on the *Max Miller Show* at the Metropolitan Theatre in the Edgware Road. After a few weeks at the Metropolitan the show was scheduled to go on a tour of the Syndicate Halls including such well-known theatres as the Chelsea Palace, East Ham Palace, Chiswick Empire and the Shepherds Bush Empire.

We were booked for eight weeks work, twice nightly, and it was a tremendous booking so early in our careers. On this show we were billed as 'Radio's Crazy Comedy Harmony Trio'. Besides the Syndicate Halls there were other circuits such as the Butterworth Theatres found mainly in Lancashire, The Moss Empire, which included Cardiff's Empire Theatre, and the Stoll Theatre which numbered Cardiff's New Theatre and the Bristol Hippodrome on their circuit. We were only booked for the Syndicate Halls but could have carried on with any of the other circuits and as they totalled over 150 theatres, it meant being good for almost three years' work. Once you completed that list, if you were good enough, you started all over again.

When television came on the scene it was totally different. You could play to more people in one night on a TV show than you did in three years travelling around the circuits. It was a real education watching a master like Max Miller working his audience. He earned himself a certain reputation for being near the knuckle, and he certainly was just as risqué in those days when we first met up with him.

'They say you can't mix business with pleasure but I know a few girls in Brighton who are doing it.' He never let his audience down and was one of the best stand-up comics we have ever had. He always came on stage looking as if he had made his suit out of curtain material and he wasn't billed as 'The Cheeky Chappie' for nothing. *Make the most of me now ladies, there will never be another.*'

It may seem strange now but Max used to end the second half of the early evening show—but then finish off the first half of the second show, just so that he could catch the train back home to Brighton in plenty of time every night. He was such a big star that he was able to write that into his contract but it made the later performance a huge strain for the rest of the acts on the bill.

He was a very quiet man offstage and always dressed in an ordinary dark suit and trilby hat when he left the theatre to go home.

> *'I went to a wedding. It was the girlfriend's.'*
> *'Did you give her away?'*
> *'No, I never said a thing.'*

Max would have two books with him on stage, one white and the other blue. Then he would let the audience know that the white book contained clean jokes while the blue book had all the others. 'Which one do you want?' he would ask, and the reply was always the same—'The blue book!'

> 'I came home the other night and there was the wife in the arms of the butcher. I thought this isn't right—it's the coalman we owe the money to!'

He was the highest-paid variety entertainer of his day, was much loved by the audience, and will never be forgotten. I actually started Max playing the guitar. He used a three string ukulele in his act but one evening during the interval he came into our dressing room and asked me to show him a few chords. It developed from there and whenever possible, wherever we were appearing on the syndicate, I would have to find time to give Max a few lessons. It didn't take him long to learn a few chords but I don't know whether he ever kept it up.

While the three of us performed twice nightly as the Harmaniacs with Max and the other acts such as Alfred Thripp, the blind pianist and vocalist, all six of us, wives included, stayed in digs in Brixton Road. It was owned by an Austrian couple who were once in the business themselves. Rationing was still on and we used to pool our ration cards and go round the local shops to see where we could get the best deal for our coupons. The trams went down the Brixton Road and we used them regularly to get about.

Ernie Cash was now earning his money by getting us jobs all over the country. We paid our first visit to Scotland and appeared at the Tivoli Theatre of Varieties in Aberdeen in a show featuring Britain's leading family team, the Logans. Their name was actually Short, and I stayed friends with Jimmy Logan until his death in 2001. Jimmy eventually broke away from the family and became an accomplished musician, comedian, actor and impresario.

From there we went to the Palladium Theatre in Edinburgh before returning in April to play at the Empire Theatre in Croydon where once again we described ourselves as 'Certified Insanely Funny' now known as our personal bill matter. The Croydon booking was in a show topped by Billy Reid and Dorothy Squires. He wrote the songs and she sang them in her own unique style. I worked with Dorothy many times and she was a lovely girl who was married to Billy at the time. Later on she married Roger Moore, the famous film star.

Ernie was now also inviting what was known in the business as 'bookers' to watch our act. Bookers were used to find good acts to fill bills in the syndicate theatres. Ernie was a booker himself and he fixed us up back at the Winter Gardens, Margate for a short season. Once again Sam Costa was top of the bill but by now we were as big a draw as Sam. Then Ernie really earned his money when we were signed up for a summer season at the Gaiety Theatre in Ayr, way up in Scotland. It was a 26 week season, twice nightly at 6.30pm and 8.40pm, and the show was called *Gaiety Whirl of 1949*.

We started the summer show at the end of May, and what an experience it turned out to be. We had to change the act every week so it was another good place to learn the business. Everyone who was a name had appeared over the years in the *Gaiety Whirl* show. They were mainly top Scottish acts such as Denny Willis, Will Fyffe and Lex McLean. Lex was funny but you had to listen to him carefully as it was difficult to understand his broad Scottish accent.

The audience took to us immediately and very quickly the Harmaniacs became the stars of the show. One week I leapt on stage wearing a kilt and bonnet and in a thick Scottish accent I began singing . . .

'There was a soldier, a Scottish soldier
One day his kilt caught fire
And boy did he perspire . . .'

Also on the bill during that summer season was a young dancer who was part of a double act. His name was Lionel Blair and he worked with his sister Joyce.

The show was such a good grounding for us because we didn't just have our own spot. All the acts were expected to join in with the entire ensemble in various 'big' numbers. Sometimes it was a Highland Fantasy and dressed in kilts, which was where the 'Scottish Soldier' skit came from. At other times it was a big dance routine where Lionel would show off his steps. Don't forget that the shows were twice nightly for six nights a week and we did at least four spots in every show. It was hard work and in America they call it 'Summer Stock' but it was how you learned your trade. There couldn't be a better apprenticeship.

Our act had become polished by now and we were doing impressions of the Ink Spots or Mills Brothers to begin our set. The Mills Brothers were very big at the time and good impressions went down well with audiences. 'April in Paris' and 'Stardust' were two of their top numbers and we offered our own style of the songs to the audience.

We would then mix up some musical jokes with a Spike Jones routine or perhaps a hillbilly selection. We used the top songs of the day and did our own version of them. I became the link man between Steve and Hal during the comedy routines. You can't buy that sort of experience.

During the run, Betty came home to give birth to our first son, Roger, who arrived on 24 September 1949. I still don't know how I managed to be funny on stage in Scotland while worrying about Betty and our new baby boy back home in Wales.

After starring at the Gaiety Theatre and being well received by a demanding audience, the summer season came to a close in October. We returned to Cardiff and I started a new life as a father, albeit very briefly.

The two lads wanted a rest from show business but there was no break for me as Ernie still wanted money from somewhere and I really did want to carry on. In any case, I now had three mouths to feed so he booked me up for my first pantomime which was at the Grand Theatre, Swansea. It was a 16-week run of that old favourite, *Red Riding Hood*. I had a partner in the panto. The only trouble being he was a midget and we played a couple of robbers—the Long and Short.

For me it was like entering Wonderland because in pantomime I was able to try out lots of visual humour routines. I also had to work hard to get any laughs in that particular show because all the audience's sympathies were with the dwarf. At least I could travel home every evening to Talygarn Street where the three of us lived with Betty's mother and father.

With the pantomime season over it was back on the road and Ernie, in his wisdom, had decided to fix the three of us up at the Empress Playhouse in Glasgow. Lex McLean and Margo Henderson, who I would later meet up with in the Minstrels, were the big names on the show and once again we had to be prepared to join in with numerous other spots besides doing our own act. Lex had been in *Gaiety Whirls* so we quickly teamed up once again and the four of us got on like a house on fire.

We toured around the music halls of Lancashire after that and I remember us playing The Vic in Burnley in the summer of 1950. It was an old-fashioned theatre but not quite as old as the one we worked at up in Paisley, Scotland. All the lighting around the auditorium in that theatre was done with oil lamps and cheeky little kids ran around blowing them out during the performances.

We were booked for several appearances in *Welsh Rarebit* and also did a radio show called *Four in Hand* which ran for about three months on BBC. That was when I got to know Peter Sellers very well as he made his first radio broadcast on our show. Also appearing were well-known pianists Billy Milton and Walter Wade, and a harpist called Mario Lorenzo. We also made an appearance on *Henry Hall's Guest Night* which was a big thrill for me as it had always been a favourite radio programme of mine. It was one of the most popular radio shows of the time.

In late July of that year it was a return visit to the Winter Gardens in Margate for a week. Joint top of the bill was Peter Sellers who was now making a name for himself in the radio programme *Ray's A Laugh* where he was the creator of crazy characters such as Crystal Jellybottom and Soppy. Peter had been a drummer in the Forces and he could also do impressions. He was wrapped up in his work even then and worked hard to get all his voices off to perfection. He was a versatile performer who could play the ukulele and banjo and there was a story that his father actually taught a young George Formby to play the ukulele. Sadly, Peter was only 54 when he died from a massive heart attack in 1980 after he had become a huge film star. Sharing top billing with him on the show was Max Bacon whose bill matter described him as the 'Heavyweight Champion of Humour'.

By October we were at Feldmans Theatre in Blackpool and for the very first time the Harmaniacs were topping the bill. We were overjoyed to have that top billing. That was so important, much more than the money. There were acts who would work for nothing just to be placed top of the bill. Orchestra Stalls and Grand Circle seats cost four shillings

(20p) including tax, while the cheapest unreserved seats in the pit stalls were the princely sum of one shilling (5p) each. Those really were the days.

Despite all our success, Steve and Hal found being away from home very difficult and they had serious misgivings about all the non-stop touring we were doing. Although they were fine artists in their own right, they didn't have the same desire of making a full-time career in the business that I did.

Another consideration, and a very big one at that, was the £100 a week salary we were earning. Shared between three families, it was not a great deal of money when working away, not even in those days. I was different though because I wanted a career in show business and Betty backed me to the hilt.

I couldn't resist the pantomime season and while the two lads rested at home, I joined the cast of *Dick Whittington* at the New Empire in Bristol for Christmas 1950. That great Welsh favourite Ossie Morris played Idle Jack while I took on the role of the Mate. Marcia Owen, later to become another client of Ernie Cash, played the lead role of Dick. She was a sort of Marie Lloyd character and a very fine performer. It was a great show with plenty of fun both on and off the stage as everyone involved was so friendly.

When the panto season was over, Steve, George and me had a lengthy, but amicable, meeting to decide the best course of action for the trio that would suit all three of us. After a long discussion it was decided that the Harmaniacs would work only local venues for a period to see how that worked out. This made it easier for Steve and Hal who were tired of all the travelling and being away for long periods.

Throughout 1951 and 1952 we stayed reasonably local by playing the Olympia and Capitol in Cardiff, the Municipal in Pontypridd, and up around the Valleys, while travelling only as far as Gloucester and other theatres within easy reach of home. Providing the lads could get home after a show, distance was no object.

Although I would have rather been touring the main theatres gaining even more experience, I was very lucky in a way because, in addition to working within the boundaries we had decided to set out, I was also able to do solo radio work with *Welsh Rarebit*. I was then offered the opportunity of appearing in a programme called *The Jones Boy* where Gwyneth Petty, the mother of former BBC personality and news reader Sara Edwards, played the part of my wife. I was Mr Jones and it was a situation comedy about a local family that was broadcast on the radio for half an hour every week. This helped keep my name known in the business, at least within Wales.

In the meantime I also returned to my job driving for Pickfords and it was back to combining the two jobs for a while. But the writing was on the wall as far as the Harmaniacs were concerned and I think all three of us knew that. After a lot of soul-searching it was decided that at the end of 1952 we would bring the final curtain down on the partnership. All good things must come to an end but I was sorry to lose my two good mates as the Harmaniacs had become a very successful trio and we had always got on well wherever we were performing. When you spend so much time together as we had then you develop a special bond so it was a sad day when we parted.

Steve opened a music shop in Cardiff with Joe Gregory and eventually bought the business outright. I introduced George to TWW, the local independent television company as he was good at making props. One of his best was a fantastic cut-out in tin-plate for one of our regular numbers, *Ghost Riders in the Sky*. A light would be shone through the cut-out and appearing on the wall at the back of the stage was the shadowy figure of a ghost rider. It went down very well with audiences and George was good at many things like that.

As for me, I had been developing my own solo act while still working with Steve and Hal so I felt that I was ready to go back to being on my own, just as I had been before the trio became a professional act.

Ernie Cash came up trumps once again when Max Bygraves fell ill while playing the role of Buttons in Birmingham. I was lucky enough to stand in for Max for a few days until he was well enough to continue. A stand-in took Max's role in the panto and I covered his solo spots. Mind you, I never received anything like the salary Max was on in those days.

Ernie had started to build up a reputation for keeping people on the telephone when he was trying to book dates for me. The impresarios all used to say 'book him'—just to save having to listen to Ernie for half an hour on the phone. He was a great character who had actually worked with Charlie Chaplin when they were both members of Fred Karno's Army in the States. Stan Laurel was another in the troupe at the same time as Ernie and Charlie. You didn't have to go far to hear some wonderful stories of life in those early days of silent films.

I was happy with the way Ernie had conducted the Harmaniacs affairs and was pleased that he agreed to stay as my agent now that I had decided to go permanently solo. *Welsh Rarebit* was such a well-loved show that it went on tour around the country and when Bernard Woolley put it on at the Hippodrome in Chesterfield for a week on 18 February 1952, I headed the bill. One of the other acts on the show doing trick acrobatic stuff was Gudzows' Welsh Collie Dogs. One of the collies was called Blacksmith because he was always making a bolt for the door. You don't see routines like that anymore.

At the end of the season I was ready for a return to the *Gaiety Whirls* in Ayr. It was July 1952, and once again three of us made the trip north, but this time I was with Betty and young Roger. They both joined me in a caravan which we were able to site not far from the theatre. I now owned a big Humber Super Snipe and so had no trouble towing the caravan up to Scotland.

Gaiety Whirls of 1952 starred Margo Henderson and once again I had my own solo spots as well as joining in with the whole company. As usual, the programme changed every week so it kept us all on our toes. The Harmaniacs had made such a good impression that Ernie was able to book my return as a solo artist and it turned out to be a great success. The reviews were tremendous and it opened up all sorts of possibilities for me.

I was offered a spot on the top radio show *Variety Bandbox* which was a regular Sunday night radio programme. Stars such as Frankie Howerd and Derek Roy alternated at the top of the bill and the Billy Ternent Band provided the music. By some strange piece of good fortune Billy and his Band were away at the time I was booked and their place was taken by the Cyril Stapleton Orchestra.

Cyril was so impressed with my act that he offered me an immediate spot on the new BBC *Showband Show* which he was in the process of forming. He was looking for a comedian who was a little different from the normal stand-ups, and I fitted the bill. It was a fantastic opportunity for me and something that would have guaranteed me at least three years' work in a top show.

Unfortunately, I had to decline the offer straight away because I was contracted to the Popplewell family who owned the *Gaiety Whirls* back up in Ayr and I was only half way through the summer season. I knew in my heart however that the *Showband Show* would put me well on the road to stardom. I travelled back up to Ayr and arranged to meet the Popplewells to let them know of Cyril Stapleton's offer.

Without even a thought for their own show they very kindly released me from my contract and I was indebted to them for that. I had been their star performer and by allowing me to leave they risked losing money for the remainder of the summer season so it was quite a gesture on their part. I have met lots of lovely people touring the theatres all over the country but the Popplewells remain amongst the nicest of all.

Now that I was to become a regular on a nationwide BBC light entertainment show I knew it would mean even more hard work as it was a top class programme with no expense spared. I was comedian/compère for each of the three nights the show was broadcast every week and I had to have new scripts available at all times.

I was still writing all my own material but Bob Monkhouse, who was also starting his career as a comic on the show, sold gags that he and partner Denis Goodwin thought up. They advertised in trade journals and a good script from them probably cost about half of anyone's show salary. I was relieved that I could write all my own stuff.

Bob listened to American radio stations and noted down all the best gags. He and Denis would then change them around to suit British audiences. In those days Bob seemed happier behind the scenes as long as his material was being used. But it wasn't long before he worked at an act and began regularly appearing as a stand-up comedian in his own right.

American joke books were available such as *Boffs Bundles* in which you could find funny stories, rhymes and songs that could be modified for the British audience. I took a great deal of interest in other performers on the *Showband Show*, particularly jazz musician and comedian George Chisholm who sadly passed away a few years ago. George could make his trombone talk and we would jam along together between programmes with another relatively unknown musician called Kenny Baker.

Whenever my name was mentioned in newspaper articles I was always referred to as the former lorry driver from Cardiff. The lead singer on the *Showband Show* right at the start when I joined also had the same trouble as he used to be a bus driver. His name was Matt Monro and he was a lovely chap with a terrific voice and singing style. He could usually be found smoking a cigarette when he was not on stage and I rather think that led to his early death.

The production team behind the show was first class and the producer was Johnny Stewart who went on much later to do *Top of the Pops*. Tom Sloan was another with a big input while Eric Maschwitz, who wrote *A Nightingale Sang in Berkeley Square*, was head of BBC at the time.

Being in the *Showband Show* didn't limit me from appearing elsewhere—I used to regularly be offered spots at other venues. At this time I wrote and produced the first light entertainment television show ever put on by BBC Wales. It was called *Look You Now* and was a series of sketches, songs and guest artists. Later on during its successful run, Terry Nation, the originator of the Daleks, and George Evans wrote a few scripts for the show. During the day they both used to work in Cavendish's, a furniture store in the centre of Cardiff.

I also did a lot of charity performances as these were useful in showing my act to the most important people in the business. I appeared at the London Casino alongside David Hughes, Archie Lewis, George Williams, who had also been in Variety Bandbox, and Jimmy 'Aye Aye! That's yer lot' Wheeler. Later on, in another charity show, I shared the stage with Janet Brown, Jack Warner, the delightful Alma Cogan and the great Gracie Fields, though of course not all at the same time. Nat

Gonella and his Orchestra provided the music.

I worked with Al Martino and Frankie Vaughan in London and also met up for the first time with that great American singing star Johnny Ray and the old black magic man himself, Billy Daniels. I opened a 16-week tour with Billy at the Glasgow Empire and we moved down the country to theatres such as the Gaumont in Bradford and the Manchester Hippodrome. We got on very well together for the whole duration of the tour.

I was now using a lot of accents in my stage act so had the advantage of sounding as though I was a local lad wherever I was performing. That was useful, particularly up in Scotland where they really hated English artists. I never had any trouble though because I let them know I was Welsh. I learned to make use of accents after watching films starring the Bowery Boys, Buster Keaton and the Three Stooges. As well as the accents I also used a lot of one-liners but they were always my own work.

I admired greats such as Jack Benny, Bob Hope, Red Skelton and George Burns who were all masters of that particular craft. I went to see Jack several times when he came to London. Whenever he stepped on to the stage there would be four or five minutes of continuous applause before he could even start his act. He was another to use a stooge and in his case it was a man called Rochester.

Those early days when I was a keen cinemagoer in Cardiff had certainly served me well. I had spent hours in the Coronet in Woodville Road, or the Gaiety in City Road. They were my locals as I was living in Crwys Road at the time but, sadly, neither exist as cinemas anymore. Cinema was true escapism, especially if the film was a Western. Whenever I saw a cowboy film I remembered the time I used to sell ice cream in the cinema in Gowerton while watching Tom Mix and the other heroes of the day.

My act had developed into good wholesome fun and I never had to stoop to smut or to ridiculing members of the audience as that would also have been wrong. You don't want to make unnecessary enemies. Ridicule yourself and people will laugh with you. Perhaps that is one of the reasons my act evolved in the way it did, so much so that I continued to be billed throughout the country as 'Certified Insanely Funny'. There was still a strict code of conduct regarding smut at all theatres around this time and don't forget, what is now known as 'alternative comedy' had not even been thought of in those days.

Butlins had a notice posted up in all their camps that stated clearly what they expected of their performers.

Parents don't want it
Children don't understand it
And we won't have it.

Sadly that has all changed now.

While still appearing three times a week with the *Showband Show* I had the biggest break of my career to date when I was booked to appear at the most prestigious theatre in the world, the London Palladium.

4

THE LONDON
PALLADIUM

*'Dorothy [Squires] had been having a difficult time . . . The
last time she had appeared at the Palladium was way back
in 1947 when she was brought in after 'Two Ton' Tessie O'Shea
had fallen off an elephant. Quite what Tessie was doing on
the beast I don't know, but the thought of it still makes my
eyes water . . .'*

* * * * *

There is no doubt that the London Palladium is one of the top
theatres in the world and only the very best acts are ever
invited to appear there. The building itself dates back to 1886
when it housed the famous Hengler's Circus. Alterations were
made and in 1910 the present building was completed and
took its present name. The theatre played host to all the great
music hall names of the day before briefly becoming a cinema
and then, in 1928, reverting back to a variety theatre.

It was July 1953 and I knew about a couple of months
beforehand that I had been booked to appear for two weeks.
I was doubly delighted when I knew Billy Daniels would be
top of the bill as we got on so well. He had liked my
impersonation of Johnny Ray which I was featuring in my act
and when his show had finished its 16-week run he asked me
to go to America to tour the States with him. I was approached

by the Music Corporation of America who wanted to represent me in the States. They would have 'farmed' me out to various syndicates over there. What that meant was that they would be paid a sum of money for allowing me to appear on a show and then they would have paid me—obviously less than they received.

I didn't want to uproot Betty and Roger so kindly refused the offer but every time Billy crossed the Atlantic to work in this country he asked me to be part of the tour. We ended up going all round Britain several times together. To play the Palladium was every performer's dream. If you appeared there and the act went down well, you had arrived.

The Palladium was the top of the tree. It was **the** place to perform. I had been there before as a paying customer to see one of my all-time favourite artists, Jimmy Durante, while on another occasion I went to see the great Jack Benny at work. If I was appearing in any of the theatres around London I would always take the opportunity of going to a show at the Palladium. This would usually be on a Wednesday afternoon when they put on a matinee performance. The front row was usually filled by old music hall professionals. It was daunting doing your act knowing that fellow entertainers were there en bloc watching you.

Your whole life changes once you are booked to play the Palladium and I am very proud to say I appeared there on a number of occasions, also doing the television version of *Sunday Night at the London Palladium*. The trick was proving you were good enough to the people at the Moss Empire. If you did that then they gave you a chance, but only after seeing how you did at places such as the Nottingham Empire, in Bournemouth, Brighton, and all the big theatres in their group. It was really a grooming for stardom. But until you conquered the Finsbury Park Empire you wouldn't be booked for the Palladium.

There was a discipline to performing in those early days of my career and providing you followed the ground rules the people at Moss Empire would do all they could to help you. One of the bookers for the organisation was Ted Gollop and another was Cissie Williams. They would always be at the Finsbury Park Empire on a Monday to watch the act before deciding if it was good enough to be taken to the Palladium.

But the toughest of all theatres was the Glasgow Empire. If you succeeded there it really was a feather in your cap. Many a good act has died a death there and I can recall Des O'Connor pretending to faint so that he could get off stage. He told me that as soon as he went on he could feel the hostility towards him and nothing he could say or do would ever have changed it on that particular night. So he fell to the floor in a fake faint, the curtains were pulled, and he was able to beat a hasty retreat out of Glasgow.

Of course, Des has since worked many times up in Scotland and he is as well-loved up there now as he is in all the other parts of the country. But in those days at the Glasgow Empire—if they liked you, they let you live. Once you had conquered those theatres, an appearance at the Palladium pushed up your value and many performers appeared regularly at the great theatre. For example the impersonator Eddie Arnold was booked almost monthly as was Max Bygraves.

Sunday Night at the London Palladium was a totally different show. We played twice nightly, at 6.00pm and also 8.15pm with a Wednesday Matinee at 2.45pm, whereas Sunday night was staged specially for television. Bruce Forsyth, my old army mate Norman Vaughan, and Jimmy Tarbuck all made their names as compères for the Sunday show. I played football with Tarby the week before he took over the job of compère while still a relatively unknown comic. I remember that time well because we played at Ashton-under-Lyne and I fell awkwardly during the game and broke my wrist. By then I was piloting my own plane and I came back home flying one-handed. If the authorities knew of my injury then I wouldn't have been allowed to sit in the cockpit.

The weekly Palladium show did not have the same format as Sunday night so had no need of a compère. Incidentally, ticket prices at the Palladium at that time, with all seats bookable in advance, ranged from 2/6d (12p) to 14/6d (72p).

Billy Daniels was an important artist with a big say in who joined him on the bill. Maybe he helped me get there, I don't know. If he did I am grateful because we all need a little help now and again. And remember, he only wanted an act if it helped the show.

American performers never minded other acts grasping the limelight because they knew they would take it back when it came to their turn. Unfortunately, a number of British artists never had that same philosophy. American stars had about 70% say in the make-up of the show. They could request artists from all over the world.

I was appearing in Glasgow when the time came for me to travel down to London for my two week booking at the Palladium. I caught the overnight train, carrying my stage suit and instruments, and took a taxi from Kings Cross to the theatre. It was 7.30am and apart from a security man the whole place was empty. I was allowed to leave my suit and instruments before going off to look for an early breakfast. I found a place called Express Dairies open and had a good fry-up before making my way back to the theatre around 9.00am.

That was the time when rehearsals started and every artist had to lay out his 'band parts' in a line on a first come-first served basis. After a chat with the Musical Director, it was Wolfie Phillips when I made my debut there, the band played through my opening music. They only needed to do it once and then I was ushered away and the next act took over. When everyone was finished it was the turn of Billy Daniels' accompanist Benny Payne who would run through the top star's routine.

I had to cut my act down from Glasgow as I was doing a longer set up there so had to be careful with what I left in as each artist had an allotted time. A live performance is very fluid and it is a fantastic feeling when it goes right and when it does, it seems to be over so quickly. But you had to stick rigidly with your script as it would put the whole show out if you over-ran.

There is no better feeling than working at the London Palladium and then knowing that your act has gone down well with the audience. It was nothing to do with money. It was all about succeeding at the greatest theatre in the world. I was paid around £300 for each week, two shows per night and so it meant a lot of hard work. Billy Daniels would probably have been earning £3,000 for a week as well as taking a percentage of the profits.

I had been given my own dressing room on the first floor as I was third billing along with a ventriloquist called Chris Cross. In second spot after Billy was an impressionist called Dave Apollon. He was also a banjo player and had first appeared at the Palladium way back in 1934. After completing my act I was coming back down to earth in my dressing room when there was a knock on the door. I opened up and standing there was a small gentleman with a moustache and dark-rimmed spectacles.

'I just thought I would let you know that you were great tonight son,' he said. It was none other than the songwriter,

Sammy Kahn.

The following evening Billy De Wolfe, who had also been in the audience, took the trouble to look me up and said, 'I just wanted you to know I thoroughly enjoyed your performance'.

But the finest accolade came at the end of the first week when Billy introduced me to his World Manager. Yes, he was that big in the entertainment industry that he also had a World Manager. His name was Rasputin, but he wasn't Russian, and he was smoking a huge cigar which I remember had a gold ring round it.

'You've got it kid,' he said and tapped me on the arm.

I still have the programme for that show and written inside is a short note from Cyril Stapleton who was also in the audience. It says simply—'Congratulations you were wonderful'. I will never forget Billy Daniels. He was a lovely man who started his career working in the clubs of America during the prohibition era. He even had to use the back doors in some of the places because of the colour bar in operation in many states. He actually came to my house for tea when we were on the same show in Cardiff and he was always interested in how my career was developing. Many times he asked me to go to the States to be on his show as he knew my act would go down well over there. He was the top guest when Eamonn Andrews did my *This Is Your Life* programme and sent over a video message from Salt Lake City where he was performing.

There were many descriptions of Billy's voice but a couple that stand the test of time and I remember are these: 'Billy Daniels sang as though he had a swarm of bees down his neck'; 'He sings in a voice of chocolate cream wrapped in silk'. Another described his facial contortions while he was singing, 'Daniels rolls his eyes, twists his face in alternate agony and ecstasy, and hugs his ear in the manner of one selling coal or buying rags and bones'. So you can see why a Billy Daniels impression always went down well during my act.

You cannot imagine what it was like to have played the Palladium and received top reviews. Doing it once would have been enough in anyone's career but I was lucky enough to have been booked there, and done well, on a number of occasions. A host of top stars were lined up for when our two week run was over. Guy Mitchell came next followed by Bud Abbot and Lou Costello, then Kay Starr, Frankie Laine and finally, the great man himself, Bob Hope.

My next time at the Palladium was a year later when Johnny Ray headed the bill. He had a huge following and his fans even broke down the stage door to try to get a glimpse of him. He was one of the first idols to have such a fan base and he certainly knew how to play to his audience.

He would walk on to the stage slightly pigeon-toed with the palm of his hand up to his ear where he wore a hearing aid. That wasn't for show, he really did have a problem with his hearing and he told me that he had worn a hearing aid since he was 14 years old. His trousers would be two inches short to show off his bobby-socks. He had his first break in 1951 with a song he wrote himself called 'The Little White Cloud That Cried'.

Once he started singing his hit numbers such as 'Just Walking in the Rain', or 'Cry', the audience would begin screaming and shouting, and it wasn't just the young girls. Johnny appealed to the older fans as well who just wanted to 'mother' him as he had that 'little boy lost' look about him. He had an emotional delivery when he sang a song and it was perfect for comedians and mimics like me. It was quite funny really because I had been doing a Johnny Ray impersonation in my act for some time and had decided to keep it in for the two weeks at the Palladium. He was amused by it and would stand in the wings watching me whilst shaking his head and laughing.

Unlike Billy Daniels, I could never get close to Johnny Ray. He always had a couple of minders to look after him and they kept him out of the way of the other acts but on a few occasions we did meet up back stage for a little chat. From what I did see of him I think he was a genuinely nice bloke even though he was cosseted so closely by his managers. He faded from popularity in the States in the late fifties but continued to shine over here and also in Australia where he toured more than any other American artist. Liver problems finally caught up with him and he died in February 1990 aged 63.

I was back for a two week stint at the Palladium in May 1955 when the Four Aces, America's top vocal group, headlined. Also appearing on the show were Kitty Kallen and the Billy Cotton Band Show. The Four Aces began when two of the lads were serving in the US Navy. After discharge they joined up with the other two in Pennsylvania but to begin with they were an instrumental combo, although they soon discovered that they were better vocalists than musicians. They sold over a million copies of their first record 'It's No Sin', although they had to start their own record label to get it off the ground. Eventually they were signed up by Decca and their second song, 'Tell Me Why' also sold a million. Perhaps we remember them more for the themes from the films *Three Coins in the Fountain*, and *Love Is a Many Splendoured Thing*.

Pretty Kitty Kallen, as she was known, began as a child performer in Philadelphia. She won an amateur talent contest doing imitations of some of the singers of the day. When she was 17 she joined the band of Jack Teagarden before moving on to the Jimmy Dorsey Orchestra where she sang on the number one best seller, 'Besame Mucho'. Later on she worked with the band of trumpet ace, Harry James.

Then she left the business rather mysteriously for two years before bouncing back to record monster hits such as 'Little Things Mean a Lot' and 'In the Chapel in the Moonlight'. She told me a rather strange story that happened to her at the height of her popularity. She had no less than three imposters who worked the music halls billing themselves as Kitty Kallen. When one of them died, it was reported that the real Kitty had passed away and she had a lot of explaining to do to prove she was alive, well and still singing.

Billy Cotton was famous for his radio shows, particularly *Wakey Wakey*. His resident singers were Alan Breeze, Doreen Stephens and Kathy Kay, and he had a 12 girl dance group called the Leslie Roberts Silhouettes. Despite getting on, Billy was about 55 when we did the Palladium together, he insisted on joining in the dance routines with the girls. He formed his first dance band in 1924 and found success through his popular radio show which ran for almost 20 years. He had been a pilot in the RFC and was seriously injured in a crash. Whenever we met we compared notes about flying. He was one of the best-liked people in the business and had a lovable personality.

Alan Breeze was a wonderful commercial singer yet surprisingly, he stuttered very badly during normal conversation and it was sometimes very difficult for him to communicate. Many artists launched their careers on the back of the *Billy Cotton Band Show* including Russ Conway, Mrs Mills, Ted Rogers and my old pal Roy Hudd. Billy liked nothing better than racing cars and he told me that his favourite tracks were at Brooklands and along the seafront at St Helier in Jersey where he used to race until early in the 1950s. He was also a useful footballer for Brentford in his younger days and he actually turned out for me briefly in one of our charity matches.

My next appearance at the Palladium was slightly different in that it was for one night only. I was to take part in one of television's most-watched shows, *Sunday Night at the London Palladium*, and the star for that night was a long time favourite of mine, none other than Bob Hope. It seemed that many years had passed since I had been privileged to watch the great man in action when he was appearing at that American Servicemen's Camp in Sully, Glamorgan during the early part of the war. Ever since that night, and watching him with Bing Crosby in the Road films, I had been a fan of his and now here I was, 24 February 1956, actually appearing on the same bill in the world's greatest theatre.

For the Sunday night TV show there was little time to rehearse. I arrived at the theatre in the morning, sorted out the music I wanted, cut my act to the time specified, and that was it. There were no recordings in those days, after all, this was live television so you only had the one chance to get everything right. Once I knew what time schedule I was allotted I was able once again to decide what part of the act to leave in, and what needed to be taken out, as of course my normal act would have gone on for much longer than would be required.

The compère for the show was Tommy Trinder, yes the same Tommy that I auditioned for at the New Theatre in Cardiff way back when I was just 17 years old. During a rest break in the afternoon we had a cup of tea together and talked about the time I parked my Pickfords' lorry outside the New Theatre in Cardiff before nipping in to do my act for him. Even though he must have auditioned loads of would-be performers during his time in the business, Tommy remembered that particular occasion when he turned me down just because he reckoned I looked like him and could put him out of work.

When the time came for me to perform I was called from my dressing room and stood waiting in the wings as Tommy made the introduction. The act couldn't have gone better. The audience played its part in full and in no time at all the curtain came down and it was all over. You get a special buzz when you know everything has worked out perfectly and that night I had the biggest buzz I had ever experienced.

I sorted myself out during the interval and then made my way back stage in time to watch the master of the one-liners, Bob Hope. One thing that immediately surprised me was that Bob made full use of what we called 'idiot boards'. They were cards placed conveniently around the front of the stage, unseen by the audience, on which were written topical gags. I could fully understand why he had to use the boards. Firstly, he was working so much that it would have been almost impossible to learn all the new material and secondly, he liked to be topical so up-to-the-minute events would be included in his act. Of course, he had a large team of scriptwriters to deliver all this new material but at the end of the day, the delivery came from the man himself and he was impeccable with that.

Don't forget, the best ad-libs are the well rehearsed ones. He was kept well apart from the rest of us in the show so I didn't get to speak to him either before or after the performance. People at that level in the profession are generally on a different wave-length to the rest of us but that never bothered me, not with Bob Hope anyway. I did eventually meet up with him, but he was 94 by then. He became Baby Rat in the Grand Order of Water Rats. The last one to join is always known as Baby Rat. Almost everyone in the business became a Water Rat but funnily enough, my old pals Eric Morecambe and Ernie Wise never did.

On the Monday after the show everyone hurried to read

the papers to see what the critics thought of the show. Fortunately, they were all unanimous in their praise and I was singled out for a very special mention in the *News Chronicle*. The headlines read 'Pupil Outgags the Master' and I still have a copy of that review in my scrapbooks. It went on to say

> *The appearance of Bob Hope on Sunday Night at the London Palladium was a special television event. It was a great pity that last night his wonderful technique was not accompanied by a better script. Our very own Stan Stennett seemed to me to be very much funnier.*

That was a personal triumph for me and while I would never suggest that I was as good as the great Bob Hope, it was pleasing to have such good reviews.

My next visit to the London Palladium was 6 June 1963 when I was privileged to be asked to join a Royal Midnight Performance in the presence of HRH Princess Marina, Duchess of Kent. The show was called *D-Day With The Stars* and was in aid of the Army Benevolent Fund of which Her Majesty the Queen was Patron. Naturally enough, there was an army theme throughout the show and after RSM Brittain had called everyone 'On Parade' the show started with the lovely Susan Maugham in excerpts from her summer show *Swing Along*. A few years later I was in pantomime with Susan and she was a delight to work with.

Then it was time for the King Brothers, a very popular act, before an amusing sketch about the resistance movement starring my old CSE pal, Norman Vaughan. He was assisted by that well-known film star Richard Todd, comedy actor Richard Wattis and Sheree Winton.

After a musical and dance interlude it was time for my spot

and I was in a funny sketch called 'Wartime Concert' where I played the part of the NAAFI comic. Also appearing with me were Alma Cogan, Reg Varney, Spike Milligan, Frank Ifield and the Forces Sweetheart herself, Vera Lynn. It all seemed to go down well with the audience despite the limited rehearsal time given to everyone.

The second half of the show was much as the first with comedy sketches and music. Harry H. Corbett and Wilfrid Brambell, now well known as Steptoe and Son, Jimmy Edwards, Eric Sykes and Hattie Jacques were all in a sketch called 'Calling Up Papers', so you see the Forces theme was kept throughout the show. The younger members of the audience, and those watching later when the event was shown on television, were pleased to see their idols Gary Miller and Adam Faith on stage before the night's entertainment was brought to a close by Anna Neagle.

As an ex-soldier it was wonderful for me to be part of a great occasion for such a good cause, and it was a fitting evening to be held at the best theatre in the World.

I was delighted to show my support for a dear friend, Dorothy Squires, by appearing in her own show at the Palladium in December 1970. Johnny Tudor was also on the bill that evening. Dorothy had been having a difficult time and for some reason wasn't getting the attention that a singer of her class should have received. Just like me, she was having a problem with television bookings, or the lack of them, and had not appeared on the small screen for nine years despite her many record successes.

The last time she had appeared at the Palladium was way back in 1947 when she was brought in after 'Two Ton' Tessie O'Shea had fallen off an elephant. Quite what Tessie was doing on the beast I don't know, but the thought of it still makes my eyes water and yes, it was true. So Dorothy decided to hire the London Palladium and put on her own production. It was a marvellous success as we all knew it would be. She almost brought the house down with her rendition of 'Say it with Flowers'.

Llanelli-born Dorothy staked £5,000 of her own money to prove she was still a star attraction and worthy of more West End and TV work, and it came off spectacularly as it resulted in an extensive tour of Britain and singing contracts in Las Vegas. She was in fabulous form and the packed audience loved all her numbers including 'My Way' and 'For Once in My Life'.

Her dressing room was packed to overflowing with well-wishers after the show, me included, but when she heard there were dozens of Welsh fans among those outside waiting for a glimpse of her before they made their way to Paddington Station for the night train home, she immediately went out into the cold to meet them. She just about made even on the night in financial terms, because as well as the huge outlay to hire the Palladium itself, she also had to pay for the orchestra, the arranger and conductor, a pianist, treat herself to a £500 gown, and pay for all the advertising.

The gown of beige chiffon with jewels, pearls and ostrich feathers failed to arrive at the stage door until the National Anthem was played to start the show, but Dorothy remained calm. While she changed, I kept the first half going in quickfire style with Johnny Tudor. My spot also gave me a chance to introduce Billy and Bonzo to the audience. They were going to be the leads in my Christmas pantomime in Porthcawl that year.

I knew exactly how Dorothy was feeling during the performance because the previous summer I had staked everything on producing my own summer show in Porthcawl. The second half of the programme lasted almost two hours instead of the scheduled one hour, yet no one left the theatre before the finale. She had a five-minute standing ovation from the capacity audience at the end and she found time to give me a special hug.

Seven or eight years later I was back on *Sunday Night at the London Palladium* on a bill headed by Guy Mitchell. Guy was a country and western singer who had moved into the pop music world. His recording of 'Singing the Blues' which he released in 1956 sold on the pop, country and R&B charts all at once, such was his appeal to a vast audience. The record sold a staggering 12 million copies worldwide and was number one in the charts for an astonishing 10 weeks. Funnily enough, Tommy Steele did a cover version in this country and that also sold well.

Guy and I never had chance for a long chat but when we did have a break for a coffee he told me that his real name was Al Cernik and it was his music producer who suggested a change. His name was Mitch Miller and as he thought Al was a good 'guy', he became Guy Mitchell. He liked nothing better than going out riding when he toured and he especially enjoyed the fields around Marshfield and Castleton when he worked in South Wales.

Also on the bill that Sunday night was a new comedian called Jimmy Cricket, the one who wore wellies with Left and Right written on them. He was a pleasant enough young lad but I have not seen or heard of him for a while though I think he is still in the business.

I am sure there is still an audience for variety shows like that, providing quality performers are used. There used to be nothing better than sitting down in a theatre, or at home in front of the television, watching a variety show with dancers, singers, comedians, speciality acts, and of course a big star. Sadly those days now seem long gone.

It was not until a few years later that I made my final appearance on the London Palladium stage. By now I had been a Water Rat for many years and the show Rats Revels was put on in June 1989 to celebrate the centenary of the Grand Order of Water Rats. The list of artists attending was a Who's Who of the music hall. Just about everybody in the business was there that night and a great time was had by all. It was particularly good to meet up with fellow performers I hadn't seen for many years and it provided a fitting end to my appearances at the London Palladium.

5

ON WITH THE SHOWS

'Ken Dodd used to say that he knew Lonnie [Donegan] when he sang in English. He also said that he knew Nancy Whiskey when she was a small tot—so you can tell that Doddy used to write his own scripts.'

* * * * *

Of course in between my Palladium appearances I carried on working all over the country. I even had my own comic strip in *Radio Fun*. That lasted for almost two years and helped keep me in the public eye. It was on the lines of the *Dandy* or *Beano* comics and had cartoon strip adventures.

In 1953 I found myself at the State Theatre, Kilburn in front of two packed audiences for the early and late shows totalling almost 7,000 theatregoers. Ronnie Aldrich and the Squadronaires were on the bill along with the lovely Ruby Murray, Audrey Jeans and Frankie Vaughan. Ruby was a quiet little Irish girl but I think she was handled wrongly and so never achieved the heights she should have. At one time she had an incredible five records in the Top Twenty including probably her most famous song, 'Softly, Softly'. She married one of the Jones Boys, Bernie Burgess who now lives in Spain. I am still in touch with Bernie and he calls me fairly regularly for a chat. Poor Ruby couldn't take the fame and adulation and died while still quite young.

I had a tremendous ovation at both houses and it was

another step for me along the road to stardom. The State was a huge place and anyone who could hold an audience of that size was on the right road. I played there a number of times and remember performing in one show when Al Martino was the star. He made the song 'Spanish Eyes' famous and was a typical American singer of the time. There were rumours that he had links with a number of American gangsters and that the character in the film *The Godfather* who woke up in bed next to a horse's head was based on Martino. Whether that was true or not I don't know but it was certainly the story going around the theatres.

Around this time I also appeared with Joan Regan and Tommy Fields. Joan had honey blond hair and sang popular ballads. We appeared together a number of times and have kept in touch ever since. I still meet up with her occasionally to talk over old times and in May 2006 we appeared together at the City of Varieties in Leeds in another show full of nostalgia.

Tommy was the brother of the legendary Gracie Fields who I was lucky enough to meet on many occasions. It was in April 1953 that I first appeared on a show with Gracie. It was at the Princes Theatre, Shaftesbury Avenue and it was an annual show in aid of the Variety Artists Ladies Guild and Orphanage of which Gracie was president. Her Royal Highness the Duchess of Kent attended.

Many top stars gave their time including George Martin, the well-known television and radio comedian, Ian Wallace, famous much later for his 'Glorious Mud' song but then just a bass baritone from the Glyndebourne Opera, and female impressionist Janet Brown. Anona Winn, who came to fame on *Twenty Questions*, sang some songs, Archie Lewis and Jimmy Wheeler went on in the second half as did Jack Warner who was famous for his acting roles and particularly for being

Dixon in the show *Dixon of Dock Green* on BBC television. Gracie herself then brought the rafters down with her own unique style of singing.

Ernie Cash, my agent, was doing a tremendous job for me and I always seemed to be in work. I was grateful for everything he did even though he slowed up in later years when perhaps I should have moved on to other agents. During the summer I became part of the Billy Daniels tour appearing at places like the Glasgow Empire, Manchester Hippodrome and Gaumont, Bradford.

I was delighted to get great reviews during the run with one from the *Manchester Evening Chronicle* that was particularly good. The critic spoke in glowing terms of Billy Daniels but then wrote: 'Good to report that running him close in the honours race is a surprisingly good dish of comedy from Stan Stennett.'

I am sure that the success of shows like that, and the reviews that followed, led me to my first appearance at the Palladium. Summer Shows followed in this 1953 Coronation year and I played at the Arcadia Theatre in Skegness before appearing in the very last show to be staged at the Shepherds Bush Empire before it became BBC TV studios.

Heading the bill was Rob Wilton while Al Monte had two spots. Rob Wilton was a well-known comedian but he was another who started out playing character parts, usually melodramatic villains. He found that he was getting laughs so decided that comedy was the path to follow. He was originally billed as 'The Confidential Comedian' but later became famous for his sketches about incompetent officialdom. 'The day war broke out . . .' is still remembered by all devotees of Wilton wit.

By October I was at the Empress in Brixton. I finished the first half of the show and Sid Millward and the Nitwits closed it up in true Millward manner. I hadn't seen Sid and the boys since our army days out in Italy.

Then it was panto time once again and I was heading for the Lyceum Theatre in Sheffield to appear in *Babes in the Wood*. I was Baron Baddun's page called Billy and the great Freddie Sales was Nurse Marryme. In true pantomime fashion, Robin Hood and his Merry Men were worked into the story. Maid Marian was played by the lovely Mary Millar, known as the girl with the golden voice. Some of you may recall Mary in the television series *Keeping Up Appearances*. She played the rather flighty sister of Mrs Bucket who wore those brief skirts and always had a whole flock of men friends hanging about.

Of course there has to be 'baddies' in any panto and that particular year was the first time I met Eric Morecambe and Ernie Wise. They were placed down the bill playing the part of a pair of robbers. My friendship with the two funny men lasted for many years until their untimely deaths. Opening night was Christmas Eve at 7.00pm and except for Christmas Day, it was also performed at 2.30pm.

In the schoolroom scene poor Billy had the blame for everything and of course I kept having beatings from the teacher. I used to receive letters at the theatre from little boys and girls telling me not to worry as they were all sticking up for me. They said that if those robbers ever came to their school they would get their own back on them. That surely meant that our audiences whether young or old were entering into the spirit of it. That is the beauty of a good pantomime.

During the run in Sheffield I was able to do other things on Sundays when the theatre was shut. Usually it was a cabaret spot at some of the night clubs around the city. In January and February 1954 I did a series of shows at various theatres but mainly in the London area. I appeared alongside Ronnie

Aldrich and the Squadronaires, Tito Burns and his Band and Joan Regan, who had by now become a well known radio and television star. I had worked with both Ronnie and Joan before and it was good to see them again.

In between working for BBC Radio in *Welsh Rarebit*, doing the *Showband Show* and other programmes, I also toured the country. For the first time I found myself appearing in Middlesbrough at the Empire Theatre where I was top of the bill. The show included a puppeteer, a mad musician, three skaters, a trampoline act and Tibor Alexander's Revue. Believe it or not, that act consisted of 20 dogs and a monkey. Don't even think about it—it's a long time since we have seen variety shows with bills like that.

I did a summer Sunday night show at the Spa Pavilion in Felixstowe in a superb location right on the sea front. The theatre seated about 1,000 and it was packed full when I was there in July. The format was one top performer plus the resident band. The band was the Jerry Allen Septet who spent the rest of the week playing at the Pier Pavilion.

Following me one week later was Benny Hill, then Tommy Trinder, and also booked to appear was Peter Brough and Archie Andrews. Peter Brough made his name on radio as a ventriloquist. I know it seems crazy but it's true. Whenever he made Archie speak you could always see his mouth saying the words. He was probably one of the worst vents ever seen on the stage but that never seemed to matter. Archie Andrews became so popular on radio that Peter Brough got away with it when they appeared on television.

Ernie Cash had me back at the Winter Gardens in Margate for a Midnight Matinee in aid of charity. Finishing the first half was none other than Hutch, who was a huge star at the time singing and playing piano. Also on the bill was comedienne Suzette Tarri who went on just before me. She was on the radio more than on the stage and usually finished her act by singing 'Red Sails in the Sunset'. It was an endless round of theatres as Ernie kept me busy all through the year. I was also often on radio and my bill matter now had 'Radio's New Star' added to my usual 'Certified Insanely Funny'.

It wouldn't have been the same without a trip up north and I was delighted when Ernie booked me for a week in November back at the Gaiety Theatre in Ayr which was still run by the Popplewells. I was so glad to be working back there even though there was also an act on the show called Tex James—with his ponies, dogs and a monkey. That combination seemed to be popular with audiences whichever part of the country they were in.

There was just time to do a Celebrity Charity Concert in Manchester along with my friend Joan Regan and Eddie Arnold before it was back to pantomime. This year's offering was *Babes in the Wood* at the Hippodrome in Derby and I had top billing playing Silly Billy while Morecambe and Wise were once again the two robbers called Marmaduke and Horace. Ernie always played the Bad Robber and Eric was the Good Robber. I just loved pantomime time.

I met the great Joe Loss early in 1955 when I guested on his Band Show along with Jack Jackson who was famous for his radio record programmes.

In February 1955 I shared the stage with the 'irresponsible' Max Wall at the Odeon in Plymouth. We were the only two acts along with the Squadronaires, directed by Ronnie Aldrich, who provided the music. I did the first half and Max completed the second half.

Before yet another visit to the London Palladium in May, I had the good fortune to be booked to appear at the New Theatre in Cardiff a few weeks earlier. It gave me the chance of sampling some rare home life. It is always a pleasure to appear in your own home town although somehow there is usually a little more pressure. People seem to expect too much from their own, and the saying 'A prophet in his own town has no honour' is very true.

Top of the bill was the glamorous Radio, Stage, Film and television singing star Frances Day while I had second billing. Further down a new comedian called Des O'Connor was beginning to make his way.

After my third appearance at the Palladium I was booked to appear at the Empire, Finsbury Park where Ray Burns, a friend of mine from the *Showband Show*, was also on the bill. He was a fine singer and recording star. The Radio Revellers and Daisy May with Saveen also entertained the full houses we played to at every performance.

Not long after that booking I met up with Ruby Murray once again at the Winter Garden, Eastbourne. She was a huge recording star with hits such as 'Let Me Go Lover', 'Heartbeat' and 'Evermore'. Jon Pertwee was also on the show and it was the first time I worked with comedian Harry Worth.

Ernie Cash couldn't resist booking me in at the Winter Gardens, Margate and it seemed like home from home when I appeared there in August. The ragtime pianist Joe 'Mr Piano' Henderson and the man with the golden trumpet, Eddie Calvert, were also on the bill. Joe called himself the 'Jekyll and Hyde man'. When I bumped into him backstage I asked him how he got that tag and he told me that he was a business man publishing music as a composer, while also being a performing artist. Sometimes he didn't know which part of himself he was using so that was why he coined the phrase.

As well as the New Theatre in Cardiff, shows were also produced at the Gaumont Theatre which was situated in Queen Street. I just had time for a trip back home to appear with the Eric Delaney Band before it was off for summer season in the Fol-de-Rols in Scarborough. It was typical good family entertainment and Leslie Crowther told a story or two while maestro of the keyboard, Semprini, played 'old ones, new ones, loved ones and neglected ones'.

It was around this time that I had the very great pleasure of taking over from Bud Flanagan in *Jokers Wild* at the Victoria Palace. Bud was nursing an injured knee so I became part of the Crazy Gang until he recovered and it was a big opportunity for me. I was even able to use his dressing room and props, and it was a great privilege to be amongst such well-respected performers.

I enjoyed that experience so much that later on I stepped in one night for Dave King at the Adelphi in London while he did a television show. I had learned quickly that you have to take every chance that you get in this business because the trouble with opportunity is that it always looks bigger going than coming. That was something Dave never considered. On the way up the ladder he made a number of enemies and just when he thought that he had finally cracked it, the rug was pulled from beneath his feet and he suddenly found work hard to come by. He began doing some straight acting parts as the variety jobs dried up but never again did he reach the heights of popularity that he once enjoyed.

Travelling up and down the country was becoming very time-consuming so in March, 1955, at the ripe old age of 30, I decided to have my first flying lesson at the old Pengam Airport in Cardiff. Flying was to become one of the loves of my life.

In January 1956 I appeared at the Trocadero Theatre, Elephant and Castle with Europe's greatest band attraction, Ted Heath and his Music. I was a guest star along with Bill Maynard from *Great Scott—it's Maynard*. The Ted Heath Band produced a great sound and Don Lusher, who became a pal of mine, was an expert with the trombone. Bill Maynard had started out as a double act with Terry Scott before going solo. He was a tall, thin lad with a quizzical expression during those early days, nothing like the character of Greengrass that he later played so well in ITV's *Heartbeat*. By a strange coincidence, I worked with Bill when I did one of the early episodes of *Heartbeat* for Yorkshire Television.

My time in the *Showband Show* was coming to an end but there was no let-up in bookings and Ernie Cash was still in the money because he was keeping me very busy. My style of comedy seemed to be back in favour. The age of radio stifled visual comedy and bred raconteurs who needed nothing in the way of costume except a lounge suit or evening dress. They didn't need to look funny, a string of gags was all they required. But now the trend was coming back to vision and that definitely suited my style. After all, my heroes were Red Skelton, Buster Keaton, Groucho Marx and Jimmy James, all people who used facial expressions to emphasise a gag.

Summer season was at the Palace Theatre, Manchester with Jimmy Young, my old friend Jon Pertwee, and a very funny lady with a thousand voices called Joan Turner. That was yet another happy show where I first came across the George Mitchell singers. Incidentally, right at the bottom of the bill was a little known comic called Ronnie Corbett just beginning to make his way in the business.

In no time at all it was September and I was in yet another Moss Empires show. This was at the Empire, Glasgow and the star was Lonnie Donegan with his Skiffle Group. Lonnie was a lovely chap who had found sudden chart success with 'Rock Island Line' and 'Lost John'. I was second billing and finished the first half of the show.

On the third night of our week playing to packed houses, one of Lonnie's guitarists injured his arm and was unable to play. There was only one thing to do—I stepped in and played the rest of the week as a member of Lonnie's skiffle group. What a great experience that was. We spent a lot of time together and although Lonnie was very sure of himself, he was still a good mate. He was not a very robust man however, and I think the strain of performing led to his early death.

Pantomime in 1956 was *Dick Whittington* at the Dudley Hippodrome. Playing the captain and his mate were my old pals, Morecambe and Wise. Ernie was the captain and Eric was the mate. As usual Ernie told the mate what to do and generally gave him a dog's life. I have never lost my love of pantomime. Betty and Roger came up to Dudley with me and we stayed in a caravan beside the theatre. We were not the only ones there as next door to us was Ernie Wise and his wife in their 'van, while further along was the principal 'boy' and her husband who were next to Dick Whittington's cat and his wife.

While we were in Dudley I decided to form my own football team with me at centre forward. We organised a match between the Dudley panto staff and the staff from the Wolverhampton Grand Theatre led by Teddy Johnson. It was all in aid of charity but they took it a little more seriously than we did, well what would you expect when Eric and Ernie were playing in your side? But we won 6–1 and it whetted my appetite for more. I went on to arrange numerous matches and meet many famous footballers and sports stars over the next few years.

Early in 1957 I was asked to go to Cyprus to entertain the troops stationed there. It was a three-week tour with the Combined Services Entertainment Unit and a few artists joined me including the lovely blonde actress, Vera Day. She was the constant recipient of wolf whistles from the lads. That reminds me of an old saying, 'A man is not middle-aged until the girl he is whistling at thinks he is calling the dog'.

I devised my own show which I called *Musical Cheers* and it went down so well that I was hailed as the best comedian ever to set foot on the island. Perhaps not so many funny men used to go there in those days. It was a fast-moving, slick, two hours of entertainment. As well as Britain's 'Pocket Venus', as Vera was known, I also had Lou Campara and Lisbeth Lennon out there with me. My greatest difficulty was getting off the stage after the shows. In one show I gave no less than 12 encores.

The trip was so well received that George Brightwell, Controller of CSE in London, actually wrote to Ernie Cash. He gave a warm description of the success of the tour and also sent a request from Cyprus that we should all be sent back to do it again very soon. Mind you, the trip did start off on the wrong foot. When I arrived in Cyprus all my luggage was searched and in my props they found my cowboy outfit and two shiny six-shooters. I protested that they were only props but I was still forced to hand the guns over. They were worried that if terrorists got hold of them they could use them for hold-ups.

After the Cyprus trip we had time for a short family holiday in Spain before it was back to work. On our return I went to Blackpool to star at the Hippodrome in a big revue called *Rocking With Laughter* which was produced by Tom Arnold. Three of us, all up-and-coming in the profession, would jointly be the stars of the show.

Besides me, there was a young comic called Ken Dodd. He had shot to stardom by providing more laughs to the minute than any other top comedian of the day. He had a good singing voice and could have been a straight singer if comedy hadn't got in the way. The previous year Blackpool had been plagued by balloons which, when inflated, revealed a caricature of buck-toothed Ken who even in those early days understood the need for publicity. There were no balloons when we appeared together but he did have a box of ashtrays with his photograph on that he gave away. Incidentally, he insured his protruding teeth for £10,000—and was forbidden to eat even one stick of rock. Not many people knew that he had finished with his long time girlfriend whose home was in Swansea. The walk home each night had begun to get him down.

The third star was the glamour in the show, the beautiful sapphire blonde Jill Day. Jill came from Brighton and her first job in show business was as a teenager in a *Tom Arnold Ice Show* in her home town. Then she joined Sid Dean to sing with his band and made her first radio broadcast. She worked in cabaret in Paris for a year before returning to England to join Geraldo's Orchestra. Her chance came in the West End when she took over from a dear old friend of mine Joan Turner in the *Talk of the Town* at the Adelphi where she co-starred with Jimmy Edwards and Tony Hancock. This led to her own TV series which confirmed that as well as being a lovely girl she was also very talented. By a strange coincidence Lisbeth Lennon, who had been in Cyprus with me, was also a member of the company.

This was my first seasonal show in what was renowned as Britain's mecca of summer entertainment. Every year a score or more of the country's top stars went to tower country to entertain the holiday crowds. I was thrilled to have a booking like this as it gave me the opportunity to look up old colleagues in the show business world as well as mingling with all the holiday makers. Betty and Roger came up with me and we lived in a roomy caravan near the sea making the most of the summer sunshine to top up the tans that the Spanish sun had given us.

I was interested in the new skiffle craze and became president of Lonnie Donegan's fan club, being a great friend of his. Ken Dodd used to say that he knew Lonnie when he sang in English. He also said that he knew Nancy Whiskey when she was a small tot—so you can tell that Doddy used to write his own scripts. Lonnie and I used to have skiffle sessions whenever we were working close to each other and I finished my set at the Hippodrome with my own version of his hit song, 'Cumberland Gap', not using the same words of course.

Lonnie began as a banjo player with the Chris Barber Jazz Band. Ottilie Paterson was their singer and she also played the washboard. He was really the king of skiffle although there were other acts around at the time such as Les Hobeaux.

While in Blackpool I met up with Charlie Cairoli at the Tower Circus. In his act the clown had three huge cream cakes in the ring with him which he had made out of three or four gallons of a creamy chemical substance. It only took a couple of minutes for him to see them off in his act. Charlie invited me to pay a visit to his home in Warley Road, Blackpool. He told me I couldn't miss his house if I knew the best residence in the road—he lived two doors down from that.

By this time Betty and I had purchased our first house at Heol Madoc in Whitchurch, well the Building Society actually owned it but at least we were now on the property ladder. When September came round it meant a return to Cardiff and the New Theatre in a Bernard Delfont show called *Rocking The Town*. It ran for a week with performances twice nightly at 6.10pm and 8.25pm.

The George Mitchell Singers were on the bill with a new singing sensation called Gary Miller. I had worked with Gary at the Palace Coliseum a few weeks earlier and he brought the house down as his fans screamed and yelled for their favourite singer. Don't forget that hero-worship, or fanmania, was only just taking hold in this country and Gary was one of the first singers to have such a following. Sadly, he became very ill and died while still a young man.

I finished off the second half of the programme and it was a good feeling to be back in Cardiff in a Bernard Delfont show topping the bill.

I have always been prepared to offer my services for charity and when that charity is the Variety Artists Benevolent Fund then you can see how I came to be performing at a Grand All-Star Garden Fete later that month. It certainly was an all-star event—also giving their time for such a good cause were my old mates Tommy Cooper, Pearl Carr and Teddy Johnson, the Four Jones Boys, Joan Turner and Nat Jackley. The event was opened by Ruby Murray.

Dear old Tommy once told me that he almost gave up thoughts of being an entertainer. He trained as a shipwright before going into the army where he was in the Horse Guards. He said he did conjuring tricks for the other lads because it was monotonous guarding horses for seven years. He became so popular as an entertainer that after he completed his military service he decided to take up a career in show business, and what a career that turned out to be.

There was nothing Welsh about the Jones Boys. They all met while they were milkmen in Doncaster. When I asked Bernie Burgess how they came to be using that name he told me the story. They started out as the Ward Brothers before becoming the Four Melomacs. Then they heard and liked the song 'The Whole Town's Talking About the Jones Boys' so they decided to change their name again, and it brought them fame.

One of the various attractions during that charity afternoon was bowling—with a live pig as the prize. Well—the fete was being held in the grounds of a large country house. But things were about to get a little bit warmer for me. Following the success of our CSE trip to Cyprus, I was asked to put a show together to take out to Malaya and Singapore to entertain our troops who were sweating it out in the jungle over there.

Before I left for the tour I bought Roger a puppy which he named Scamp. It wasn't his only pet as he also had a tortoise called Whirlwind who had already gone underground for the winter. Roger was now a pupil at Eglwys Wen Junior School in Whitchurch and he was often chosen to tell the rest of the class a story. His teacher told me later that his stories usually contained half my act.

We left on 7 October, but not before I had asked for any messages and parcels for the lads over there to be sent to my home in Heol Madoc so that I could take them with me. I didn't know what I let Betty and myself in for as the letters kept pouring in by the hundreds. I was even sent a tin of salted nuts for personal delivery to one soldier.

Joining me in Malaya on the five week tour were my old Aussie friend pianist-accordionist Lou Campara, Wally Dunn, soprano Lisbeth Lennon and dancer Shirley Gordon. The joy and delight I saw on the boys faces as I handed out almost 3,000 letters, parcels and messages made it a worthwhile trip despite the heat and I am pleased to say that I personally delivered every item I received.

The shows were well received everywhere we went and I even had time for a game of football with the South Wales Borderers, scoring four of the goals in a 5–0 victory. By a strange coincidence, I also had a reunion with Captain Butch Jenkins. My last six months in the Royal Artillery were spent under him at Newport Barracks so we had much to talk about. The trip was not without mishaps. On one journey, the jeep I was travelling in from a jungle outpost to Johore overturned. Fortunately no one was injured.

I returned to this country with a tan, and went straight into a show at the Glasgow Empire before starting rehearsals for my 1957 pantomime *Mother Goose* at the Grand Theatre in Leeds. We opened on 23 December and George Lacy played the lead role. Throughout the whole run of the panto we swapped ideas and gags to mix up the show and vary the laughs. George was probably the finest Mother Goose ever seen in pantomime. We also found that we had something in common because when George had been out entertaining the troops in Malaya in 1956, he had also travelled in a jeep that overturned into a ditch.

The run at the Grand coincided with round three of the FA Cup and Cardiff City, my home team, had beaten Leeds United 2–1 at Elland Road. It was a great thrill for me when the City players came to my dressing room during the evening performance after knocking Leeds out of the cup. As ever with pantomime, I regarded the children as my most important audience. If they laugh at you then you know you are being genuinely funny because they take you at face value. Reputation means nothing to children.

I did have a very embarrassing moment during the panto's run, though fortunately it was back stage. I had lent one of the chorus girls a long-play jazz record and wanted it back. Being me, I just couldn't go up nicely and ask for its return. I waited until I was dressed in my cowboy outfit, bristling with guns, ready for my next sketch. Instead of knocking on the door I stuck one of my guns through the opening and shouted 'Stick 'Em Up'. Unfortunately for me, the girls in the dressing room thought it was the real thing and one of them let out a piercing scream that was heard in the auditorium. Other members of the cast and back stage staff rushed to see what the commotion was about and I was left holding my gun in sheer embarrassment. It was quite a time before the panic subsided—and I never did get my record back.

The pantomime proved to be one of the most successful

ever at the Grand by doing the most business in the theatre for 31 years, but it was good to be heading home after a couple of months in Yorkshire.

6

TAKING TO THE SKIES

'Two caterpillars were sitting on a leaf when a butterfly flew past. Said one to the other, "You'll never get me up there in one of those contraptions".'

* * * * *

On the air in radio shows—on the screen in television—or in the air in my own aircraft—it was all the same to me. I became known as Cardiff's flying comedian, amongst other things, and I really did fly myself on variety dates from theatre to theatre.

As a boy I had always been keen on becoming a pilot, in fact I was just as keen to fly as I was to become a professional comedian. Yet if I had not become a funny man I would never have taken to flying. I felt that the best way to learn to fly was to join the Royal Air Force but that wouldn't have been possible because my eyesight wasn't good enough.

Early in 1955 I was chatting to a few friends about flying because they were also interested and they advised me to join a flying club. That was how I came to take my first flying lesson on 25 March at Pengam Airport on the eastern edges of Cardiff. I enjoyed flying from the word go and worked hard in my lessons. That meant I didn't have to wait too long before passing my pilot's test and gaining my wings. I made my first solo flight on 30 April after clocking only five hours dual air time.

My only setback was knowing that although I could now fly, I didn't have the most important commodity—an aeroplane.

Fortunately I was able to hire one from the flying club whenever I fancied and so I began, at first, to make short trips.

Fellow comic Jimmy Edwards offered to sell me his well-equipped Auster which had finished second in the King's Cup a few years previously, but I preferred to wait and buy an aircraft similar to the type I was using at the aero club. I felt it was better to start out with a machine I was familiar with.

I found it almost as cheap to fly to engagements as it was to motor there. My big Humber Super Snipe did 18 miles to the gallon. A light single-engined plane used four gallons to the hour, during which you could travel a distance of about 120 miles. Having worked it out for yourself you will see that the figures proved the undoubted benefits of air travel, and that was without allowing for the time-saving aspect of flying.

Mind you it didn't always work out as planned. I was asked to open an air display at Squires Gate in Blackpool but the arrangements came unstuck when the aircraft developed a wheel-brake fault. So when I should have been flying over Squires Gate announcing the opening of the display, I was hurriedly repairing the faulty wheel. I eventually arrived there one and a half hours late and opened it by making my speech from the air on the intercom.

News soon got around that I was a fully-fledged pilot and when I flew to Blackpool for a summer season in *Rocking With Laughter* at the Hippodrome I was surprised by how many of my fellow artists were interested in my new hobby. The first person to collar me was a good friend of mine, Tommy Cooper. He asked me to fly him to London on business. When I eventually took him up for a spin we had a load of laughs because Tommy had never been in a light aircraft before and really didn't know what to expect.

The lovely singer Jill Day, who was also at the Hippodrome, went even further by asking if I would give her flying lessons. Of course I said yes and one afternoon a very nervous Jill heard me shout 'Contact' and saw a mechanic twirl the propeller. Yes, the Biggles books were correct—the pilot really did shout 'Contact'.

Jill was horrified when she saw what the mechanic was doing but I assured her that this was no rubber-band powered machine and he was not winding up the elastic. She didn't seem too convinced. So the myth of the rubber-band supplies was born.

I purchased my first airplane in 1957. I was in Great Yarmouth for the summer season and bought a second hand Auster for £1,000. I had it christened as well. I called it The Jolly Roger. It might seem a strange name for a plane but I almost spent the money on a boat. After all we were close to the Norfolk Broads at the time and they were certainly inviting as it is a beautiful part of the country. If you believe that you believe anything because, of course, it was really named after Roger, our little boy.

Ruby Murray officially christened The Jolly Roger. I decided that for some fun during the summer I would form my own Air Force. That's how the BAF came into being. The Burks Air Force! A Burk was an idiot—and anyone who flew with me must have been an idiot. Soon I had loads of members and naturally I became chairman of BAF.

Derek Franklin, one of the Hedley Ward Trio and also the husband of Beryl Reid, was lance corporal. No air force anywhere had such an unusual rank. And no air force anywhere had such crazy members as Tommy Cooper, The Hedley Ward Trio, Ruby Murray, Nat Jackley, Jill Day and myself. And later on I enrolled even stranger recruits. Incidentally, did you know that Hedley Ward had never been a part of the trio even though he formed it himself back in 1948?

One afternoon, after my show's football team had been beaten in a friendly game by a side from a local holiday camp, we decided that it was time to call upon the BAF to avenge the defeat. We painted black crosses on the wings of The Jolly Roger, loaded her with flour bombs, and then I flew over the holiday camp's dining room with lance corporal Franklin in the passenger seat and we bombed it.

Unfortunately, this was the one and only bombing raid carried out in The Jolly Roger as I didn't keep it long before selling it and purchasing an American Taylorcraft in the summer of 1958. I only kept that for a short time as well, although I did quite a bit of flying around the country in it. But then I fell in love with another American plane called a Cessna PVS which I bought a few months later.

That was a beautiful aircraft and at the time there were only a few of them in this country. They cost around £6,000 new in the States but I bought mine from an American pilot who had been living over here and decided to sell it before returning to America. The aluminium on the fuselage glistened and the engine sounded like glorious music. What a wonderful hobby. I wouldn't have changed those times for anything.

I had a couple of scares mind you. Once I was flying over the Thames Estuary and had to come down low to avoid a troublesome storm. Any lower and it would have made my plane a submarine. I thought I would never see the Bristol Channel coastline and dear old Cardiff again, but it turned out alright in the end and I did eventually reach my destination safely.

I was very comfortable flying the Cessna and began chalking up the air miles on a regular basis. I was always available to give lifts to my fellow performers when they needed to get to a destination quickly. Amongst others, I flew Val Doonican down to London when the singer needed to pay a quick visit to his agents, probably to get a new supply of woolly jumpers.

But I will always remember a flight from Aberdeen when I

brought Sue Williams, one of the Television Toppers, back to Cardiff. She had been unwell all week so to save her a long road trip I offered her a lift. It was fortunate for her that she accepted, as it turned out she had appendicitis and if it had been left much longer it could well have become life threatening. We still keep in touch even now and I was delighted when she came on as a guest during my *This Is Your Life* with Eamonn Andrews.

I did have one narrow squeak when I was giving Trevor Ford a flying lesson in the skies over Bridgend. We were at about 2,000 feet when the carburettor iced up. I contacted Rhoose Airport to let them know I was in trouble and made a forced landing at Llandow, a disused RAF airfield near St Athan. We were relieved to land after a five mile glide and skimming a boundary fence. An airport mechanic came out from Rhoose to carry out some repairs and once completed, we took off again and made our way back home. Going straight back up is the best way of dealing with something like that, but Fordy took a lot of persuading before I had him strapped in next to me.

In June 1960 Harry Secombe asked if I could help him get from Blackpool, where he was appearing in a show, to Soho Square in London where he was to be a guest at Tommy Steele's wedding. I would have been delighted to help but it was not possible as I was travelling to Scarborough that day to begin rehearsals for the Minstrel Show.

It was while I was up in Scarborough that I became politically involved. Well, not quite. I was told that Wilf Proudfoot, the Tory member for Cleveland (Yorks), who was also a Scarborough grocer, had a problem. He wanted to show his new agent his constituency in as short a time as possible. There was only one way to do that, by air, and so I flew Wilf to Redcar racecourse where we met Reg Allen, his agent, and we did a quick tour around the district. They enjoyed the flight so much

Chapped lips and harmonicas

1940 suited and booted

The Modernaires in 1941. The backdrop was a sheet pegged on Olive Guppy's clothes line

With my Army pal, Steve Merrick, in Germany

Where's my Fyffes?

The Harmaniacs

There was a soldier

In my demob suit 1948

Back to driving

With Johnny Ray at London Palladium in 1954

Jon Pertwee and me holding the baby with Jon's wife, Jean Marsh, behind him, 1953

Babes in the Wood, 1954 with Mary Millar

The 'eyes' have it

Johnny Stewart, me and Lonnie Donegan in Dudley 1960

First day of Babes in the Wood rehearsals, Sheffield 1953–54. Left to right: Morecambe and Wise, me, Mary Millar, June Bishop, Freddie Sales and Frank P. Adey

Babes in the Wood, 1953–54 at Hippodrome, Derby. Me, Rex Holdsworth, Eric and Ernie

Barney Colehan, me and Harry Corbett in Leeds 1957

Lunchbox with Noele Gordon and Three Monarchs 1958

Workers Playtime with Petula Clark 1948

Summer Stars 1953. Jimmy Young, Jon Pertwee, me and Joan Turner in car

My first pantomime at Swansea Grand in 1949. Ossie Morris in fur coat and I am on left with my robber pal, the Long and the Short

The first Good Old Days at City of Varieties, 1953

My collapsible bike

Babes in the Wood, Swansea Empire 1955. I am behind Eric on right and Ernie is next to Reg Holdsworth on left

In a Scarborough field with Frank Weir, Teddy Foster and Joe 'Mr Piano' Henderson

I'm the one on the left

The Black and White Minstrels

With Penny Nicholls in the Black and White Minstrels Show

With Margot Henderson in the Black and White Minstrels Show on TV

Martian Magic

Leslie Crowther, George Chisholm, Val Brooks and me in a Latin number from the Black and White Minstrels TV Show

that I was invited to visit the House of Commons next time I was in London. This was not to take part in any debate on air defence or anything serious mind you, just to have a cup of quaint English tea.

I sold the Cessna in February 1961 and bought a Bonanza a month later. That was another beautiful plane, a little more expensive but, as in all walks of life, you get what you pay for. Although I smoked cigarettes at the time, I was not a drinker so flying was my only hobby and it was a wonderful release to be up above the clouds away from the pressures of performing twice nightly on stage.

On one occasion my good deed of offering lifts badly back-fired. I was doing summer season in Morecambe and my usual drill was to do a recce over the area to find a suitable landing strip with a house not too far away that I could rent for the family. After an initial inspection I chose Farmer Burkett's field as it looked flat and well-trodden by cattle. After returning to Blackpool where I kept the plane, I telephoned him for permission to use his meadow and he readily agreed.

When I came to use the strip for the first time I reduced height so that I could see which way the smoke was coming out of chimneys to help me gauge which way the wind was blowing. That is very important for landing and taking off. Then I made my approach to the strip but just as the undercarriage touched the ground I could see that there was a bull in the field.

Now the fact didn't escape me that my Beech Bonanza was bright red, and thoughts of a charging bull came into my mind as I brought the plane to rest about 20 yards from the beast which, I found out afterwards, was well tethered. The farmer had seen my approach and came out to meet me before moving the bull to one side of the field. Once landed, I contacted ShellMex who delivered a windsock and 50 gallons of high octane fuel so I was well set for the summer.

That incident reminded me of a gag I sometimes used in the act.

Two caterpillars were sitting on a leaf when a butterfly flew past. Said one to the other 'You'll never get me up there in one of those contraptions'.

Anyway, back to my back-firing good deed. A charity football match was organised for Stanley Park in Blackpool and of course, if it was football, I was definitely going to be there. Ronnie Corbett and Fred Mudd of the Mudlarks also wanted to play for our All Stars XI but they had a problem as they were in summer season down in Great Yarmouth. I had first met Ronnie in summer season in Manchester back in 1956 and we had also been in pantomime together. I didn't know Fred but I was always ready to help out fellow artists.

It was one and a half hours' flight time from Morecambe but that was no problem for me so I readily agreed to fly down, pick the lads up for the match, and then take them back home afterwards. I flew to Caistor Airstrip and they were waiting by the side of the runway for me. After they boarded, I turned the aircraft round and flew straight back to Blackpool.

I was aware of the airstrip at Caistor after doing summer seasons at Great Yarmouth so I knew exactly where to go. It wasn't the question of following an AA road map like I sometimes had to do. The airstrip was run by a pal of mine called Gordon Wright, known by everyone as Wilbur.

When we arrived at Blackpool the boys rushed off to get a taxi to the ground but I was stuck, because I realised then that I had forgotten to pack my boots. So, it was back in the air and a quick flight to Farmer Burkett's field followed by a small drive in the car to the rented house to collect the missing kit.

I was as quick as I could possibly be, but that was my undoing. The engine was still warm and in my haste when I got back to the plane, I flooded the engine and was unable to start the motor. I spent ages re-winding the propeller to get rid of excess fuel and it was a full hour before I was back up in the air. When I finally arrived at Stanley Park the lads were just coming off the pitch at the end of the match.

So I collected Ronnie and Fred, flew them back to Great Yarmouth, and then made the return trip to Blackpool, all without kicking a ball, or a member of the opposition, in anger.

I also introduced Jimmy Logan to the joys of flying. I had worked with Jimmy many times up in Scotland where he was a member of the Logan family. Eventually he bought a British-made plane called a Miles Messenger. We would occasionally arrange to meet in the skies over Whitby, communicating to each other on the intercom, before going on to Scarborough and Oliver's Mount where we would land.

It didn't matter which way the wind was blowing at Oliver's Mount. You took off down the hill and landed up the hill. The area was a well-known spot for motor enthusiasts who were into hill climbing. Looking down on the cliffs falling into the sea as I used to take off or land I remembered what a coastguard had once told me. He said a visitor had asked him whether people threw themselves off the cliffs very often. 'No, only once,' he had replied.

My dear old friend Eric Sykes was another keen pilot and we used to spend hours talking about flying when we met up at various theatres. Last year for his birthday I organised a painting of Eric sat in his favourite Tiger Moth aircraft. We had a great time chatting about the old days when I presented it to him.

Another good pal was Fred Kirk, once a bass player with the John Barry Seven. Fred gave up the music business to become an aircraft engineer and he made me a beautiful model of a Buccaneer. Eventually he became chief pilot for McAlpines, the construction company.

I still have all my flying log books and it was only after looking through them that I realised quite how many aircraft I had owned. I seemed to change aeroplanes more often than I ever changed my cars.

I cannot recall which model I was flying at the time but an emergency sprung up while we were in Blackpool with the *Black and White Minstrels Show*. Would you believe it—they ran out of Negro No. 2 Max Factor make-up. Of course, the show couldn't go on unless the singers were made up, so I flew down to one of the theatrical make-up depots in London, collected a batch of the missing cosmetics, and rushed back to save the show.

My flying career could have ended in March 1964 when I had to appear in court in Reading accused of endangering a man's life by negligent flying. It was an offence I was supposed to have committed during a small air display in Reading the previous November.

I had been given permission to enter the take off strip while an RAF twin Pioneer was circling above. The prosecution claimed that I was given a red light for 10 seconds to stop me from taking off until they found out whether the Pioneer was going to land. When I didn't stop, as I never saw any red light, a marshall was supposed to have run out and waved at me to halt. I never saw him either but he later claimed that I eventually took to the air only three feet above his head.

The case was thrown out because the lamp they used was proved to have never worked properly due to its batteries failing on a regular basis, while the person whose life I endangered admitted during the case that he wasn't really in any danger. I was cleared of both charges, quite rightly, yet I still had to pay all my costs and that didn't seem to be fair. After all, if you are innocent and it has cost you money to prove it, then you shouldn't end up out of pocket.

By now I had painted the Bonanza black and white and renamed it The Minstrel. In the summer I had a rather adventurous trip doing a favour for George Inns. He had been told that his father was critically ill in London so I immediately offered to fly him from Morecambe, where we were appearing with the Minstrels, to Gatwick where he could get a car to his father's home in Eastbourne. The flight down only took us an hour and a half but the return journey was very different.

I flew through some of the worst electrical storms I had ever experienced over the Midlands and I had to keep in constant touch with Birmingham Airport. Having to fly so low to avoid the worst of the storm, I lost my bearings and the airport couldn't pick me up on their radar screens to pinpoint my location.

I was beginning to get very worried and I had just about given up hope of getting any help from the control tower when I suddenly saw the name of a firm on a factory roof below me. I still remember the name even now, it was Herbert Morris Cranes. I immediately called up the airport and asked them to tell me where I was. I was told to hold on while they looked the name up in the telephone directory. When they were able to come back and tell me it was in Loughborough, I knew exactly how to get back on course. That return journey took me almost three hours but I still made it back in plenty of time for the evening performance.

It was always a priority to check the weather forecast before going up. Mind you, I knew a weather forecaster who was sacked because he kept getting the weather wrong. He told his colleagues that he was surprised to be leaving under a cloud.

When the summer season at Morecambe ended, I flew the family back home to Cardiff but it was important that it wasn't a bumpy flight or else I may have upset the VIPs on board. I'm not referring to any politicians or top stars, I was talking about the family pets. The fussiest guests flying that day were not Betty, Roger or Ceri, but Scamp the dog, Bill the budgie, and VIP-in-chief, Ceri's pet goldfish. Happily, everyone arrived back home safe, sound and in good heart.

When the Minstrel Show went to Leeds, it gave me the opportunity of teaching some of the Television Toppers how to fly. Every Tuesday and Friday mornings we would gather in my dressing room and out came charts, maps and navigational aids for a two-hour session. Some of them became so good at the theory side of flying that I couldn't teach them any more. When the weather was fine I would take them up for short flips to whet their appetites even more.

In January 1965, I took ventriloquist Neville King from Newcastle to London for a special dinner. It was an occasion organised by the Water Rats to honour none other than the great Stanley Matthews. My old pal Trevor Ford was also going but I would meet him there. It was a wonderful evening to celebrate Stan's 50th birthday and as well as all the artists belonging to the famous Grand Order, there were many famous footballers like Trevor all wanting to pay their respects to a fine player and gentleman.

During the summer I had a bit of a drama flying over the Welsh mountains. I was on my way from Cardiff to Liverpool but found myself running short of fuel. I contacted Speke Airport and remained in constant touch with them. Low cloud, driving rain and strong winds had slowed my flight and, over Wrexham, I realised that landing in Liverpool was going to be a close-run thing. The controller in Speke wanted me to change course and head for Hawarden but I didn't know the area and so decided to press on, even though I only had about 10 minutes flying time left. The airport officials became very anxious for my safety and all the emergency services were placed on alert. But they did a wonderful job of guiding me on the last stages of the flight and bringing me in to land safely. With the amount of fuel left in the tank, I wouldn't have wanted to do another couple of circuits around the airstrip.

Having beaten the traffic jams by taking to the skies, I came up with another idea to make life even easier. I bought a collapsible bicycle. I would park the car, take out the bike from the boot, cycle to the plane out on the tarmac and then stow the bike on board for the trip. Afterwards, it was out with the bike, on with the bike clips and off to the waiting car. Now I really was a mobile minstrel.

Every now and again the Bonanza needed a service which usually cost me about £2,500 but that was a small price to pay for knowing that you were safe up above the clouds. By the middle of 1966 I was well on the way to clocking up 250,000 air miles.

The Bonanza went in August 1967 and I bought a twin-engined Cessna 310. It cost me £14,000 but was worth every penny. It was capable of speeds up to 230 mph and had 23 different dials on the instrument panel. That was the good thing about small aircraft. You were the captain, pilot, navigator and engineer all rolled into one. The dual controls were fairly simple to operate with pedals to go left or right and a steering-wheel shaped joystick for going up or down. My call sign was Golf Alpha Tango Charlie Romeo but I was known as Charlie Romeo at aerodromes all over the country.

By now, the BAF had grown in size and I had to co-opt someone to look after all our 'supplies'. Harry Secombe fitted the bill and he became Quartermaster with the direct responsibility of looking after our mountain of rubber-bands in a cave up in North Wales. Jill Day didn't know what she started when we were together at the Hippodrome in Blackpool. Later on I promoted Harry to Defence Minister, mainly because he was big enough for all of us to hide behind.

Just before I took delivery of the Cessna I was honoured to be voted Pilot of the Year by the Royal Aero Club. I received my citation on 21 April 1967 together with a trophy known as Mike's Mug. It was named after the racing driver Mike Hawthorn who had originally given a cup to the club for annual presentation. The year before I was honoured Jimmy Edwards won the cup—he had flown Dakotas during the war. In 1968 the cup went to Hughie Green who ferried aircraft across from Canada in wartime so that was another vital job.

No matter where I was working, there was always someone who needed to get to a destination fast and when I was appearing with Frankie Vaughan in Leeds I heard he wanted to go to Glasgow. He was grateful when I offered to fly him there and back, and while he did his business I hung around the airport and took him back well in time for the evening show.

Frankie was a singer of popular ballads and his career in the theatre began in the late 1940s doing variety song and dance acts. He was known as a fancy dresser even in those days. He is probably best remembered for his signature tune 'Give me the Moonlight, Give Me the Girl'.

By now, flying to and from theatres was not enough for me and in 1969 I bought a single-engined Cessna 172 so that I could go racing. Being part of the Royal Aero Club meant that racing was just something you ended up doing.

I had one or two scary moments but in general, provided pilots followed common sense and obeyed the rules, it was a safe sport. Everyone usually started off from the same airstrip and there was a handicap to allow for the different classes of aircraft.

I entered the Round Britain race in 1970 but it turned out to be a disaster. I was booked to start from Rhoose with a few other entrants but the weather was so bad that none of us could even take off, so that was the end of that. There was a popular race at Ha'penny Green near Wolverhampton. In that one I was up against Second World War air ace Douglas Bader who was flying a Beech Travelair. During the race the Duke of Kent overshot the runway and was killed.

I did another race from the famous Second World War base at Biggin Hill and was going along quite well when my nearest competitor developed engine trouble and was forced to land in· a field. I went down to offer what assistance I could and that meant another early finish.

On another occasion, King Faisal of Iraq was introduced to all the competitors when we were assembled in Coventry at the start of a race. A few months later I was in Iraq on the day he was assassinated. We were on a Combined Services Entertainment tour of Middle East bases and we had to leave the country in a hurry. All eight of us with the CSE just managed to get places on the last Viscount to leave.

We were put up in hotels while we toured those bases. Some of the hotels were good while others were in need of attention. In the best hotel it was so fancy that they made you wear a tie in the shower. I wouldn't say it was exclusive but even room service had an unlisted number. In another, my room was so small that when I put the key in the door I broke a window. Joking aside, we were all glad to put a little entertainment into the lives of the troops stationed out there.

I also raced in my next plane, a Piper 180 which I bought in 1971 and kept for a year but my racing days were over in March 1973 after I decided to purchase an Azdec six-seater. It was perfect for taking passengers but not so good when it came to racing.

I found that aircraft a little too big, but in any case I now had an expanding family to take around and a two-seater was not a great deal of use as family transport anymore. Within the next couple of years I owned and flew a Comanche 250, the type of aircraft Sheila Scott flew round the world, an Apache, another Piper, another Bonanza, until finally in July 1983 I bought my last plane which was an American Mooney that I kept and flew regularly until 1988.

If I was home in Cardiff I kept my airplanes at Rhoose Airport, although of course for much of the time I was working all over the country and they were parked at the nearest landing strip. It was important to have each machine serviced by experts so I always flew them to the main concessionaires for any work. The Beechcraft was taken to Belfast, the Pipers were serviced in Biggin Hill or Denham, and the Cessna was only worked on in Blackpool.

I have piloted planes since 1988 but the Mooney was the last one I owned. Most of them were top of the range aircraft with retractable undercarriage, variable pitch propeller and all the latest instruments. I loved flying although 90% of the time a pilot is looking for somewhere to land in case anything goes wrong. There are only two sorts of pilots, the old and the bold— and you don't see any old, bold pilots. As long as you remember certain rules such as checking all instruments and turning back if you are flying into bad weather, then the enjoyment of being free as a bird up in the sky is absolutely marvellous and one I certainly will never forget.

I still like to get up in the air even now and as recently as November 2006 I flew a plane from Haverfordwest to Swansea for an old pal of mine.

7

HOME AND AWAY

*'... I fixed up a three week trip to Cyprus to entertain the troops
stationed out there. Between shows there was a little bit of time
to soak up the sun but as I have said many times—sun bathing
is only a fry in the ointment.'*

* * * * *

Performing in *Mother Goose* at the Grand Theatre meant
there was little time for anything else that winter season of
1957 in Sheffield, but we did manage to have a little fun with
other artists working in the city. Between shows I found time
to organise a football match between the Grand Theatre cast
and the Sheffield Lyceum pantomime cast who were
captained by my good friend, Ronnie Hilton.

Poor Ronnie scored two goals for his side as the Lyceum
beat us 9–4 but when he got back to the dressing room he
found that he had a swollen ankle and had to be treated by the
Sheffield Wednesday masseur. Fortunately it was not serious
enough to keep him out of that evening's performance. I made
them accept a rematch and this time we were ready and won
4–1. Ronnie wisely decided to sit out the second match and
become non-playing captain.

Before leaving Sheffield however I had to spend a day in
court. My car had been in collision with a van while I was on
my way to a matinee performance at the theatre. It wasn't my
fault though and the driver was fined the princely sum of £1

and ordered to pay £4 costs for driving without due care and attention.

Early in 1958 I appeared in the *Dickie Valentine Show* on ITV. It was my first appearance for ITV since doing Sunday Night at the London Palladium two years previously. I had two spots, one a skiffle duet with Dickie, then I went out west with Ragtime Cowboy Joe. I was quite happy with the way my act was received and hoped it would lead to even more television appearances.

There wasn't much of a New Year rest for me with the family because in the second week of March I was booked to appear on an all-star variety bill at the Gaumont Theatre in Cardiff. Joining me on the show were singer David Hughes and a dear old friend of mine, Gladys Morgan. Well known for her performances in *Welsh Rarebit*, Gladys had that heart-warming quality that made us think of our favourite aunt, or if we didn't have one, she made us wish she was one of our own family, and you cannot pay a higher compliment than that.

There is always something special about appearing in your own home city and whenever I played in Cardiff it definitely gave me an extra thrill because there is nothing quite like performing in front of your own people. After the Gaumont I never had far to go because I did a midnight matinee down the road at the Capitol in aid of the Red Cross. Wyn Calvin joined me at that venue and the compère was Alun Williams who also played the piano. The Welsh premiere of *Tale of Two Cities* starring Dirk Bogarde and Dorothy Tutin was shown later in the programme.

Memories were recalled when I appeared on television's *Show Band Parade* in May, for it was Cyril Stapleton that gave me my first big break in the business and it was quite a reunion. Cyril and I had plenty to talk about when we met up backstage.

I decided that part of my act would consist of a number called 'Whole Lotta Woman', a song that had been a big hit for Marvin Rainwater. Marvin always boasted of his Red Indian ancestry so I decided to daub myself up in woad and go on as an ancient Briton.

No sooner was that show over it was back overseas entertaining the troops again not only in Cyprus, but also in Aden and the Persian Gulf. Once again my old chum Lou Campara was with us on that trip. Providing the lads on army service out there a little bit of fun and relaxation was great. Wherever we travelled, and we covered a lot of ground on that tour, everyone was delighted to see us, and as well as watching the shows, they all wanted to know the news from back home. All of us would go out among the troops after the show to chat to them and talk about home.

In the summer of 1958 I was at Great Yarmouth in a Tom Arnold revue called *Top of the Town* in the newly built Britannia Theatre. Nat Jackley and Joan Turner were also on the bill along with Mr Desmond 'Penny Whistle' Lane. It is amazing when you think someone can make a good career out of playing a simple instrument like that.

You only had to see Nat coming out on the stage to start laughing. He was as thin as a rake and always looked old even when he was young, but his dance routine was hilarious. Many have tried to copy his antics but there will only ever been one Nat Jackley. We did pantomime together and worked up a good double act as we both had the same sense of humour.

It was in June that year when I lost the chance of becoming a major film heart-throb. Well, not quite. I did actually pass a screen test but commitments prevented me from taking up an offer to play a part in the Kenneth More, Jayne Mansfield film, *The Sheriff of Fractured Jaw*. Quite what part I would have played I never found out. Perhaps I was the fractured jaw.

That same month I decided to become an impresario by taking over the lease of the Savoy Theatre in Clacton. My first show at the venue starred Lonnie Donegan as top of the bill. Also appearing at the Savoy for me during the summer were Derek Roy, Ronnie Carroll, Andrew Ray, Jimmy Young, Eric Delaney and Humphrey Lyttleton.

I was pleased when Lonnie agreed to do the first show for me because with any new venture, you need a good start and he certainly gave me that. After all, by now he was a big recording star and his records were selling like hot cakes. Deep down Lonnie was really a jazzman. He was always tense and unable to relax as much as he should have. Unfortunately I couldn't be there in person because I was in the *Top of the Town* show in Great Yarmouth.

In August, excerpts from *Top of the Town* were shown on BBC television. I arrived at the theatre in a seaside pedal-car, did my cowboy act and sang 'All the Monkeys Aint in the Zoo'. The six-shooters I had holstered on my hips were the very guns confiscated by the Security Forces when I toured Cyprus. I mixed in a few one or two liners such as:

> *Said one woman motorist to another, 'The thing I hate most about parking a car is that awful sickening crunch!'*

Everyone enjoyed the show and it had good reviews.

Meanwhile, business at the Savoy was fair, but not great. It takes a while for people to come to terms with anything new, and the shows at the Savoy had to earn their audiences and that would take time.

The stars I had booked all worked hard to help that first venture of running my own theatre, and what I learned during those few months would stand me in good stead when I later moved into producing my own shows and pantomimes.

Derek Roy, who appeared at the Savoy for me, was an interesting character with Welsh connections. His real name was Derek Saunders Thomas and his great grandfather was the famous Welsh poet, John Saunders. Derek wasn't interested in poetry however. He was more concerned with looking after the welfare of retired greyhounds. He also had a pet St Bernard called Nero and was always looking for foster parents for the dog during the summer season, usually without success as that brute could eat for Britain.

While at Yarmouth for the summer I kept my aircraft at the North Denes airfield and was able to fly home and spend Sundays with Betty and Roger—now nine years old.

I met up with Shirley Bassey backstage after one of the shows and asked her if she had passed her driving test. It turned out to be a touchy subject as she had been a learner for over two years and was still waiting to take another test having failed on her first two attempts. But luckily for me she was in a bubbly mood and showed me how she relaxed by lying back on a couch with her legs up against the wall. She told me that her favourite song at that time was 'My Funny Valentine' because it made her feel both happy and sad. It was a great show that summer in Yarmouth. We played to full houses every night and all the reviews were good.

In November I appeared at the Theatre Royal in Dublin for a week in an all-star variety concert called *Shake Hands With the Irish*. It turned out to be a never-to-be-forgotten experience as the show was brought to a finale by the Yankee Doodle Dandy man himself, James Cagney. He had caught the public's attention as a tough-talking gangster in the 1931 movie, *Public Enemy*, and also in *Angels With Dirty Faces*, but he was originally a song and dance man in vaudeville having spent much of the 1920s on stage in New York.

It was his singing and dancing in *Yankee Doodle Dandy*, made in 1942, that earned him an Oscar for Best Actor. He retired from the business in 1961 but returned 20 years later to star in *Ragtime*. Most remember Cagney for his portrayal of bad guys in those black and white movies and few will recall that he was a brilliant dancer. It was a great experience for me to see the master at work even though I was surprised at how small he was. In one respect it was like the films he appeared in as he was always surrounded by his minders and no one was able to get close to him during the short time he was in the theatre.

While in Dublin I took the opportunity of doing some riding at the Bel-Air stables run by famous steeplechaser, George Wells. I came a right cropper one day when my mount decided to stop and I didn't, resulting in a nasty fall. But nothing was going to stop me appearing in that evening's performances and in true tradition, I dusted myself down and went out on stage as if nothing had happened. Mind you, afterwards I was as stiff as a board and it was two or three days before I was back to my normal self.

I had a short break from work at the end of the month so Betty and I flew to Holland to spend a few days with my dear pal Trevor Ford and his wife, Louise. Trevor was playing for PSV Eindhoven at the time although they both wanted to come back home as soon as possible. I don't think he ever really wanted to leave Wales but Fordy was Fordy and he had little time for those controlling football in this country. In any case, he didn't have much option after he was suspended along with some Sunderland colleagues from playing in the English leagues.

Pantomime was once again at the Leeds Grand but this year I was playing Buttons in *Cinderella*. First things first, I needed a very large pumpkin. Well you know how important pumpkins are in *Cinderella*. I mean, Cinders would never have arrived at the ball if it had not been for a pumpkin.

I read in one of the papers that a woman in Bristol had grown a super-duper pumpkin so I arranged to buy it from her. Sadly, it started to rot before we had even finished rehearsals. Luckily, a grower near Worcester came to my rescue with a 52 pounder which I promptly insured for £10,000.

Of course, there were a number of conditions attached to the policy.

(1) It must not be sat on.
(2) It must not be placed within smelling range of a pig or any other animal with a taste for pumpkins.
(3) It must not be taken on a bus.
(4) It must not be placed near heat.
(5) It must not be thrown about or eaten before the end of the pantomime season.

It never lasted the course and started to go rotten towards the end of the pantomime season so I claimed on the insurance. They wouldn't pay out but I got them to donate money to charity instead.

Of course, it was all a gag to publicise the pantomime. The insurers had their bit of publicity as well because there were plenty of articles about the pumpkin in the papers, so everyone was happy with the end result.

A different disaster struck one night when part of the house scenery fell on to the stage during the show. The chorus girls were doing a routine out front at the time and luckily saw it about to fall and rushed to the side of the stage. Like real troupers they kept on dancing while I hurried out from the wings to tell the audience that it was the first time I had ever known the opening scene bring the house down.

I had my biggest break on television when I took over the job of master of ceremonies in the final show of the series of *Black and White Minstrel Shows* on 11 April 1959. I replaced Kenneth Connor who had to drop out because of film commitments. It was my 12th appearance on television but the first time I had been given the role of compère.

This was my chance to show what I could do and I knew that if it went well, it would give my career a huge boost. I had turned down offers of summer shows to be available for any television work that may come my way so there was a lot riding on this one show.

The opening number was 'Basin Street Blues' and that gave me the chance to play the trumpet. Later on I played guitar while also appearing in sketches, doing a solo spot, singing two numbers and acting as compère, so it was a busy evening for me. Also on the show besides the Mitchell Minstrels were Benny Lee, Rosemary Squires, Glen Mason and Lou Campara while Kenneth Connor made a guest appearance. Straight from the Minstrels I went to the Hippodrome, Birmingham for a week, happy in the knowledge that reviews for the television show had been good.

Television was a strange phenomenon. Every artist wanted to be seen on it as much as possible but for some, particularly comedians, it was a double-edged sword.

A comic had to be careful about appearing on the box. Once a gag was used on television it was finished, just like it was on radio, and couldn't be repeated in the theatre.

Many a comic's act has been pinched after appearing on television. I once met up with a comedian from Barnsley who said he enjoyed my act on television so much that he used some of the material in his own performances and it went down well with his audiences. I didn't know whether to be pleased, or to hit him.

Much later I also had a bit of a row over the same thing with a comic called Digby Wolfe. He was given a hard time by the critics for pinching a lot of my cowboy act. He reckoned that he had always used it and had never even met me but that was wrong because we had worked together. He later went to the States to continue his career.

A week or so after the Hippodrome I appeared in a star-studded variety bill at the Welfare Hall, Llanharry in aid of a miner injured in a colliery accident. It was the first time I had joined up with Steve Gibson and George Hodge to re-form the Harmaniacs since we called it a day all those years ago, and it felt as though we had never been apart even though our reunion was only for this one show. We just found that the act rolled along as though we had never been apart.

Also appearing were Cardiff singing star Dan Donovan, a young vocalist called Maureen Evans, a rhythm group from Ely called the Hot Rocks, and television personalities Maureen Staffer and Colin Bower. The show was a sell-out and achieved its purpose of helping the injured miner.

On May Day I was in a Midnight Matinee at the Davis Theatre, Croydon. The show was in aid of the Variety Artists Benevolent Fund and a host of top stars gave their time for this worthwhile cause. Appearing on the bill that evening, fairly early in the programme, was a young singer called Cliff Richard. He already had a big following of young girls who screamed and shouted so loud that you could hardly hear what he was singing. Cliff was a quiet, polite young man off stage in those days and he has looked after himself well and deserves all the success that he has achieved.

He was followed by a dear friend of mine Roy Castle, who was starring at the Palladium at the time. Roy was a good dancer and no mean trumpet player. We got on well and it was a great tragedy when he died so young. Roy had started off as a stooge for Jimmy James but soon blossomed into an excellent all-round entertainer. Then came the glamorous singer Alma Cogan, another who was with us for only a short time, and Peter Brough.

Mr Acker Bilk and his Paramount Jazz Band closed the first half of the evening. I had many a jam session with Acker over the years when our paths crossed. He once told me that his real name was Bernard but he had the nickname Acker from the Somerset slang for friend. He learned the clarinet while serving in the Army and by the mid-1950s was playing professionally. He has had loads of hit records but his most famous is probably 'Stranger on the Shore'.

Performing after the interval were Bob and Alf Pearson, Bernard Bresslaw, who had made his name in the television comedy *The Army Game*, Des O'Connor, the lovely Joan Regan, and I finished the evening off. It was a good show and a lot of money went to the Benevolent Fund.

In July I appeared on Lonnie Donegan's TV show *Putting on the Donegan*, and it was the first time we had worked together since I became a stand-in member of his skiffle group. I used to say I was related to Lonnie Donegan—my name was Soon-To-Be-Done-Again.

Funnily enough, I was on several pieces of sheet music about that time and one of them was Lonnie's big hit 'Cumberland Gap'. I was on the cover because I used to sing it in my act. Other sheet music I was involved with were 'This Is My Mother's Day' which was a Dorothy Squires hit written by Billy Reed, and 'The Good Old Days of Ragtime'.

The Lonnie Donegan show had been originally scheduled for the end of May and so because I had some spare time, I fixed up a three week trip to Cyprus to entertain the troops stationed out there. Between shows there was a little bit of time to soak up the sun but as I have said many times—sun bathing is only a fry in the ointment.

Every time I went abroad to entertain the lads who were doing a difficult job stationed far from home I felt that I was doing my little bit to keep morale up. They were always so pleased to see the shows that we usually tried to pack in a few extra performances wherever we could.

My gamble of refusing a summer show to concentrate on television finally paid off after Ernie booked me to appear at the Theatre Royal in Dublin. I had a hard act to follow as the previous week the star of the show had been none other than the famous American singer and dancer, Danny Kaye. Danny made his film debut in 1935 in a comedy titled *Moon Over Manhattan* but he is probably best known for his roles in *Hans Christian Anderson* and *White Christmas*.

It was an unusual arrangement at the Royal as the performances were non-stop. Alternating with the stage show was a film—in my first week it was *The Sullivans* starring Barry Fitzgerald, and as soon as the film finished the stage show would start. This was known as cine-variety. When the show reached its finale, the film was shown again. I was booked for two weeks but it went so well that I was kept on for a further week.

The reviews were fantastic and in some I was even compared to Danny Kaye. At no time then, or even now, would I compare myself to Danny as he was a wonderful entertainer known all over the world, but I was still delighted to be given that sort of praise.

During my first week I received some visitors at my dressing room door. Two young lads were brought back stage by their parents to meet me. They were the Cluskeys and they had brought their sons to the theatre to see my act as both lads were keen on a stage career. They must have been only about nine or 10 years old then but they worked hard at their singing, along with their cousin John Stokes, and made a superb career for themselves selling millions of records. It was of course Con and Dec Cluskey, who with John became known worldwide as The Bachelors.

Unknown to me, during the show's successful run, Ernie Cash had been in contact with George Inns, the producer of the *Black and White Minstrels Show*. George had read the show reviews and arranged to fly over to Ireland to see my act. He came to my dressing room after a performance and told me that he had enjoyed my routine. Then he asked if I would be interested in joining the Minstrels on a full-time basis. He said he was looking for a comic who was musically involved, I fitted the bill, and I had been a success deputising for Ken Connor on the show earlier in the year. Of course, he knew I could do what he wanted after that one Minstrels show and he was well aware that I had also been in the *Show Band Show* for three years. Despite all that I am still convinced that if I had not done so well in Dublin he wouldn't have booked me.

As soon as I said my farewell to George I was on the telephone to Betty to tell her the news. I usually rang two or three times every day anyway but I wanted to share my excitement with her as quickly as possible.

Ernie and Joe Cash rang to offer their congratulations and they carried out the contractual side with the BBC as normal agents would—I had now become their top client.

All was set for a big change in the Stennett family's lifestyle. Just like my flying, my career was about to take off but I didn't want all my eggs in one basket so whenever possible I accepted bookings around the country. Even though I put my heart and soul into making my appearances on the *Black and White Minstrel Show* a success, I still found time to do radio work. I appeared in Sunday concerts with both Joe Loss and Ted Heath while in November 1959 I joined Dickie Valentine and Janet Brown in a series of lunchtime shows on the Light Programme called *How About You?* The show included sketches, vocal spots and a weekly situation comedy. The scriptwriters were Dick Vosbrough and Brad Ashton and I am still in touch with Brad even now.

Poor old Dickie had no acting experience whatsoever, yet he rehearsed like mad and easily pulled it off. In all, the three of us mustered up nine different voices so that was more than enough, and with Janet's uncanny impressions, my usual zany style of comedy and Dickie's singing, it made for a good show that ran for six months.

I didn't have far to go for pantomime in 1959. It was back to the scene of my very first panto 10 years earlier at the Grand, Swansea when I played one of the robbers. This time it was *Mother Goose* and I needed an egg, a very large egg and I wanted it sprayed golden so that I could use it in the show. Well, anything for a yoke!

In the end I found an egg practically right on my doorstep. It belonged to a lady in Swansea and was 10 inches from tip to tip, six inches across and had been laid many years previously by an ostrich. The egg had been presented to the owner by an American serviceman who had stayed with her during the war.

Mother Goose was a traditional pantomime with a bit of slick humour for the adults but first and foremost, it was for the kids. If the parents see the children laughing then they are happy as well. I played the part of Sammy, and appearing as the squire was a well-known television personality at the time called Alan Taylor, later of *Mr and Mrs* fame. Eddie Henderson was the dame and the goose was played by Tony Snape who had been playing geese for about 30 years. What a way to earn a living.

We played to full houses almost every night and I was sorry when the run came to an end. It also meant that I would be back travelling all over the country with the Minstrels Show although there was a week in Bristol so I was able to get home each night when we appeared at the Hippodrome. It used to take me 10 minutes to fly straight across the Bristol Channel in my Cessna. The road journey in those pre-Severn Crossing days would have taken a couple of hours.

There was some sad news in May 1960 when the death of Mai Jones was reported. Mai had given a helping hand to many artists, not just me, including Harry Secombe, Albert and Les Ward, Wyn Calvin, Ossie Morris and Gladys Morgan. She was a good friend to all of us.

Later that month I appeared in a charity show at Merthyr Tydfil on behalf of the World Refugee Fund but I wasn't the only one to be dashing around the place. That superb singer David Hughes, another who was helped by Mai, had to drive down from Wolverhampton after a week's variety there. The day after the show he set off early from Merthyr and headed for Chepstow where he boarded a ferry for Torquay so that he would be in plenty of time to report to the Pavilion Theatre down in Torbay by noon.

Also in the charity show at Merthyr, besides David and me, were Ivor Emmanuel, Patricia Bredin, that great actor Stanley Baker and a lovely singer called Yana. She was a glamorous ballad singer who rose to fame through television. She collected dolls and even had a giant teddy bear over six feet tall. The Phil Williams-Sybil Marks Professional Formation Team from Cardiff also put on a display.

You can never stand still in this business so I was always on the look-out for something new to do. When I was invited to London to record a few songs I jumped at the chance, anything Dickie Valentine and Frank Sinatra could do . . . I had already visited a recording studio to make a record a few years before but not a single copy was sold. It was a new recording company and they had forgotten to put the hole in the middle.

Dickie suggested that I record a version of 'Tennessee Stud', a number I featured in our radio series *How About You* on the BBC. We made the demo disc but sadly I was never going to become a new singing sensation so the project was shelved. The BBC then decided on a new idea, and that was a programme showing the stars off duty at the Candlelight Club in Scarborough. The first programme started at 10.30pm when we had all finished at our various theatres and went out live to the watching television audience. Also with me on that first night were Dickie Valentine, Max Jaffa, who I knew when he was a tangerine, Dennis Spicer and the Geoff Laycock Quintet.

The joint was really jumping as I played trumpet and sang a jivey duet with Dickie. Max then came out of his shell by playing some violin boogie and Dennis Spicer and others danced as if they never meant to stop. In truth, going to the Candlelight, or places like it, was a way of winding down from the buzz of performing. On my first visit to the club, I went to the rostrum and entertained the guests non-stop for two hours, joking, singing and playing the trumpet. The session didn't stop until 3am but of course events for television were strictly limited to just 25 minutes on screen.

Due mainly to the success of the Candlelight Club, I was given my own show on BBC Television in September. It was called *Stan Stennett Says Meet The Boys* and it was on for half hour from 6.30pm. Dai Francis, John Boulter and Tony Mercer from the Minstrels were my guests and I sang 'Gone Fishin'', the popular Crosby-Armstrong number with Tony, and followed that with 'Tie Me Kangaroo Down Sport' and 'Basin Street Blues'.

I was pleased with the whole presentation and hoped it would bring even more television work my way. Although I was now making some appearances on the box, I still wasn't on TV as much as I would have liked.

8

THE BLACK AND WHITE MINSTRELS

'That Christmas I made a New Year's Resolution. I promised to give up being a chain smoker and try tobacco instead.'

* * * * *

The slickest programme on television returned to BBC TV on Thursday, 10 September 1959 and I was booked as Master of Ceremonies for the complete series of 16 shows. The Minstrels had a huge following and a reputation for putting on a fast-moving show.

Fortnightly, for 45 minutes, they would rip off one tuneful melody after another. Many were songs that had stood the test of time but others were right up to date. All had one thing in common, they were the sort of tunes that everyone liked to hum, whistle or sing and we rehearsed the whole programme in Earls Court.

The Mitchell Minstrels, conducted by George Mitchell, were the backbone of the programme wearing their familiar boaters, blazers, big bow ties and blacked-out faces. I had my own spots between the songs and linked up each act. George started in the business during the war writing music for army concerts, forming his first choir from ATS and military personnel and naming them The Swing Group.

In 1948 he conducted and arranged a BBC series of negro

spirituals called *Cabin in the Cotton* and from there stemmed the idea of the Minstrels. In the very first show I did a country and western piece with jazz trombonist George Chisholm and we had great fun rehearsing and performing 'We've Gotta Get The Shoes on Willie'. Believe it or not, that was a number originally recorded by Perry Como. I was dressed up as a real hillbilly dad while George was rigged out as my 'hick' son. He was a superb trombonist, so good that when the great Louis Armstrong toured Britain he always asked George to join him.

Other artists appearing that evening were a 12-year-old pianist called Roy Budd, who later became a fine composer, along with Dai Francis, Tony Mercer and John Boulter, all of them resident Minstrel soloists. All three were top class singers. Tony was a Yorkshire lad who had been interested in music since he was a young boy. He went to school with Wally Stott who became a leading musician and orchestra leader. Like me, Tony toured with a services show. His show was called *Hello from SEAC* and we spent many an hour reminiscing about our time entertaining the troops. On leaving the forces he sang with the Roy Fox and Eric Winstone Bands before becoming a founder member of the George Mitchell Minstrels.

John was a tenor who originally wanted to be an opera singer but was told that his voice was too light. He worked with Cyril Fletcher and Betty Anstell in several productions before linking up with the Minstrels a few months before I joined the show. Dai was from Seven Sisters, near Neath, and he did an uncanny impersonation of Al Jolson. Everything he knew about Jolson came from his father who was an expert on the songs of the old-time music hall. With three such talented singers there was no way the show could fail.

I even found an old pal amongst the Minstrels. I first met Glyn Dawson at a talent contest in Ynysyngharad Park,

Pontypridd not long after coming out of the army. Glyn was with the Mitchell Singers before going into the Minstrel Show and he was one of the longest serving members with 24 years as a Minstrel before retiring.

The make-up of each programme suited me down to the ground as I was able to play the trumpet and guitar, tell a few gags, become the only country and western Black and White Minstrel, and even try my feet at tripping the light fantastic. The three-quarters of an hour show meant a constant rush for me to change for each item, none of which lasted longer than two minutes. I would race off the set, up a passage with a couple of steps, and by the time I reached my dressing room most of my clothes would be off. I would then change with a stop watch in my hand ready to race back for the next announcement. My one trouble was to make sure I stopped breathing heavily and looked as though I had all the time in the world when I was back on stage. In one show I could be a guardsman in full regalia then one minute and 20 seconds later I was a hillbilly complete with beard.

I had enjoyed watching the programme before I was ever invited to take over from Kenneth Connor and now it was a big thrill for me to be working with such accomplished entertainers. Not many people will recall that when the show first went out even the ladies were blacked-up. Producer George Inns then made a number of changes including introducing a girl dancing troupe, the Television Toppers, while replacing the 'Poor Old Sam' type of Victorian melody with the latest hit-tunes interlaced with the evergreens. Only the male singers were now blacked-up while the stars kept to their normal make-up. I believe that the Black and White Minstrels were the ultimate answer to rock'n'roll. Nostalgia was what people wanted, and probably still do. The further back the songs came from the better, and I was out to prove I could go back further than anyone.

It was a stroke of genius when Margo Henderson was booked to appear in the second Minstrel Show. We did a double act together that went down so well that Margo was promptly booked for the rest of the series, provided that at some point in the show we would do a duet together.

I had a bit of a setback after five or six weeks though. During November my doctor advised me to take more care of my throat as I was in danger of losing my voice. The cause of the trouble was all the noises I made during my act from the clopping of horses hooves, doors creaking, and cats fighting to the sound of trees being felled. The doctor rationed my noises to six a week to avoid permanent damage to my vocal chords. I was also advised to cut down on my smoking. That Christmas I made a New Year's Resolution. I promised to give up being a chain smoker and try tobacco instead.

It was a real blow to me as of course I had been making sound-effect noises since I was a schoolboy. I was told that I could make those sounds because of a freak jaw formation—Frankenstein had nothing on me. There was nothing else I could do but follow the doctor's advice so for a while I kept the noises down to around six screeching brake sounds and a couple of horses at the gallop per week.

I had turned into more of a comedy-song man since appearing with the Minstrels whereas I used to think I was just a gag man with an unusual ability to make funny noises while occasionally strumming a guitar and singing. Before I joined the Minstrels I only sang in the bath but after a couple of months on the show I was so confident I could sing in the garden as well.

Margo Henderson joined me in 'On Mother Kelly's Doorstep'. If that had ever been done before by a Welshman and a Scot, then I was an Irishman. Our duets had now become an established part of the show. I stepped down temporarily early in December to go into pantomime at the Grand Theatre in Swansea, but before I left I did my impression of Louis Armstrong and followed that up with my version of 'Mack The Knife'.

The fact that I could briefly leave before returning at the end of the panto was a big achievement for me because it gave me a certain standing in the show. Kenneth Connor resumed as compère in my place while I played Silly Sam in *Mother Goose*. Ken came from an old show business family and his father was a singer in the music halls.

My spell away from the show meant that I didn't have to fly from Cardiff to Denham Airport for rehearsals, something I had been doing since the start of the series. I used to leave on a Monday and stay with friends of mine named Bill and Betty, also known as the Skating Meteors, until the Friday. Bill would meet me at the airport and let me use his car while I was in town.

It seemed no time at all before I was back for the last three Minstrel shows. The summer was going to be a busy one, for such was the popularity of the Minstrels that we went on tour around the Moss and Stoll circuit after the final programme in the series on 29 March 1960. We started at the Hippodrome, Bristol for a six week run. Funnily enough, that show opened the very night the final programme of the *Black and White Minstrel Show* was shown on television. That was possible because the TV show had been pre-recorded. After Bristol we went on to the Empire, Liverpool and the Palace Theatre in Manchester. On 23 May we were up in Edinburgh. Each show would be twice nightly. It took six girls one and a quarter hours to make-up the minstrels and a staggering 130 new costumes went into each show.

While we were in Scotland it reminded me that every time a Scotsman was seen on the telly he was either wearing a kilt, singing in front of tartan drapes, or smiling at chorus girls wearing plaid shorts while the bagpipes were being played. What was the need for all that fuss? I have performed in front of many Scottish audiences and I have never found them lacking in appreciation just because I wasn't wearing a sporran. When I was home playing in front of Welsh audiences they didn't expect me to have a leek in my hair. I spoke to my mate Jimmy Logan about it and he told me that the Welsh were just as bad with their male voice choirs and songs such as 'We'll Keep A Welcome In The Hillsides'. Perhaps that was a fair comment but anyway, enough of the serious stuff.

After Edinburgh it was on to the Hippodrome, Birmingham before moving to the Theatre Royal in Hanley and the Winter Gardens in Morecambe. It was a busy time for everyone connected with the Minstrels with all that travelling before we could settle down with the show in Scarborough for the summer season from June right through to September. Incidentally, usual prices at most of the theatres was 2s 6d (15p) in the Upper Circle while best seats would run to as much as 8s 6d (42p). Now that was value.

My new duet partner on tour was Penny Nicholls as Margot Henderson had gone into the London version of the Minstrel Show along with Dai Francis. Penny was very experienced in the business and had sung with the Henry Hall Band and also the Billy Merrin Band before linking up with the Minstrels. She first came to prominence with her own radio series called Penny Serenade. As well as her duets with me, Penny took part in many of the big production sequences along with the Mitchell Maids and the dancers.

Before we reached the Liverpool Empire however, she became ill and was admitted to hospital in Bristol with suspected appendicitis. A young girl called Johan Banks took over her spot at a moment's notice. We sat down together and read through the sketches shortly before the show started and she did very well as cover for Penny throughout the week.

I had something else on my mind besides worrying about Penny's replacement. I had been on tenterhooks for a couple of weeks as Betty was due to give birth to our second child. I finally received the call on 27 April and John Boulter came with me as I paid a flying visit to the maternity hospital in Cardiff to see Betty and my new son. It was just a flying visit because I had the Cessna back in Liverpool in time for the two performances later that day. I kept in touch with Betty and baby Ceri by flying home whenever I had a few hours to spare.

After Liverpool we went to Newcastle so that meant a three-hour flight but it was well worth it. By starting off at nine in the morning I could spend most of the afternoon with Betty and the baby and then be back up north in plenty of time for the evening performances.

Everywhere we went on tour we played to packed houses. It was the first time in history that a television show had been successfully transferred to live theatre and it proved that a good television programme could give new life to theatres everywhere. The vivacious Penny Nicholls recovered quickly and was soon back giving the show her own brand of vigour, verve and wit and reviews were good whichever part of the country we were playing. We were now dueting with songs such as 'You are my Honey, Honeysuckle' and 'I Can't Give You Anything But Love, Baby'. I thoroughly enjoyed working with Penny as she was a talented girl and had the right sort of personality for the show. In our hillbilly routines she would wear a long blonde wig and clutch a washboard. Her teeth would be blacked out and she was cross-eyed as we did our routine. Not many pretty girls would be prepared to look like that on television, show business or no.

It was all looking good for our summer season at the Futurist in Scarborough starting in June. Incidentally, the Futurist was bought by impresario Robert Luff from the proceeds of the *Black and White Minstrel Show*.

I did not want to be away from Betty, Roger and Ceri for the whole summer so I arranged for all three of them to come up with me. We always made a point of being together as a family whenever possible even though it meant vacating our home in Cardiff for a while. Long separations due to theatrical work have been the cause of many an upset marriage.

Of course to do that I had to find a suitable landing strip for my Cessna and then rent accommodation within easy distance of the landing site. I eventually found one and arranged for a pal of mine to fly the Cessna up from Rhoose Airport, near Cardiff. Then I realised that John Hollingsworth, that was my pilot pal, would have difficulty in recognising the right field from the air. Well you have to admit that there are quite a few fields in Yorkshire and many of them look the same. John was an air traffic controller at Rhoose Airport and had been a fighter pilot during the war.

I thought about using a mirror to guide the plane down but gave that idea up in case I attracted the wrong aircraft and ended up being accused of spying. Then I hit upon the idea of purchasing a dozen rolls of wallpaper and with John Boulter and some others from the show, we set about papering the field. When John flew over and saw the wallpaper he knew he had arrived at his destination.

The show in Scarborough cost £25,000 to mount and it looked just like a lavish production of the television programme. There was even a walk-round between the orchestra pit and the audience which added to the effectiveness of the presentation. The one thing that took the show out of the ordinary was the singing, and yet as far as the Minstrels were concerned, it was all pre-recorded. You couldn't describe it as miming though because it was obvious, especially to the audience closest to the stage, that the Minstrels were also singing their hearts out even though the bulk of the sound that came over was recorded. This allowed greater movement on stage and singers did not have to be static in front of a mike. Of course, there was no pre-recording of my spots.

Tony Mercer and I shared dressing room accommodation at the Futurist and he had a nasty habit that took some getting used to. Every time he entered the room he would shout 'Stand by your mirrors!' Now having served in the army during the war, I was rather allergic to such sounds. Naturally I would never have believed it of Tony until I discovered his secret. The man who possessed the voice thousands of viewers admired for its rich soothing qualities had been a Sergeant Major in the army.

We had a wonderful party after our opening night. Dickie Valentine and Thora Hird, who were also appearing at theatres in the town, both came to enjoy themselves after completing their own performances nearby. As part of the entertainment, I joined in a jazz jam session on the rostrum with Ossie Noble, who was from Treforest, Dai Francis and Frank Weir. Dickie went up on stage and joined in by singing a bit of jazz.

In any spare time that we had, Ossie and I would play a round of golf. He talked all the time we played so I found out a little about his life. He was a drummer in Harry Roy's band and when war broke out, he joined the RAF and was stationed at Cranwell. It was then that he realised he had a flair for entertaining. He organised dances and concerts and even formed his own band and his career just took off from there.

He had a unique routine where he dressed up as a clown and his only prop was a clay bust. He would then throw bits of clay which landed on the bust at strategic points. Ossie never said a word on stage, he just growled, babbled and clowned. His humour was all visual. Perhaps he learnt that from his younger days as both his parents were deaf and dumb.

As well as my solo spots I also worked with a number of other stars who appeared on the show. I did a 'Bavarian peasants' routine with my mate George Chisholm and an up-and-coming trumpeter called Eddie Calvert, while another skit was called Four Backbones of the Empire and included Valerie Brooks, George, myself and Leslie Crowther. The interludes provided by the comics brought a bit of light and shade to the production. Non-stop singing for 45 minutes would not have held an audience, hence the manic outbursts from yours truly and the others.

Leslie was a lovely chap who spent around eight years doing *Crackerjack* for BBC television. He was seriously injured in an M5 car crash in 1992, developed a blood clot on the brain, and was forced to retire from the business having made a great success of *The Price Is Right* for ITV. Four years later he died in hospital in Bath after a heart attack.

It was hectic for me during the show as my dressing room was up three flights of stairs and I had to dash up and down 24 times a night. The weather was good that summer but I had little time to enjoy the sun. In the spring of 1961, the BBC entered a filmed recording of a *Black and White Minstrels Show* in the first international contest in television light entertainment. The contest was held in Montreux on the banks of Lake Geneva and the first prize came to be known as The Golden Rose.

The opposition from 17 different countries was formidable and included shows starring Fred Astaire and Sammy Davis

Jr, a Soviet entry featuring the famous Kirov Ballet, a spectacular Italian revue and a German entry that was reputed to have cost over £30,000 to produce. George Inns wanted to make sure that the panel of European judges understood the style of the show, so he arranged for all the Continental visitors he could think of to watch and pass judgement. Fortunately, they assured George that the black-faced entertainers would be understood on the Continent.

For three days the judges sat in a darkened theatre watching all the entrants and on the fourth day the winner was announced. The first Golden Rose of Montreux was awarded to the BBC's *Black and White Minstrel Show*. It was a fantastic achievement and every one of us who played a part in winning that award was proud.

By now the television show could almost guarantee an audience of at least 16 million, and frequently managed to top 18 million viewers. It established itself as one of the world's greatest television musical programmes. The music from the show broke sales records and the stage show was equally popular. Later on, in 1969, the production at the Victoria Palace Theatre in London would enter the *Guinness Book of Records* as the stage show seen by the largest number of people.

Big-hearted Arthur Askey was in Scarborough that summer appearing at the Floral Hall. I met up with him and asked him to write something about himself for my weekly column which I used to write for the *Yorkshire Evening News* whenever I was in that part of the country. This is what he wrote for me.

> *Arthur Askey was born in Liverpool at the turn of the century—and that's what gave the century such a nasty turn. As a boy he sang in the choir at*

Liverpool Cathedral. He was called up for the Army in 1918 and saw service in the Far East (Great Yarmouth). After that he went back to the Tonsils and Adenoids Department of the Liverpool Education Offices. Eventually he gave up his job, and pension, to work on the stage and appeared in almost every medium of entertainment.

I suppose it served me right for asking. But I can remember thinking at the time that if Arthur was ever awarded a knighthood he would most certainly be the shortest knight of the year. In July 1960 the Minstrel Show was again shown on television. It had been recorded at the Futurist a little earlier but not without a few problems. The audience in the theatre for the tele-recording had longer entertainment than they expected when the 35 minute excerpt was delayed because of a technical hitch. Ossie Noble did an act, I came up with a little impromptu material, and some community singing from the Jackpots filled in the time until the fault was fixed. The last number in the show and the finale had to be done again because of the fault.

While I was in Scarborough I took time out to meet up with the popular beat singer and musician Don Lang. Yorkshire-born Don, whose real name was Gordon Langhorn, had come to the resort to do a Sunday concert. He regularly made the trip from London to Halifax to meet up with his parents. On that particular trip however the wires must have been crossed because he told me that his parents had gone to stay with his wife and two children at their home in Wimbledon leaving him up north on his own.

After a record-breaking season in Scarborough it was time to move on, but not before I made a presentation on stage to the Futurist's managing director, Mr Catlin. The gift from the whole company was wrapped up and when I gave it to him he said that the first record he would get for the record player would be the Minstrels debut long player. At that point I clutched his sleeve and quietly whispered to him that it was a tape recorder and not a record player. Unfortunately, I was right in front of the mike when I told him so everyone in the audience knew. Fair play to him, he said we had better provide him with a tape recording of the show instead.

The show at the Futurist had been an outstanding success, breaking all records after being seen by over 250,000 people during its 12-week run. But we didn't travel too far after Scarborough as we were booked to do the show for a week at the Empire Theatre in Leeds. It was the start of nine weeks' touring that would take in the Globe Theatre, Stockton-on-Tees before moving down to the Theatre Royal in Nottingham and then further south where we would play such places as Shrewsbury, Cardiff and Brighton.

When we moved on up to Teeside I travelled by car because my Cessna had to stay in Leeds undergoing a mechanical check-up. It was November by the time the show reached the New Theatre in Cardiff and it had played to full houses all along the way. Unfortunately for me, we were only booked in for a week but at least it gave me a taste of living at home for a short while before it was back on the road again heading for Brighton.

I hadn't spent a week at home with the family since April so I had almost forgotten what to do with my time there. Usually approaching the festive season, I was involved with pantomimes but for the first time in almost 10 years there was no build-up and it took a little getting used to. Normally there were rehearsals up until the last minute, Christmas Day at home, then I would be off early on Boxing Day for the first show. It was alright when I just thought about Christmas, but if I thought about show business, I felt a little redundant and maybe that is why I am still producing pantos at Christmas now.

There was a small break for me when I appeared on BBC television in Joan Regan's Saturday night show, *Be My Guest*. I sang a comedy number to my own accompaniment and then did a duet with Joan. Little did I know then that over 45 years later I would be singing another duet with Joan at the City Varieties in Leeds.

There was no time for pantomime in 1960 because we were busy rehearsing for a Christmas edition of the Minstrel Show for television. Having the Minstrel Show on television at Christmas was becoming almost as traditional as eating turkey and mince pies. Straight after the festive period, starting in the middle of January, there was a new series of the show which would run for 18 weeks.

My act had changed a little for television in that it had become more subtle. In theatres I could be a facial comic but in front of the television cameras I had to curb my grimaces letting the flick of an eyelid be sufficient. That was all part of the learning process and you are never too old to learn new tricks in show business.

For the Christmas Show I had devised a few new routines but only used the 'see-saw' on the show, as I preferred to hold the others back for the new series starting in the New Year. That was the routine where Penny Nicholls would be dressed in a gymslip and I would have small trousers and big boots and be holding a bunch of flowers. We would sit astride a see-saw and as we alternately bobbed up and down we would sing 'I'll be your Sweetheart' and I would desperately try to pass the flowers over to her. It was a good routine that always went down well with the audience.

The hour-long television programme contained loads of

new ideas, a new look in costumes, and more gimmicks like those that had made the show such a sell-out success during the long summer and autumn season. Teamed up with me were Leslie Crowther and former *Television Topper* Valerie Brooks who was making her debut as the Minstrels' new leading lady, while George Mitchell had sorted out nearly 100 separate melodies as the programme made a monster attempt at the world song-speed record. In an odd scenario, minstrel John Boulter was specially 'whitened-up' for the Prince part in the Alice in Wonderland number. My old mate George Chisholm and his Jazzmen provided a musical interlude.

From the opening number 'Parade of Pretty Girls' right to 'Jingle Bells' at the end, the whole show sparkled and when Leslie and Valerie joined me in our hillbilly sequence it went down very well. It was certainly a good forerunner for the new series which started a fortnightly run on television from 14 January 1961 and would run until April. The programme alternated with the Billy Cotton Band Show and Benny Hill, having changed from a Friday position in the schedules to the peak-viewing Saturday evening slot.

There was no solo spot for me, or any of the other stars, in the programme because after all it was a team show and a single act would not have gone down well after one of the Minstrels song and dance routines. Leslie, George, Valerie and myself worked together all the time and we were quite happy to play our parts in that way.

I sang 'Leaning on a Lamp-post' in that first show and then we joined together to do our usual hillbilly routine. Once again, George Inns produced a marvellous show and he told me that he followed the advice given to him by a famous radio producer named Harry S. Pepper. This was 'start bright—get brighter—slow it down a bit—and finish with a bang'. No one could say that the new series didn't do all that because for the first show we drew an audience of over 10 million viewers—don't forget that not every household owned a television set in those days.

George had given himself double trouble by making the show fortnightly instead of monthly. He used to work long into the night with George Mitchell smoothing out any problems. Fortunately, they lived close to each other so they were able to get together regularly. One small flaw in the planning could have thrown the whole schedule out of gear and they had to go through everything with a fine-toothed comb to eliminate any possible snags. It wasn't just on stage that they had to thoroughly plan, there were the costumes and make-up which all had to be carefully organised. The costumes alone cost about £500 for each television show and the make-up was applied by an enthusiastic team of six make-up girls.

Costume changes were laid out on chairs placed in the wings and the cast literally changed within range of the television cameras. The timing of the programme was calculated right down to two minutes of applause per show. If the audience looked like clapping too long, band leader Eric Robinson would get a signal to start playing the next number.

During rehearsals, stop-watches were put on each item and seconds trimmed off if necessary. Some songs only lasted 15 seconds. A hitch could have meant a whole scene was scrapped. George would rather do that than risk botching up the overall show. Once some walking sticks failed to arrive and at other times there were broken zips, burst seams or missing hats.

Funnily enough, when the show first started the men were asked to change into different trousers for each number. This caused such chaos that it was decided very early on to let the men wear the same pair of trousers throughout each show. During one performance, viewers were watching a sketch about Alice in Wonderland, blissfully unaware that there was a fire raging in the studio. A magnesium flash was used as part of special effects and the burning powder set fire to Alice's chair. The assistant producer Len Mitchell had to rush across and beat out the flames with his bare hands.

Later on in the series along with Leslie and George Chisholm we were seen as convicts behind bars singing 'Are You Lonesome Tonight?' and I was a Foreign Legion minstrel in another sketch. I once had a friend who joined the Foreign Legion. It took ages to fill in all the forms and by the time he was recruited he had forgotten what he had joined to forget.

It was a successful run and finished with a special programme on Easter Monday before going on another tour round the theatres, starting in Bristol at the Hippodrome in May. But it would not include me as I was taking a well-earned rest before heading for Blackpool and Bernard Delfont's summer production *Show Time*.

9

STILL A MINSTREL

'. . . in double quick time I was Al Jolson, a policeman, an old man, myself, a Martian, a railway porter, a hillbilly, a schoolboy, a folk singer not unlike Donovan, and a pilot. Hence all the face washes which definitely made me the cleanest comedian in show business . . . I was surprised no enterprising soap firm ever approached me to do a TV commercial.'

* * * * *

It would be December before I rejoined the Minstrels along with my old hillbilly partner, Margo Henderson. We were to be in a seven week season at the Royal Court, Liverpool starting three days before Christmas and I was back in my old job as comedian/compère.

Once again George Inns and George Mitchell had succeeded in devising a show to suit all tastes and the reviews were exceptional. Margo and I combined as though we had never been apart and the costumes and scenic effects along with the fabulous Minstrels helped the show once again prove to be one of the most popular ever devised. It was so highly thought of that in 1962 it was put on at the Victoria Palace in London, while at the same time I was in Morecambe for the summer season, starring in the show with Penny Nicholls. And at the end of the year another production would head for Australia where they expected to stay for 18 months.

The beauty of my Minstrel 'appearances' was that I didn't

have everything in one basket. I was constantly working other theatres between my spells in the show and really I had the best of both worlds. After taking time out to play Buttons in *Cinderella* at the Pavilion Theatre in Bournemouth, I was the featured guest star on the Minstrel Show on television at the end of January in 1964. The Black and Whites had BBC's top variety spot on a Sunday night and it was a great pleasure to make my return to the show on television.

As well as my solo spot I joined up with Leslie Crowther and George Chisholm and we did a marvellous skit on the popular television programme *Z Cars* that went down well. Following our show on TV that evening was *Perry Mason* and after he had solved the 'Case of the Hateful Hero', it was the turn of *Dr Finlay's Casebook*. Sports lovers had 30 minutes of Winter Olympics at 10.00pm.

Soon after the show was over I was told that I would be starring in a new £50,000 stage edition of the Minstrels Show for the summer season at the Winter Gardens in Morecambe starting in June. It would be my third summer season and after our last visit to Morecambe proved to be a sell-out at every performance, we all had our work cut out to make this one even better.

Betty and the boys came up with me for the summer and we found a nice cottage to rent just outside the main town. I would again be acting as comic and compère but I would also feature in the big Jolson spot on the show and I was looking forward to that. Just a few hours before the show was to open in front of an invited audience that included the mayor and mayoress of Morecambe, we lost the services of our musical director Gordon Rolfe. His father was taken critically ill so I flew Gordon to Gatwick where a fast car was waiting to take him to Eastbourne and his father. I delivered him safely and then flew back with minutes to spare before the curtain went up.

It was a wonderful production with non-stop action and breathtaking colour and at the end of over two hours, the whole cast had to respond to curtain call after curtain call from an audience that would have willingly sat through the show again. The sets for the show were impressive and often I could hear the audience burst into spontaneous applause as the curtain rose to reveal a new scene.

The singing of the Mitchell Minstrels was top class as usual and the three vocalists, Don Cleaver, Bob Clayton and my old pal Glyn Dawson put on excellent performances. Ventriloquist Saveen with Daisy May and Micki the talking dog made a big impression, and once again Kris Keo worked some great routines with me.

Before every show could start there had to be a ceremony that the public never saw. It was the most fantastic ritual in show business and happened before the curtain went up. It was known by everyone involved as the spellbinding, pagan, hoodoo ceremony of 'Dib-Dibs'. It had been going on for as long as anyone in the show could remember and was started by a superstitious Topper to ward off evil spirits allegedly caused by electricity in a television studio. Once started, the ceremony couldn't be stopped in case it brought bad luck to the show. Even George Mitchell himself went along with it.

In truth, it was just a way for the cast to allay their pre-show nerves but it seemed to do the trick. The magic certainly rubbed off that summer as advance bookings reached £25,000 and there was always a long queue at the entrance to the Winter Gardens. Each night 5,000 people watched two shows, and that added up to a 30,000 audience every week.

There was another comedian in the show, Reg Thompson, and his slick patter and harmonica playing endeared him to the audience. During the first week, Reg's wife presented him with a daughter in a Middlesbrough hospital so I flew him up for a surprise visit. The stork delivered the baby, and I delivered the father.

I was the only one of the principals from the previous summer season to be back in the show and I worked hard at bringing new ideas to my solo spots. I devised a flying routine with a cinerama-type background and effects and it became one of the hits of the show. The comedy was changed around a lot and I frequently added to it. In this type of fast moving show a comic had to work his insides out because it was not the easiest one from a comic's point of view as it was so fast-moving. At the beginning of the season enough material was submitted to the Lord Chamberlain to allow for these changes to be made when necessary.

I managed to stay fit and well throughout the 13 week run but the show was anything but injury free. During the first half of the season rarely a week passed without one or other of the Minstrels or Toppers reporting sick. Slipped discs, injured toes, sprained ankles, pulled muscles, sprained fingers and eye trouble, along with bouts of 'flu and tonsillitis, all contributed towards some degree of absenteeism. This put a strain on all the fit members of the crew because as everyone knows, the show must go on. So the ritual at the start of every performance which was intended to ward off bad luck didn't seem to have any effect.

In no time at all we came to the end of our run and once again we had broken all records. But there was to be no let up as we all went north and opened a four-week season at the Kings, in Edinburgh. I took Betty and the boys back home before flying up to Edinburgh and leaving the plane at Turnhouse during my stay there.

It wasn't the same show that we performed in Morecambe so there were new routines to learn. As compère, I had to know the exact order of the show. I joined up with Reg

Thompson for some madcap tomfoolery dressed as Martians which we called 'Lunar Lunatics', and Neville King was a ventriloquist with a difference—he had a dummy you couldn't see. But I did manage to keep my airplane skit in the show to send the audience careering skywards in a crazy flight around the world.

You really had to be a Minstrel to appreciate the happy atmosphere within the show. If anyone ran into trouble, everyone tried to help out. For instance, Kris Keo wanted a day at home in Liverpool so I flew her down to Speke, and went back later to pick her up. And while she was gone, one of the boys even offered to look after the budgie she kept in her dressing room.

It was now the Scottish audiences turn to see a show that was breaking records everywhere. Record sales were now well over six and a half million, the West End production was into its third year and booked well into the next, and television audience figures were in the hundred million bracket.

Midway through our second week we were already sold out, and don't forget it was a twice nightly show. One of the secrets of the Minstrels success was that everyone in the cast got a tremendous kick out of it, and that came across to the audience. In many shows there was friction between personalities behind the scenes but with the Minstrels there was no attempt at personality building—everyone in the show was a star. The result was a happy and contented atmosphere. Only one thing really counted and that was to get out there in front of the audience and give them your best. Nothing succeeds like success and that was the way with us. We knew we were appearing in a great show with a great reputation, we liked being in it, and we all tried to give just that little bit extra at every performance.

After delighting all our Scottish friends, we went to the

Lyceum Theatre in Sheffield for a four-week season starting in October. On the opening night I made an appeal to the audience for digs for seven of the chorus girls who had failed to find lodgings. The show had a cast of about 50 and some of the girls had found it difficult to get somewhere to live at a reasonable price. Within minutes of opening up the stage door the following day, we had received 18 offers of accommodation and in no time at all everyone had been fixed up in temporary homes.

Although we were to be at the Lyceum for a month, our opening night saw the centre of Sheffield brought to a standstill by a huge traffic jam, such was the interest in the Minstrels. Many claimed it was the finest musical show ever staged in the city.

During the second week I was kidnapped and held to ransom but it was not as bad as it sounded. As I was leaving the theatre I was bundled into a car along with Kris Keo and lead singer Malcolm Hilbey and we were driven off at high speed to a University Hall of Residence where we had to spend the night. Our abductors were Rag students and the kidnapping was an official stunt that the authorities had been made aware of beforehand.

They told us they would release us in time for the night's performance providing we presented prizes for one of their crazy capers. It appeared that they were trying to break the world record for the number of people in a bath at the same time. At least we didn't have to climb in there with them. From Sheffield we went up the road to the Leeds Grand Theatre and once again played to packed houses.

It was building up to a Christmas Spectacular at the Theatre Royal in Newcastle where we would perform twice nightly, 6.15pm and 8.45pm for a total of 15 weeks. These shows would take us through the holiday period and into 1965.

By now, Kris Keo had become an important member of the show. She was not the first girl to be pulled out of the chorus line and given a starring role and neither will she be the last, but her elevation was well deserved as she was a superb dancer and had a natural flair for comedy. It was at my request that she was given a chance and she never let me down. We appeared in theatres all over the country with, and without, the Minstrels, and toured abroad, and she was always a great asset to the show.

She started out as a Littlewoods Songster when just 16 years old, and after four years of singing became a Television Topper. She had a bubbly sense of fun and a rare way of coaxing tunes from a guitar, piano and bongos. Her chance came when Penny Nicholls went sick while we were appearing in Morecambe and Kris took her opportunity well. Coming from Liverpool she was a good friend of Cilla Black, George Harrison and Paul McCartney so that was another claim to fame for her. She eventually returned to Liverpool to get married and it was a great loss when she retired from the business.

The Newcastle stop was the longest we had been in one place, apart from our summer season, for over a year. While moving from theatre to theatre fatigue never struck, but if you relaxed for a little it would hit you hard, especially as it was a hectic and breathless show. At least it gave me a break from juggling with transport. Every time the show moved I had the problem of shifting a car, a caravan and an aeroplane.

With Roger at school it was difficult for Betty and the boys to join me so every other weekend I flew home to Cardiff for my Sunday dinner with the family, and then back in time for the show. It only took me two hours from Newcastle to Cardiff but by road in those days it would have been more like 10 hours of driving.

We managed to make arrangements so that Betty could occasionally come up and stay for a few days. I brought a caravan up and parked it at Birtley. Let me explain how I managed to get my plane, car and caravan all in one place in Newcastle. We were still down in Leeds with the show so I asked a friend to drive my car and tow the caravan from Leeds up to Birtley. That same morning I flew over in my plane and waited at the airfield. My friend arrived, parked the van, and then drove to the airport to meet me. I flew him back home to Leeds and then carried on to Cardiff for my Sunday lunch. When I eventually flew to Newcastle for the show, my car was at the airfield and my caravan was all ready for use. Like most things, all it needed was a little planning.

Life wasn't just performing, resting, sleeping, and then performing again. We still had time to visit local hospitals like the Fleming Memorial Hospital for Children to bring a little laughter into the little ones' lives and of course I managed a few games of football. One of those was against a Jackie Milburn XI in aid of under privileged children and my pal Trevor Ford came up for the match which was held at Brough Park in Newcastle.

After the Newcastle run finished we went to the Alhambra in Bradford. This time I had the caravan moved to Lower Shelf where it was sited with a good view. I flew down to Cardiff, picked up Betty and Ceri, and brought them back for the short season in Yorkshire. This time Roger stayed behind and was looked after by relatives as he was busy with school studies and we didn't want to take him away from them.

We played to full houses almost every night in Bradford, and then again at the New Theatre in Hull. It seemed that the popularity of the Minstrels was never-ending although the strain of it all was beginning to take its toll, not least on my face which had to be washed a dozen times a show to allow for all the make-up changes.

From Hull we went to Stockton-on-Tees, and then further north to Aberdeen where I had first appeared with the Harmaniacs way back in 1949. Although the show had visited almost every key town in the British Isles, our season at Her Majesty's Theatre was the first ever in the Granite City. I had also played there in the late Fifties when I appeared with the Lyon family—Bebe Daniels, Ben Lyon and their children Barbara and Richard. I missed rehearsals for the two-week season on the first day because of poor weather conditions which delayed me flying from Stockton up to Aberdeen. Once again my Al Jolson routine went down well as I moved to the front of the stage and sang 'Sonny Boy' during one of my solo spots.

It was now time to look forward to the summer season and the summer of 1965 would see us at the Opera House in Blackpool. I liked to have everything organised in plenty of time so I took the opportunity of a free day to fly to the seaside town in my Beechcraft Bonanza, now called 'The Minstrel', to look for a suitable site for the caravan. I also used the visit to sell my Mercedes as I was keen on purchasing a new one.

We were the last of the Blackpool shows to open but quickly became the resort's best family offering. In order to keep the Minstrels in its rightful place at the top of the tree, someone from behind the scenes always took a seat in the stalls, not just for opening night, but at every performance. Six people usually took turns as the watchdog—promoter Robert Luff, general manager Osborn Whittaker, company manager Douglas Freear, production manager Lawrence Bloom, producer George Inns and ballet mistress Jackie Griffiths. They believed that every night was a first night for the paying customers. Too many shows slacken off towards the end of a run and that was something they, and all us performers, were keen to see would never happen. The fact that someone from the company was out there watching every night helped keep everyone up to the mark.

It was a simple formula after all, with pretty girls, good voices, excellent dancers, lots of well-known songs, and good comedy. But it was also a success because there were no pauses to allow people's attention to wander. Just from my point of view in double quick time I was Al Jolson, a policeman, an old man, myself, a Martian, a railway porter, a hillbilly, a schoolboy, a folk singer not unlike Donovan, and a pilot. Hence all the face washes which definitely made me the cleanest comedian in show business. Don't forget there were even more facial scrubs every day when we had afternoon matinees. I was surprised no enterprising soap firm ever approached me to do a TV commercial.

My secret was that I used baby cream to soften my skin. I came up with the idea after thinking that babies must get pretty sore with everything they have to put up with, so I figured that if it worked for them, it was good enough for me. Every time I put the make-up on in my dressing room for one of my characters I could feel the character building up inside me. When it was time to go on I could walk on to the stage as the old porter, the airman, or whoever I was made up to be. When the routine was over I literally changed into someone else in my dressing room.

I was a natural Walter Mitty and it was great getting paid for something I loved doing. I had been playing other people ever since I was a kid, trying to mimic the great Jimmy Durante, Rob Wilton or others like that. Being someone else was just a matter of observation—and a sense of humour.

I was looking forward to the start of the school holidays when Betty and the boys would be coming up to spend a few weeks with me. Years back I remember when I did my first summer season in Blackpool and we lived in our caravan all the time, touring from town to town in shows. Roger, who by now was 14 years old, was only a toddler then.

In between shows I managed a few rounds of golf with Donald Peers, Eric Morecambe and Ernie Wise, and Freddie Garrety, of Freddie and the Dreamers, who were all appearing in the resort. I also enjoyed addressing the Blackpool Rotary Club on flying and it was a pleasant change to be able to talk about a serious subject although I couldn't resist the odd gag or two.

It was soon time to be on the move again as the show was booked to appear back in Scotland at the King's in Edinburgh for a five-week season before playing in Sheffield and then returning to Glasgow for a 15-week season. Fortunately, I had time to put my feet up at home in Cardiff for a week before linking up with the show in Edinburgh.

It was while I was at home and had a few quiet moments to myself that I decided my time with the Minstrels was fast drawing to a close. I had been tied to the show for over six years so I felt that I needed a change. The skin on my face was also beginning to show the effects of those daily scrubs to remove make-up and that also helped me make my mind up. I thought it was time to do more television, and to perform in clubs and theatres as a solo artist. I had been touring for 17 or 18 years and really needed a long spell working from the comfort of home instead of travelling around the country.

Another factor that helped me reach my decision was the change in some people's perception of the Black and White Minstrels. Certain newspaper theatre critics began calling the show a hang-over from the past, pushing forward a pier-end caricature conception of the negro. Despite still playing to packed audiences there was a sense amongst some of the critics that the show was no longer suitable. It had never occurred to me, or the other performers, that there was anything racial in the show and I couldn't understand why they had to bring that into it.

I was already committed to appear for several months and there was no way that I would pull out of my contract but when we played Edinburgh and then over Christmas in Glasgow, I knew in my heart that my time as resident compère/comedian was coming to a close. Christmas in Glasgow, in a caravan, had nothing to do with it. I had been caravanning along with Betty and the boys for a number of years and many of the show-biz personalities working in Glasgow at the time were also staying in trailers. Minstrels' ballet mistress Jackie Griffiths had a 22ft luxury model out west which she festooned with Christmas decorations. Like me, she preferred the freedom of living in a caravan to taking up lodgings. Australian-born acrobat Leslie Warren was on a site in Drumchapel with his wife Maisie and daughter Lorraine, who were all in the show at the King's.

While I was performing I never once thought that this could be my last Christmas season with the Minstrels. There was so much to do that there wasn't time to think of anything other than being on time and delivering lines. I wasn't sad or unhappy. All this business about comedians being sad souls is a lot of malarkey. After all, footballers get upset when they don't score goals and comics get depressed when they don't get laughs. If you give a comedian a big reception he is the happiest guy in the world. I was always a happy character and I thought most comics were the same.

While I am on my soapbox perhaps I can get something else off my chest. 'The show must go on' line is another joke. Sure the show must go on—not because a theatrical type is dedicated, but because unlike an ordinary worker, a doctor's note doesn't do him any good. It's no work, no pay—that is why performers make an appearance even if they have to crawl on. I think there is too much talk about how somebody or other made a sacrifice and did a performance when he or she should have been in bed. What's the odds—thousands of people go to their jobs when they should be in bed.

Take what happened to me while we were in Glasgow. I travelled 900 miles to Cardiff and back, got mixed up in floods, went two nights without sleep, and still appeared on time at the theatre to do the show. Sure it was tough but there is no use in beefing about it. I was doing a job just like anyone else and I just had to get on with it.

By now I had been doing the show for so long that it had become a way of life. The routine of it was so regular that I just couldn't get out of it. I would light my first cigarette in my dressing room at exactly the same time every night, kick my shoes into the same corner, act each night as I did before, everything was precision, just like the show. It had been a good vehicle for me, although I hadn't made a fortune. In fact I could have earned more on the cabaret and variety circuit.

Funnily enough, to ease that monotony, we had a new act join us during the Scottish section of the tour. Never seen before on television they were called 'The Wychwoods', a husband and wife team named Jack and Audrey Shaw. They somehow managed to conjure up poodles of all colours, shapes and sizes from thin air. The act was so new to Britain that the dogs were all still in quarantine and had to be rushed back to the kennels after every show.

Edinburgh, Sheffield, and Glasgow all played to packed houses and from there we headed south to Nottingham and the Theatre Royal where we started at the end of March 1966 and went right through to the end of May. Once again, my jet flight around the world brought the most laughs, even though I was in an aeroplane that stayed motionless on the stage against a back-drop of trick film sequences projected onto a wide screen. The routine was called 'Round The World In Five Minutes' and the audience really got the feeling that they were flying with me.

Dressed as an aviator, I started off by pushing the plane on to the stage. The lights went down and the plane's engine roared into life as we were off along the runway and zooming up into the air. Next moment we were going through clouds towards mountain peaks that we seemed to miss by inches, then we were out over the sea and shooting straight down towards the briny. After evading a wetting and giving the audience time to catch their breath we flew up Oxford Street and then suddenly onto a railway track at zero feet with a tunnel straight ahead.

Quickly we would soar away over the countryside before coming down on the roadway where a man is pedalling a bicycle. We would give him the fright of his life before heading back out to sea and coming in to land. But who was that on the runway? Only the man on the bicycle again so I would pull out one of my six-shooters and shoot him just as we came to a stop in the back of the hangar. The audience would sit back heaving huge sighs of relief, sore from laughing, but mighty glad to be back on land in one piece.

The last of the songs the Minstrels performed to finish the show was always 'When The Saints Go Marching In'. It should have been 'When The Cash Comes Rolling In' because even though we did two shows a night, there were queues of people for weeks eager to purchase tickets and I doubt that at the end of our eight-week season at the Theatre Royal there would ever have been even one spare seat.

My finale as a Minstrel came with the last performance in

Nottingham. I had spoken to Bob Luff, the producer, and told him that I wanted to finish as resident compère/comedian so that I could go on to do other things. He was understanding as he also knew of the problems I had been having with a sore face. After all, I had stopped shaving on Sundays to give my face a rest and had to constantly apologise for my unkempt look whenever making personal appearances.

He wished me well, thanked me for all my efforts in the six years I had been a minstrel, and then told me that I would always be welcome on a Minstrel show. I had one more task as a member of the Minstrel family before I left, and that was to appear in the BBC television version of the show, something I hadn't done for over two years. It was a pleasant change from the fast-paced version I had to do on stage.

Even now looking back, I believe that leaving then was the right decision to make, although at the time I wondered how much I would miss all the camaraderie and friendship of being a part of the most successful stage show of all time. But I wanted something else. I wanted to do more television and a bit of character acting, maybe in a straight play or something like that. Now was the time to find out what the future would hold. I was in my 40th year and a new part of my show business life was about to start.

I had grown tired of holding the team together. In show business you must play out in front. Of course I was grateful to the Minstrels as without a doubt, my seven year stint had brought in good money. But as well as a sore face I also had a seven-year itch to end the marriage of convenience and get cracking again out on my own, and it didn't take long for the offers to start rolling in.

10

SUMMER SEASONS
AND PANTOMIMES

*'Did you hear about the cowboy who walked into a German car
showroom and said 'Audi'?'*

* * * * *

The Black and White Minstrels kept me busy right up to
Easter 1961 when the television series ended. That left me
free to join Bernard Delfont's summer show *Star Time* at the
North Pier in Blackpool. But before that, I was able to fit in
a family holiday in Majorca with Betty, the two boys, and a
couple of friends. I would have liked to have flown everyone
out there as I am a terrible back-seat pilot but I only had a
four seater. To make matters worse, it cost me £120 more
than it would have done in my own plane. We had a good
break in the sun though and it was great to be together just
enjoying our own company.

Still, I was able to fly the family up to Squires Gate
Airport, Blackpool in my new Beachcraft Bonanza for the
start of the summer season. I was at the controls with Betty
beside me while Roger, now aged 10, and one year old Ceri
were on the seats behind us. It turned out to be quite a
landing. We also had another passenger in Scamp our pet
dog. Betty and I were more concerned about Scamp than we
were for the baby. After all, Ceri had flown about five times

previously but Scamp had never been up before. The family were safely billeted in a rented home on the South Shore of the resort.

Also appearing at the North Pier with me were Michael Holliday, Terry Hall and Lenny the Lion, The Allisons, Doreen Hulme and Des O'Connor. In a throw-back to the old music hall days there was also a speciality act called the Roberts Bros Chimpanzees presented by Sylvano. Bernard Delfont had devised a cunning plan for his summer season. Instead of having one headliner, he put together the six of us in top billing with the main object to 'keep 'em laughing'.

Michael Holliday had a lazy, relaxed style of singing and his record 'Story of my Life' was a big hit. He went on to star in his own show on television but sadly took his own life and was a great loss to the business. He had an easy-going attitude that his fans found fascinating. Singing came naturally to him so he had the advantage of putting over his songs with little or no effort.

The Allisons were two likeable young lads who were not brothers at all. Bob and John represented Britain that summer in the *Eurovision Song Contest* in Cannes with what turned out to be their only big hit, 'Are You Sure?' During rehearsals one morning they told me that while they were in Blackpool for the summer, they wanted to take driving lessons as they were hoping to buy their first car. I advised them not to go out on the roads until after the Whitsun Holiday weekend.

The summer season that 1961 must have been a record breaker as there was a wonderful array of talent appearing in the theatres around the resort. Shirley Bassey was at the Opera House for the first half of the summer with Cliff Richard taking over for the latter half, while Ivor Emmanuel and Mr Pastry would star throughout the whole run. At the

Hippodrome, David Whitfield was starring in *Rosemarie*, my old pal Lonnie Donegan was *Puttin' On The Donegan* at the Winter Gardens Pavilion, and Tommy Trinder was topping the bill at the Central Pier. For a complete change, Arthur Askey and Betty Driver were going straight in a play at the Grand Theatre.

I was delighted to be back for the summer, as there was no place to touch breezy, busy, bouncy Blackpool. When I met ventriloquist Terry Hall a year previously, we were both going through a nervous time in a man's life. We were both expectant fathers. I already had a son, and Terry a daughter. When the new babies were born, I had two sons and Terry had two daughters. If that wasn't a notable double, I didn't know what was. I had been friends with Terry for years and during that summer our families had many get-togethers during the run of the show. How many of you remember that besides Lenny, Terry also worked with Jeremy the dopey giraffe?

It was around this time that I took a big decision and became an employee of a company. But there was a catch— the company was called Stan Stennett Ltd. Betty and I were directors and we started with a capital of £1,000. That meant I could draw a weekly wage from the company and if I wasn't working for any reason I could still get a pay packet. Mind you, I had been brought up not to expect handouts of any kind so I was certainly not going to sit back in my armchair, do nothing, and wait to be paid. We also had to put up a little plaque on our front door at Heol Madoc to show that it was the address of our company. Apparently, it is someone's job to go round and check these things. Betty found an unobtrusive little corner for ours.

While in Blackpool I had also arranged to do a series of Sunday concerts throughout the summer. These were mainly at Butlin's Camps situated at Filey, Skegness, Pwllheli and Clacton. Working in the camps was always good fun. Well, it was a captive audience after all.

I took my six-shooters with me to Blackpool but hoped nobody would challenge my claim to gun-slinging fame. The last time that happened I found myself in a gunfight on Clapham Common. Seriously, this did happen to me. The gunfight was arranged through the English Westerners Society who had heard of my sharp-shooting fame and decided to match me with a slick cowboy from Billy Smart's Circus. It must have been an unusual sight as the circus sent a load of Indian braves to ride bareback around the common on their horses while we got down to business. We used blanks, of course—and I won't tell you who won—but I'm still here ain't I? Did you hear about the cowboy who walked into a German car showroom and said 'Audi'?

Shooting my gun on stage one night started a romance. I unearthed this tale on phoning a home-heating equipment firm in Cardiff when I wanted a job done in the house. When I told the girl on the switchboard who was calling she yelled out, 'Oh, Stan Stennett, my good friend!' She explained that she had been to see me a few months earlier and when I fired my gun she had jumped up and grabbed a young man sitting next to her. Conversation followed and they were now engaged. When I told my wife about it she said I ought to buy them a wedding present. Phone calls were expensive even in those days.

On the opening night of the show I received many telegrams and good luck messages. One was from my Defence Minister, Harry Secombe. The telegram read, 'Keep the standard of the Welsh Air Force flying—and don't fall in the water love'.

A couple of weeks into the show I took time out to top the

bill in a Workers Playtime radio programme broadcast from the Northbridge Works of Joseph Lucas in Burnley. It wasn't my first visit to the East Lancashire town as I had played there about nine years previously when I was way down the bill. Denis Goodwin and Pat O'Hare, who used to sing with the Dallas Boys before branching out on his own, also appeared. We performed in front of about 200 people in the works canteen during lunch hour for the show which was on air for 30 minutes.

I mentioned earlier that also appearing in *Show Time* were the Roberts Bros Chimpanzees and one of them almost stole the show one evening. The audience thought it was all part of the act when Sinbad the chimp ambled on stage from the wings in the middle of my double act with Des O'Connor. The errant chimp grabbed the mike and went straight into a riotous number. He then adopted the expression of someone who knows he has impressed before shuffling off.

The chimps had been the act before us and Sinbad must have slipped back through the tabs—that's what we call the curtains—to turn our double act into a trio. If we thought he could have done it again, Des and I would have kept him in the act.

It was good to have the family up in Blackpool with me for most of the summer season. Apart from not having to travel down to Cardiff to see them whenever possible, it was great being able to spend time with them before going off to the theatre. They were able to stay until the end of August when Roger had to be back for the new school term. The resort was full to the brim with holidaymakers proving that it was a great attraction despite all the overtures even in those days for overseas holidays. I have always said that if we could guarantee good weather in this country then nobody would consider overseas holidays.

I was reading the papers sat on a deckchair at the front when I spotted a headline which screamed out 'Man In Space'—then I realised that it referred to the Blackpool holidaymaker who had managed to find somewhere to park his car.

Just before a show, I had a shock when I heard that Ceri had fallen down and a fractured skull was suspected. We took him to the hospital as soon as possible to be checked over but fortunately it was nothing serious. He soon recovered but I was amazed at how kind and considerate everyone could be during our worrying time.

The show continued to play to full houses every night and the reviews were consistently favourable yet poor old Terry Hall received a lot of stick from the public. He had letters from all over Lancashire complaining that Lenny the Lion's mouthing of the National Anthem on stage every night caused the audience to snigger and titter. Terry couldn't understand the fuss and he rightly said that it would have been disrespectful for Lenny not to join in singing the National Anthem as the children watching the show considered Lenny to be a real personality.

One Sunday in September I made a special flight in my aircraft and ended up spending the day in three countries. I had breakfast before flying from Blackpool to Leeds where I had time for a coffee before picking up George Inns. From Leeds we flew up to Prestwick in Scotland to meet my old Minstrels partner, Margo Henderson, for lunch. George wanted to discuss Margo's return to the Minstrel Show after completion of her season in Glasgow. Once business had been concluded it was back in the air to London where I left George before making a flying visit to Cardiff to see Betty and the children for supper. The whole day gave me a lot of pleasure—and indigestion.

The thoroughly enjoyable summer season finally came to an end early in October but it had finished a little earlier than that for two of the stars. Michael Holliday was already out of the show after suffering from strain while Terry Hall was waiting to go into hospital for a small operation on his nose that had been troubling him for some time.

Twice nightly, for the full run of the season, Des O'Connor and I did a routine with an egg which ended with him smashing it over my head. In the final performance we almost dried up as instead of the usual hen's egg, Des came out with a huge goose egg. He said that he had tried to get an ostrich egg but just couldn't find one anywhere. That was one skit that finished in a messy way but I'm sure that all the audience could see the yoke.

After Blackpool I had time to fit in another CSE tour to Cyprus, Malta and North Africa, all places I had already visited on similar entertainment sprees. During my spell overseas I took part in a three-way *Family Favourites* programme from Cyprus. It was the first time I had ever been a DJ but it was fun bringing pleasure to the lads serving abroad and to their families back home. The trip was arranged so quickly that this time I had no opportunity to accept parcels and letters as I had done on previous visits.

After the three-week tour I was booked to appear at a club in Bristol for four nights. And that fitted in well as it was an easy matter flying across the Bristol Channel every evening. Well it would have been if the weather had been kind. After the first night I had to catch a train because the conditions were a bit dicey. It did seem wrong though that it took me eight minutes to travel by air from Bristol to Whitchurch in Cardiff where we lived, yet after landing at Rhoose Airport I was left with an eight mile car journey to get home.

But it was a good way of winding down because Christmas 1961 was going to be hectic. The new series of the Minstrel Show was due to start in December at the Royal Court, Liverpool for a seven week season so straight after my week in Bristol it was into rehearsals.

I heard some disturbing news from back home while up in Liverpool perfecting the show. The New Theatre in Cardiff was in grave danger of closing because of lack of support. If a large industrial city like Cardiff had to close its leading theatre what hope was there for other provincial cities? Television was blamed but my view then, and even now, was that theatres could still be filled provided the shows staged were capable of drawing people away from their firesides.

I wrote to the *South Wales Echo* and pledged my support, along with other Welsh performers, in order to help the New stay open a little longer and perhaps win back those missing audiences. I spoke to Wyn Calvin and Ossie Morris about the possibility of Cardiff's main theatre closing and they both agreed that something had to be done. It seemed a pity that the Welsh were not as proud of the theatre as the Scots who kept their venues thriving with shows featuring their own stars. My own personal gripe was that I had been involved in pantomime for 12 years but not once had I been approached to star in a panto in my own home town.

Christmas Day was very special as I was able to fly down to Cardiff and spend it at home with Betty and the boys, and it turned out to be our last Christmas at Heol Madoc as the Stennett family would soon be on the move. When Ceri arrived, our home in Whitchurch suddenly seemed a little on the small side so Betty and I began looking around for a bigger house. We saw one on Rhiwbina Hill that we both fell in love with immediately but it was a little too expensive for us at the time. In any case, while we were doing our sums, it was sold to a charming couple called Norman and May Humphries. It had been advertised by well-known estate agent Harold Greene as a 'house fit for a film star'. We were terribly disappointed but it was beyond our means at that time.

Of course, with the success of the Minstrel Shows, I had earned myself a top contract of around £500 per week. That was before stoppages which also included paying my agent, so when suddenly we were given another opportunity to buy the house we were in a far better position to proceed. It seemed that Mrs Humphries was a little lonely left in the house all day and wanted to move back into the centre of Cardiff.

We had another look over the property and in no time at all we agreed a sale. The Stennett family, complete with 12-year-old Roger and Ceri aged two, a dog, a budgerigar, a large shooting-brake, and Betty's mini, moved lock, stock and guitar into Craig-y-Nos in the first week of March 1962.

What a spot and what a view. This was the only place for us—lots of trees, the mountain, and plenty of fresh, healthy air. When I woke up in the morning I could hear the birds coughing. It was a stone-built dormer bungalow set in half an acre of ground, unique in design and with views clear across the Bristol Channel. I had a room for a den where I could type out scripts and generally keep all my show business paraphernalia which was something I couldn't do in Heol Madoc. The best part was that we now had the house that we had always wanted from the moment we first set eyes on it. All the hard work building up the act had paid dividends.

There was no time to wallow in deep-pile carpets or gazing across the channel. I had a show to put on at the New Theatre. I put up £1,500 in a bit of a gamble to prove that a show of good quality could be produced to bring people back into the theatre. But a one week show wasn't all that I had in mind. I had plenty of ideas that I know would have turned the loss-maker back into a vibrant theatre once again but trying to convince the powers-that-be was proving to be difficult. The council turned out to be a real stumbling block which was surprising when you think that a lot of people in the entertainment industry were prepared to do their bit.

Eventually, it had got to such a stage with Prince Littler losing £300 to £400 a week that he snapped up my offer of promoting the *Stan Stennett Show*. In turn, I hoped that it would pay for itself otherwise I wouldn't be retiring for a very long time. I contacted artists who I knew were available for the week and who I had worked with before. I was lucky to be able to call on two very good friends of mine, Malcolm Vaughan and Kenneth Earle. They were a singing comedy duo whose offbeat humour was moving them quickly up the show-biz ladder. Malcolm was from Troedyrhiw and his singing was gaining a huge following particularly after he sold over a million records of 'St Theresa Of The Roses', one of my favourite songs of the time. 'More Than Ever' and 'My Special Angel,' were two other big hits for Malcolm. Kenneth provided the gags in the act but he could also manage a song or two.

Also on the programme were the Peter Crawford Trio, ventriloquist Roger Carne, Jill and Terry who were comedy singers and comic Wally Dunn. I also arranged for a juggling act and the Gibson Girls so there was plenty to please everyone. It was a well-rehearsed show which had good reviews. For the Friday night performance, the management of Leslies Stores, a big South Wales concern, took 600 seats in a block booking and that helped us no end.

When the curtain finally went down, I hadn't lost any

money. I hadn't made any either but at least all the cast had been paid and the audiences had seen a quality show at the New Theatre. It had been a good week considering the weather and it would have been even better but for a disappointing Saturday evening when we only had two half-full houses.

Sadly, when the curtain went down on our show, it stayed down and the New Theatre was closed. It seemed that the council were sat back waiting for Prince Littler to return from America before holding discussions about the fate of the building. I estimated that my publicity calls on local stores and factories resulted in an extra £500-£600 in takings, proving that you have to publicise events if you want them to be a success. That is something I take into every show I produce even to this day. If people are unaware there is a show on, how can you expect them to turn up?

I worked out at the time that if everyone in Cardiff gave 2s (10p), there would have been enough money in the pot to buy the New Theatre. My disappointment at the outcome with the New had to be put to one side as I needed to turn my attention elsewhere. I was off to Torbay to appear on a bill with the gorgeous Beverley Sisters. It was a Bernard Delfont production at the Princess Theatre in Torquay, right on the sea front and, as usual, no expense was spared to put on a show that included Kenny Baker, one of the finest trumpet players I have ever heard. The Bevs had the audience in the palm of their hands singing 'Sisters', crooning love songs, or engaging in leg-pulling cross talk on the theme of love and marriage. They kept the same act going for year after year so all credit to them.

In March 1963 I flew from Cardiff to Prestwick on a special journey. It was to say thank you to the Popplewell family who were celebrating 50 years as owners of the Gaiety Theatre in Ayr. I would have gone almost anywhere on earth for the Popplewells who I thought were the most wonderful people in show business. I first played the Gaiety back in 1949 as a member of the Harmaniacs and the following year I returned as a solo act.

I was only six weeks into the summer season when I received the offer to join the *Show Band Show* and they didn't hesitate to tell me to take up the offer and grab the chance. I shall be eternally grateful to them. I was delighted to have a 15 minute spot on television from the theatre to meet Leslie Popplewell and let the family know just how I felt about them. After all, not many theatre owners would have allowed me, or anyone else, to tear up a contract and leave a successful show. While there I was able to recall the time 13 years previously when Roger was born. Half the audience must have sent presents and the front of the stage was covered in them. The Popplewells were a lovely family and the family atmosphere was to be found everywhere in the theatre.

I was back in the plane the following month flying to Stansted Airport where I boarded a jet bound for Singapore. I was on another overseas trip to entertain the troops over a three-week period. This time it was Singapore, Malaya and Borneo. The fact that there was trouble brewing in Borneo didn't worry me because when I went to Malaya in 1957, Communist guerrillas were causing problems, as they were in Aden when I entertained the troops. I was accompanied by Kim Brown who was a singing, swinging trombonist from the Arthur Haynes Show

We wanted to go right into the centre of the tension close to the front line but the authorities wouldn't allow us to get too near the action. We were worth a lot of money to them because of the insurance premium they had to take out on us, so they were right to be careful. While in the jungle I saw a monkey with a tin opener. I said, 'You don't need a tin opener to peel a banana'. He said, 'No, this is for the custard'.

I did another three-way *Family Favourites*, this time from Singapore and I know it gave the lads out there a boost. I only wished someone would cause trouble in the Bahamas so that I could be sent there for a few weeks. We pre-recorded the *Family Favourites* programme in London before we left so that if anything went wrong with communications in the Far East, they would still have a show and no one would have been disappointed. We flew back in a troop carrier and within an hour of landing, I was aloft flying home to Cardiff.

With the Minstrels taking a well-earned summer break, George Inns had devised a new programme called *Country and Western* which was to be shown on television on a fortnightly basis. I was delighted to be asked to take part along with pianist Van Doren and Canadian singer Gordy Lightfoot.

In no time at all I was rehearsing for Tom Arnold's summer show *Come Inside* at the Britannia Pier in Great Yarmouth along with my good friends the Beverley Sisters and those musical clowns, the Three Monarchs. They were three harmonica players. The big one in the middle was the funny one and the other two would try to push him out of the way. They all had different size instruments with Cedric, the big guy, having the largest.

I loved working in Great Yarmouth because the airfield was so handily placed for access to the resort. It was easy to collect the family and fly them in to spend around six weeks there with me. You would think that it was fairly easy to gather everyone and whisk them up into the clouds but our dog Scamp had other ideas. We missed our first flight time because he ran off as we were waiting to board and I had to chase after him.

As usual, I rented a house in Gorleston, near the resort, and it seemed that most theatre folk did the same thing as there is nothing like having your family with you. Joe Brown, who was starring at the Windmill Theatre, had rented a cottage for the season about 20 miles out of Yarmouth and he wouldn't tell anyone where it was because he wanted some peace and quiet. I take it that the Bruvvers weren't staying in the same cottage with him. Ken Dodd and Rosemary Squires, who was in Doddy's show at the ABC Regal, also rented cottages for the season.

Jimmy Saville was among the stars performing that summer in Great Yarmouth. He had a story about Elvis Presley that he would tell to anyone at every opportunity. Jimmy reckoned that just standing next to Elvis was like standing next to a charge of electricity. He was such a powerful personality that any girl would faint if he suddenly walked up and stood in front of her.

While I was at the Britannia, I was also booked to do concerts around the country so the airplane really came in useful. I worked in Ayr, Filey, Clacton, Margate and Bognor Regis doing Sunday concert engagements. It was hectic, but enjoyable. It seemed that I rarely had a Sunday off but it was all good stuff and the concerts went down well, as did the summer show and it was a shame when the time came to say goodbye. Great Yarmouth with its eight major theatres showing top class entertainment throughout the summer was beginning to rival Blackpool.

I had a bit of bad luck playing football and broke my wrist. It was fortunate that it happened when it did because any later and my appearance in pantomime at the Pavilion in

Bournemouth could have been in jeopardy. I had it strapped and used a sling whenever possible but still managed to fly the plane when needed and without the powers-that-be finding out about my injury.

The 1963 pantomime was *Cinderella* at the Pavilion Theatre and I was playing the part of Buttons. My first task was to find another giant pumpkin, just as I did for the Leeds panto a few years earlier. Always with an eye for publicity, I placed an ad in the *Times* for a pumpkin 'prepared to take a certain amount of pummelling'. The search was on.

Before *Cinderella* started I appeared in some other quality shows. I was a guest star in the televised Christmas edition of the *Black and White Minstrels* which was shown three days before Christmas, and also did a *Good Old Days* show from Leeds which was put out on Christmas Eve. There could have been nothing better for putting me in the mood to play Buttons. I had appeared in the very first *Good Old Days* show from Leeds in July 1953 and at the time the producer promised me a return booking. I was pleased that he was able to arrange it so quickly! My old mate Frankie Vaughan, complete with straw boater, was also on the bill at the City of Varieties.

Cinderella was given a new look when it opened on Christmas Eve. Although the story was told as it had been for generations, the production was given a really modern treatment with zippy and rhythmic songs and music—even including the Twist—and it was a refreshing boost to the most charming of pantomimes. Scenery and costumes were full of colour with ultra-violet lighting used in the transformation scene to great effect, and the gags ranged from the likes of *Coronation Street* to the Beatles.

My performance as Buttons included my impression of the lads from Liverpool and that part of the show appeared to go down well with young and old alike. Danny La Rue and Alan Haynes played the Ugly Sisters and what a pair they made. Their costumes were fabulous and I doubt whether there has ever been better Ugly Sisters than those two that year. Of course, I was hampered for the early performances because of my broken wrist so the guitar had to be left in the dressing room along with my six-guns until I had the plaster removed.

I had my aircraft at Hurn Airport, Bournemouth so I was able to fly back regularly to Cardiff to be with Betty and the boys. Luckily enough, the weather was kind to me most of the time although I did run into a snowstorm over the Bristol Channel on one occasion and had to land in a Somerset field. I eventually arrived in Cardiff over five hours late.

The pantomime was so successful that it was held over for an additional week and I was sorry the season came to an end because it had been a happy show with plenty of laughs.

11

BACK ON THE CIRCUIT

'A man walked into a new revolving restaurant in London to order a meal—he got the meal but it took him three weeks to hang up his coat.'

* * * * *

In February, 1964, the new BBC Wales television service opened to give Welsh viewers an alternative of 14 hours of special programmes each week, seven hours in English and seven hours in Welsh. Every Friday evening there was a 45 minute programme called the *Capital Show* from the Astra Theatre at the RAF base in St Athan showcasing Welsh artists. I was one of the first performers along with Newport-born Johnny Morris and my old pals Albert and Les Ward. Others to appear during the series were singers David Hughes, Geraint Evans and Maureen Evans, and comedian Derek Roy.

The programmes were pre-recorded before a live audience and introduced by Alun Williams supported by Ray Bishop and his orchestra. At the time it was the biggest get-together of Welsh or near-Welsh entertainers ever seen on television. There was just time for me to appear at Reading Magistrates Court to successfully defend myself against the charge of dangerous flying before it was summer season at the Winter Gardens, Morecambe with the Black and White Minstrels.

Naturally, that took up most of my time that summer but I still managed to make an appearance on BBC's *Club Night* for what was only my second television show of the year. I did a stand-up comedy spot as a change from my usual comedy songs.

Later in the year I did a radio show called 'Mid-Day Music Hall' on the *Light Programme* so although the Minstrel Show was taking up the majority of my time, I was still able to squeeze in other engagements.

Though I always seemed too busy to play football, I did manage to get in a few rounds of golf. I first started playing back in the early days when the Harmaniacs were working up in Scotland and I was quickly hooked. I have played serious stuff with Morecambe and Wise, Donald Peers, and anyone from the shows who had a little time to spend on some recreation. After all, it was good to get out in the fresh air and unlike many people, I never thought that golf was a good walk ruined.

I finally called it a day touring with the Minstrels when I began getting spirit messages from Al Jolson—only joking—and so I was able to accept cabaret engagements with the first being in Manchester at the Queen of Hearts Club. I followed this with an appearance on television in the *Chan Canasta Show* and that was exactly what I wanted to do—be seen on television more often. I had done so many stage shows that I felt I should now be on the small screen more regularly. I also had ambitions to become a character actor as well as being a comic but more about that later.

Of course I didn't want to change my image. You don't change an image that has proved to be so successful, particularly financially, although the money always came second to me. It was making the audience laugh that drove me on. Laughter's like toothpaste—even in a sophisticated age of clever-clever humour—nobody should be without it. A good laugh is better than 10 visits to the dentist.

And what made people laugh has never changed. I once tried a more sophisticated approach but when the audience had to think too much they just didn't want to know. I had learned that you can be too clever and while the satirical comedians made their jokes ever more obscure, mine became simpler. I believed that you had to give it to the audience on a plate. In truth, the golden age of comedy had gone with the passing of the likes of Laurel and Hardy, Max Sennett and Buster Keaton. They were the gods.

People had forgotten how to laugh yet it was, and still is, the best release for frustrations. You still can't beat the old one or two liners:

> *A man walked into a new revolving restaurant in London to order a meal—he got the meal but it took him three weeks to hang up his coat.*

I topped the bill in 'Blackpool Night' on the BBC *Light Programme* in July 1966 and in the same show came a commentary on the second half of the England v Mexico World Cup match. There was nothing like making sure you captured both the mums and the dads. Two days later I flew to Scarborough to appear at the Floral Hall.

In no time at all I was quickly signed up by TWW, the Wales and West of England ITV company, for a new six-week show called *Stan at Ease* which was to be screened in the autumn of 1966. There was an audience of about 700 for each show and in the programme I introduced newcomers under age 15 to the world of show business. I was also able to film all kinds of comedy situations which were fitted around the various acts.

It was another big break for me because I had always wanted a show like that. I introduced a friend as a guest star each week but the basic idea of the show was to find new talent. I began auditions by flying from Cardiff to Bristol, Reading, Swindon and Swansea and there were hundreds of clever and talented children all wanting to be on television. TWW were looking for unusual and imaginative performers rather than more conventional pop groups.

In Swansea alone, I auditioned 60 children all under the age of 16 during a six-hour session at the Dragon Hotel and before the week was out I had seen over 600 dancers, singers and musicians. There were over 100 waiting for me at the Town Hall in Swindon after I flew my plane to Vickers Engineering, South Marston where I landed on their airstrip before hurrying to the auditions.

While attending at every venue, I also had a three day engagement at Arnos Country Club, Bristol so that fitted in well with my other commitments.

Finally, between myself, Derek Clarke the show's producer, and TWW's musical director Leonard Morris, we selected who we thought were the best of the youngsters but even then red tape raised its ugly head.

We selected two young girls from Gloucester to dance on the show but they were banned just before tele-recording was to begin. I picked them to demonstrate old-time dancing but then the Board of Amateur Ballroom Dancing stepped in. They decreed, in their infinite wisdom, that if the girls took part in the show their amateur status would be endangered. I was astounded because they weren't even being paid. It was surely taking rules and regulations too far but despite our protestations, the 11-year-old girls had to be excluded from the show and so missed their chance of being in the limelight.

For the first programme I was joined by the Jerry Allen Trio, Bob Giles and my dear friend from the Minstrels, the talented Kris Keo. Liverpool lass Kris and I were so successful doing comedy routines together on the Minstrels Show that I requested her for every programme of that first series of *Stan at Ease*. The former Television Topper had planned to join her brother in Canada but when I asked her to be on the show she jumped at the chance.

I first met Bob when we were both members of concert parties entertaining the troops in France, Holland and Germany around the end of the War. When I found out that he lived in Long Ashton, Bristol, I gave him a ring and asked him to join us for the series. It was good to meet up with him after such a long time. He could fit into any sketch situation that you could think of and was a fine comedian.

Don't forget, this wasn't strictly a talent scouting show. The youngsters were only on stage for about 10 minutes out of the 30 minute programme. What we were after was a family show but I made all the children feel at home and no one showed any trace of nerves. The back-drop was a theatre setting so that also helped put the young performers at ease. I was on stage for almost the whole 30 minutes, chatting to the children, introducing the guests and taking part in the sketches.

In the second show, each one of which was shown on television on Fridays at 6.30pm, Olive Guppy's Tiny Tots danced and gave the programme added appeal—and charm. As all the shows were pre-recorded, I was able to accept bookings elsewhere and in October I starred in the *Birthday Show* at the Coventry Theatre which ran for an eight-week season. Mike and Bernie Winters topped the bill and also appearing were comedian Johnny Hackett, ace guitarist Bert Weedon and Kris Keo.

While in Coventry I persuaded the stars to come down to Cardiff to play in a football match in aid of the Aberfan Distress Fund. In the evening after the game, which was played on a Sunday, we held a star-studded gala performance at the New Theatre in Cardiff, again for the distress fund.

More than 1,400 people packed the theatre to see the show compèred by top disc jockey, Pete Murray. Parading their talents were the Clark Brothers, Albert and Les Ward, Bert Weedon, The Tornados, Victor Spinetti and of course, yours truly. A big disappointment however was that Hollywood actor George Raft was unable to appear because of a bout of 'flu. To add an extra Welsh flavour though we also had the Aber Valley Male Voice Choir and young Cardiff pop singer, Deano Wilson.

The good news from TWW was that they wanted me to do another series of *Stan at Ease*. It was scheduled to start in January 1967 and run for 13 weeks. As over 1,000 young artists were seen for the first series, we were hoping for even more this time, especially as parents had seen the shows and were happy with the way we looked after the youngsters.

I was seriously considering an offer to do pantomime and also tour South Africa with Matt Monro but when I heard about TWW's decision I put those plans to one side so that I could join producer Derek at the auditions in Bristol, Taunton, Swindon, Swansea, Cardiff and Barry. No pantomime also meant that I could spend Christmas at home with Betty and the boys so that was an added bonus.

The week before Christmas however, I was up in Blackburn playing the clubs. That meant a hectic few nights for me. I was on stage at the 77 Club, which was a converted cinema in Brierfield, at 8.15pm. When I finished my act half an hour later I made a rapid change in the tiny dressing room I shared with a Scottish singer and then hurried out to my car. I had about 20 minutes to reach the Starlight Club and after another rapid change (to change quickly I had to have another set of stage clothes already waiting in my dressing room) I stepped on stage to face my second audience in less than an hour.

The previous evening the dash had taken place in the opposite direction and somewhere along the road between Brierfield and Blackburn I would pass the other half of the bill going in the opposite direction. Sometimes the next act appeared as I was leaving the dressing room and that was the way it was on the club circuits. It was hard work but satisfying.

Most of the clubs in East Lancashire started out as cinemas, and as cinema lost a lot of its appeal, so the clubs took off. Some were very good, and some not so good. The Blackburn circuit management took a very professional attitude and would give artists all the help they needed with a minimum of fuss. In other places the conditions were poor but you learnt to take the rough with the smooth.

The customers in some clubs were little short of animals. They would give artists the bird before they had time to start their act. I could take it but I regarded boozers bawling 'shurrup' and 'geroff', and in a lot of cases something much worse, an insult to the profession. Sometimes, if it was happening to me, I would take out my gun and fire off a blank to shock them into silence. And sometimes I wished that the gun was loaded.

I wanted to participate in as many entertainment fields as possible—television, radio, theatre, summer shows, clubs and pantomimes. I felt it was my insurance policy, I suppose. I got a lot of pleasure from playing the clubs although I found it strange at first. It was a completely different atmosphere. After all, people go along to a theatre to see you, but they are already in the clubs. The entertainer goes to them and into the audience. It was a harder life than the theatre but a rewarding one.

Auditions for *Stan at Ease* went well and we eventually saw even more acts than we did for the first series. Appearing on the first show was a girl French horn player and a boy acrobat while the speciality act came from that brilliant ventriloquist Saveen with Daisy May. My old Minstrels partner Kris Keo was also back with us for the series along with Bob Giles and once again the reviews were good.

I was delighted when yet another old Minstrels pal, George Chisholm, agreed to do a spot during the run. For a quarter of a century George had been one of the country's most brilliant jazz trombonists and I had enjoyed many a jam session with him when we were together in the Minstrels. He had developed a comedy routine during his act but his musicianship always shone through, even though many of the younger viewers watching the programme probably thought he was a funny man who also played the trombone.

I wore a different type of hat when I was part of a protest meeting in February, 1967 at the Lavernock Point Caravan site. The owners had pushed up the rental from £42 a year to £52 a year, and also wanted it paid early January and not as previously agreed in March. A meeting was organised for a Sunday but the owners refused to open up the site. They reckoned that as they didn't normally open up on a Sunday they saw no reason at all to open it up for us. Feelings ran high and members of parliament and the Secretary of State for Wales, Cledwyn Hughes were approached to intervene. I had only been on the site a week when all this blew up and I had already forked out £62 but it was not just the additional money, it was the complete lack of goodwill on the part of the management that I didn't like.

When *Stan at Ease* finished its successful run, TWW's programme controller Brian Michie went to the studios to present me with a brush drawing of a landscape by the eminent Welsh artist, Kyffin Williams. I was pleased when he also presented Kris Keo with perfume as she had worked hard throughout the series.

The troops were now calling so it was off to Cyprus for two weeks in April entertaining the forces. It was my seventh overseas tour but my first for a couple of years as I had been so busy. We were billeted with the lads in little housing blocks on the perimeter of the base.

I came straight back from Cyprus to head north to the Alhambra Theatre, Glasgow for a short season with none other than Shirley Bassey. It was a cracker of a bill as apart from us, Joe Baker and Malcolm Roberts were also appearing along with good support. I didn't fly up to Glasgow as the weather wasn't suitable. In any case I wanted to play some golf as my handicap was now down to 16 and I had to keep persevering to see any improvement.

Shirley was always one to dress for the occasion and she didn't let her Scottish fans down. She had a much-publicized 'peek-a-boo' dress with a heart shape top, no middle, and the rest just poured on. She belted out all her hits including 'Hey Big Spender' and 'What Now My Love'. What a performer she was, and still is.

I did a short season at Pontins in Weston before a fortnight's return to the *Black and White Minstrel Show* at the Victoria Palace in London. I made a conscious decision to limit the amount of engagements I would accept for the summer so that I could spend a little more time with Betty and the boys. I was still able to fit in a series of short engagements in Blackpool throughout that summer because by using my Beechcraft Bonanza I could come home after each one. I reckoned that it was my first summer in more than 19 years that I hadn't been fully booked, but I was determined to be at home with the family as much as possible.

I also put in an appearance on BBC's *Dee Time* which was shown from Manchester. Remember Simon Dee? He was a performer who became too big for his boots and soon sank without trace. It was my first BBC appearance for over a year but of course I had been seen on TWW.

It seemed no time at all before we were all thinking about the pantomime season and I was delighted to sign up for *Babes in the Wood* at the Bristol Hippodrome. Joining me on the bill were Edmund Hockridge, Billy Dainty and Wyn Calvin. Ted

Hockridge played Robin Hood, I was the King's page, Simple Simon no less, Billy was the Babes' nurse, and Wyn was one of the robbers. Also taking part in the panto, reputed to have cost £50,000 to put together, were the Morton Fraser Harmonica Gang.

The star of the Harmonica Gang was Tiny Ross who was a comedian as well as an accomplished musician. In fact all the members of the Gang were multi-instrumental and fine vocalists. The production came from the London Palladium and had 14 scenes emphasising comedy in the spectacle that could only be pantomime.

My old pal Billy Dainty had the audience in stitches with his striptease routine in the babes' nursery and the Flying Ballet went down well on the large stage. We even had room for an archery tournament which was just as well because the panto went on for almost three hours. It was good fun while it lasted, and I was to join Ted Hockridge during the summer of 1968 as we played the Floral Hall, Scarborough, along with another old friend of mine, Joan Regan. Ted was a Canadian who rose to fame in a musical called *The Pajama Game*. He had a big hit with one of the songs from the show called 'Hey There'. There was a pickpocket on that show called Mark Raffles. He was great—cleared your pockets and removed your watch without you ever knowing. At the end of his act he even managed to whip off the braces from a member of the audience.

South Africa now appeared to be the place to perform so in April 1968 I was off on my travels. There were some splendid theatres, particularly in Cape Town which boasted the magnificent 2,000 seater, 3 Arts Theatre which in addition to its vast staging facilities also had the largest Cinerama screen in the world.

On my return I appeared on the 50th *Be My Guest* radio programme. In July of 1968 I was proud when I saw Roger, now an 18-year-old, provide Wales with their only victory at the British Schools Athletics meeting at Connahs Quay. Roger, who attended Whitchurch High School, won the high jump with a leap of 6ft, one inch less than his own height. Afterwards, one of the meeting officials told me that we now had a celebrity in the family. Roger was especially pleased to win after only managing a week's training all summer because of working on his A-levels.

It was about this time that the Director-General's job at the BBC became vacant so I wrote off my application. I told them that I had 20 years experience in show business, and as so much of the BBC's output was connected with light entertainment then I felt I was perfectly capable of running such a vast organisation. After all, football players become managers, and variety artists often become agents later in life. It was only tongue-in-cheek though, and I gained a lot of publicity from the application, including a short paragraph in the *New Statesman*, so it was well worth the cost of a stamp.

When I did a week of cabaret shows in and around Sunderland, I stayed with Trevor Ford and his wife Louise so there was plenty of football chat whenever we had time for a sit down. I had a week at the Starlight Club in Blackburn and flew up in the Cessna.

Happy memories were brought back when I guested on the *Black and White Minstrel Show* in a Sunday concert at the Futurist in Scarborough. Principal tenor on the show was Glyn Dawson who had, by now, been a minstrel for nearly eight years.

I was back on *Be My Guest* in September but this time there was a big difference. I introduced the programme from my plane up in the skies over Jersey. Flying with me was Jimmy Henney who chatted about flying and my career and then I introduced recordings from some of my favourite artists such as Billy Daniels, Frank Sinatra and Count Basie. It was a novel idea and perhaps another slant on an outside broadcast.

By now, TWW had given way to Harlech Television but that didn't stop the new powers-that-be offering me a new programme in November which we called *Stanorama*. It was basically a comedy show devised by George Bartram, but we decided that a serious interlude would go down well with the audience. One of my first guests was MP Sir Gerald Nabarro and he was fantastic, coming across so funny that I wanted to ask him who wrote his scripts. We also had ITN newscaster Gordon Honeycombe. Another to come on the show was George Western, formerly of the Western Brothers, and together we recreated the Western Brothers piano and singing act. By an amazing coincidence after talking to George, I discovered that with Kenneth, who was actually his cousin rather than his brother, they had flown to engagements before the Second World War using a two-seater Swallow. George brought a picture of the machine which we were able to show the viewers during the programme. Apparently it was in constant use between 1935 and 1938. And I thought I was a theatrical pioneer in the flying line . . .

If you think bomb hoaxes are a new phenomenon, don't you believe it. I was appearing up in North Wales at a club in Wrexham just before Christmas when the club received a phone call and a man's voice said that a bomb was planted inside the club. I was actually on stage at the time as the first half of the show was nearing the end, and the audience had to go outside while the premises were searched. Nothing was found but the incident did have an unsettling effect on the clubgoers although I did manage to use it to my advantage and get a few extra laughs.

After the lack of success with my application to become Director-General of the BBC I set my sights a little lower when I applied for the job of chairman of Aston Villa FC. Once again it was tongue-in-cheek although I did say that if appointed, my first job would be to try and persuade Trevor Ford, a former Villa player, to take over the running of the club. Once again I achieved what I set out to do as there was plenty of interest in a number of papers, even the *Belfast Telegraph* which I read when I crossed the Irish Sea to take part in the Royal Artillery Association concert at the Ritz Cinema in December.

It was soon time to spend Christmas and the New Year down in beautiful Torbay. I was playing the part of Will Atkins in *Robinson Crusoe* at the Princess Theatre in Torquay. It was another lavish spectacle, as you would expect from a Bernard Delfont production, and it included a fabulous Neptune's Grotto and the famous Curries Dancing Waters which had to be seen to be believed. Tommy Rose was Mrs Crusoe and he gave her an elegance and penetrating voice that provided one long laugh. When he was in the navy, Tommy used to sing with a fellow sailor at the piano. That sailor was none other than Russ Conway. As well as comedy, Tommy had also 'gone straight' with a part in the Robin Hood series for television. He had also been a stuntman and had written scripts for other comedians.

I was given plenty of scope for my own brand of humour and I was able to take advantage of every situation to keep the comedy flowing. The story followed the traditional Robinson Crusoe lines with everyone setting out on the good ship Saucy Sally in search of fame and fortune but naturally there were a number of detours on the way. One of the most impressive scenes took the audience underwater to see Neptune and the Dancing Waters.

For a while, it looked as though the weather would lead to a fall in audience numbers as snow and ice made travelling difficult but it soon cleared up and the Princess Theatre had another record-breaking season. My only complaint about working in Torquay was the lack of an airport close enough to park my airplane. It turned out to be quicker driving down in the car.

In February 1969 I was in Derby for the Press Ball at the Pennine Hotel. It was a rather grand affair which was one of the highlights of the local scene and the six-hour ball included a carved buffet meal and chances to win top prizes such as air trips and holidays. Then I was off north to appear for a week at a club in Carlisle before moving around doing cabaret spots back in Derbyshire and in Lancashire.

My plane came in handy early in the summer when I gave Val Doonican a lift from Squires Gate, Blackpool to Leeds where he was opening an agricultural show. He had with him 3,000 autographed photographs of himself and a dozen of his LPs which he sold at the show for charity. I took him back later in the afternoon and then continued to Coventry for an evening cabaret spot.

During the summer I did a series of Sunday concerts at the Morecambe Alhambra but still found time for an appearance on television's *Golden Shot*. I hadn't been doing much television so it was quite an occasion for me. It appeared that producers talked so much about finding new talent that they forgot to use experienced performers. It wasn't too bad however as I had just completed a pilot for a BBC children's show.

There was a major breakthrough in club entertainment up in Scotland where a Miners Welfare Club, just outside Edinburgh, decided to stage Scotland's first resident week of variety, and I was booked to head the first show. Johnny Kildare, an ex-bandleader and agent, was the man trusted with booking the right artists and as I always went down well with Scottish audiences he obviously thought it was a safe bet to have me on the show to start things off.

By a strange coincidence, I was asked to do a TV Roadshow

from Southport while I was up in Scotland and luckily for me I was able to fly down to Southport after the show, land on the sands, appear on television, and then fly back up to Turnhouse. Fortunately the weather was favourable or there would have been a lot of unhappy miners waiting for me back up north.

In August I made a rare appearance in Cardiff with a week in Tito's night club. It seemed that I was in demand everywhere—except in Cardiff—and that did upset me. Because I was a local boy people just didn't seem to take much notice of me, and that seemed to have been the case ever since I started in the business. Wherever I went all over the country people enjoyed my act and I was repeatedly asked back, but in my own back yard I was virtually ignored.

What hurt me most during that summer of 1969 was that I was overlooked for a place in the cast of the pantomime at the New Theatre. My name had been put forward but nothing came of it and that disappointed me a lot. If I was known as anything it was as a children's entertainer and that was just what pantomime required. I know that may sound big-headed but plenty of other theatre managers and audiences had found me good enough so why not in Cardiff? It was all part of the same trouble—I was local and as such was overlooked. Martin Williams, general manager of the New Theatre, claimed that the bookings were handled in London and that I had not been mentioned in any of the correspondence he had received from there. Still, I wasn't short of offers and was pleased to accept the starring role in *Robinson Crusoe* at the Grand in Swansea.

One place I never stopped getting bookings was up in Scotland working for the Popplewells. I had three exciting weeks at the Pavilion Theatre in Glasgow for them in a revue called *Stan at Ease*. It took a day or so to take off and then we played to packed houses for the rest of the time up there.

So, after an absence of 10 years, I was back in Swansea, at the

Grand Theatre, playing Billy Crusoe in a production of *Robinson Crusoe* over the Christmas period. It was good to link up once again with my old pal Johnny Tudor who played the part of Crusoe, and Ronnie Coyles, who once again was the dame. It was my fourth pantomime at the Grand after first appearing there in *Little Red Riding Hood* way back in 1949. The very first panto staged at the Grand was also *Robinson Crusoe* but I am sure it was a different production back in 1897, and in case you are wondering, the answer is no, I never appeared in that opening show.

I loved playing at the Grand because the audiences were homely and easy to get on with. I could relax in Swansea and I always found that I could perform better in my own surroundings. Mind you, the place had been closed earlier in the year for a complete refurbishing. The seats were taken out and sent away for reupholstering, the internal wiring was all renewed, and the Victorian ceiling was restored to its former glory. At the time it probably made the Grand the smartest and brightest theatre in Wales.

As it happened, while we were enjoying a great season in Swansea, the Cardiff pantomime of *Babes in the Wood* and the Festival Circus at Sophia Gardens were losing thousands of pounds. Not because they were poor quality shows, far from it, but on account of a 'flu epidemic and a ban by busmen on late-night services. The block on services after 9.30pm was imposed by the city's 900 bus personnel after a series of assaults by young passengers on conductors. Nothing changes does it?

Our pantomime finished in the first week of March 1970 and I am glad to say it broke all records. A huge amount of work went into the production with over 15 scene changes, superb costumes, and Curries Waltzing Waters were seen for the first time in Swansea. We were all pleased with the outcome.

12

KICKING AROUND

'. . . Tommy Cooper strung a line of washing between the uprights and Jimmy Jewell came out wearing a Davy Crockett hat, a monkey skin and cricket pads. To add to the fun I was wearing my six guns and 'shot' poor bewildered Stan, the referee.'

* * * * *

I have always been keen on football but when I first had the idea of combining pleasure with making some money for charity I never realised that it would eventually grow so big. At first it was total fun but gradually it became more serious as winning became ever more important.

I had organised numerous charity matches over the years but perhaps the edge I needed came when I was in summer season at Great Yarmouth. We lost the match against a local holiday camp and I was so disappointed that I decided to go up in my plane and flour bomb their dining hall. From that moment on it was still a pleasure to play—but I also wanted to win.

At first I had to cajole people to give their time but after a while I had a list of artists ever ready, whenever available, to take part. Some of them were good footballers like the singer Glen Mason who once played for Falkirk, and Ronnie Carroll who was an Irish schools international. Ronnie claimed that he once turned down a television date as he didn't want to risk injury before one of our games. Even Des O'Connor showed some pretty footwork but that wasn't surprising as he had been on Northampton Town's books as a youngster.

We became known as the Show Biz XI and the crowds were large at some of the grounds we played on as they all wanted to see their favourite stars. Glen became a big recording star with numbers such as 'Hot Diggity' and 'Glendora' and he was seen every Saturday at the time on *Jack Jackson's Television Show*.

Just before the start of the 1957–58 football season we played a charity match at Bloomfield Road, the home of Blackpool FC, in aid of the Water Rats. Our team was made up of comedians performing in the seaside town and our opponents were the local football side minus the famous Stanley Matthews who was the referee.

All-in rules applied on the day with free fights, tripping, water throwing and even tying down the goalkeeper to his own post. The attendance was an amazing 10,070 and they thoroughly enjoyed the spectacle, donating no less than £1,398 to the charity. The score was 4–4 at half time but after that nobody was able to keep count of the number of goals.

Tommy Cooper strung a line of washing between the uprights and Jimmy Jewell came out wearing a Davy Crockett hat, a monkey skin and cricket pads. To add to the fun I was wearing my six guns and 'shot' poor bewildered Stan, the referee.

We started with the likes of Ken Dodd, Ernie Wise, Tommy Cooper, Eric Morecambe, Jimmy Jewell, Ben Warriss, Bob Monkhouse, Robert Earl and Kenny Baker but when a count was taken we had another five players on the field. Half way through the second half, four of our side brought a table on to the pitch and began playing cards. Incidentally, Ben Warriss told me that he attended no less than 160 schools during his last five years as a schoolboy. This was due to him starting his career as a nine-year-old and then continually being on tour.

Lonnie Donegan would pester me to find out when the next game was coming up and he was in the side that played at the Belle Vue Stadium against a Manchester Sports Guild XI in March 1958. This was a benefit match for the dependant relatives fund following the Manchester United plane crash in Munich the previous month. Also with us that day were Billy Cotton, Cliff Michelmore, Andrew Ray, Pete Murray, Kenneth Wolstenholme and the former Arsenal and Wales footballer Wally Barnes. Wally's appearance gave me another idea because I thought that if we could combine former players with the stars of show business then we could get even bigger crowds and raise even more money for charity.

I was able to help Lonnie when I found that he was being 'farmed' out. This meant that his agent was leasing him to other agents so that they were both taking slices of Lonnie's performing fee. It all came about when I asked him to play in a game. He refused because he never had enough money to pay the £3 for a pair of football boots. It turned out that Lonnie was being paid about £1,000 for appearing at the Glasgow Empire and out of that money he had to pay the members of his skiffle group, digs, and all the transport costs. Really, he should have been paid about £6,000 as he was playing to full audiences every night. Not very happy with the situation after I explained 'farming out' to him, Lonnie refused to go on stage until they gave him a far more favourable deal.

Less than a week after the Belle Vue Stadium match, we were at Shepherds Bush in London playing a game in aid of the Queens Park Rangers players benefits. It was our way of saying thank you after the club allowed us the use of their facilities while we trained on their ground. Tuesdays and Thursdays were training days and kids used to climb over the walls just to cheer us on.

The following month I even played against the Show Biz boys when I appeared for Cardew Robinson's Cads along with Dickie Henderson. It was a crazy game because playing left back for the Cads was the one and only Tommy Cooper, complete with his trademark fez. That was played at the Maccabi Stadium on Watford Way and the British Empire Cancer campaign received a tidy cheque thanks to all those who came to watch the antics.

In no time at all we were at West Ham's ground, Upton Park when the Show Biz XI took on the Boxers and Jockeys. What a star-studded list of sportsmen were in their side that evening. Lester Piggott, Harry Carr, Henry Cooper and Brian London were up against our usual array of talent although we had brought in skiffle man Chas McDevitt and comedian/singer Dave King, while Mike and Bernie Winters were there to put the sportsmen off their game. Incredibly, over 25,000 supporters were in the ground to watch us win 6–4 and swell the coffers of the Sportsmen Aid Society. I was quite pleased with the way the game went because I was marked by none other than Joe Erskine, the Welsh heavyweight boxer.

There were a number of occasions when I was too busy to take part in a game but once the idea had started, there was always enough goodwill amongst the artists and performers to arrange matches and the list of charities we helped began to grow.

I now had an extra incentive to appear for the Show Biz XI. In December 1958, my great pal Trevor Ford announced his retirement and gave me his football boots. When he came back to this country from Holland where he had been playing for PSV Eindhoven, he did reappear for Newport County but I wouldn't let him have his boots back and he had to buy himself a new pair.

Early in 1959 we played at the Withdean Stadium, now the home of Brighton Football Club, and a week later my pantomime team played at the Harrogate RUFC ground. It was a big thrill for me that day because in goals for the opposition was none other than the famous Sam Bartram.

In no time at all we were in Bradford playing against a Sportsmen's XI including the miler Derek Ibbotson, cricketers Ray Illingworth and Phil Sharp, and a number of former Bradford and Bradford City football professionals. I was playing at centre forward in those days, probably because I was still using the kit given to me by Fordy, one of the greatest centre forwards ever to play for Wales. Up front with me in Bradford were singing star Ronnie Hilton and comedians Don Arrol and Charlie Chester. We never forgot the referee either. This time it was Barney 'Give him the money' Colehan.

I made a poignant return to Cardiff on 7 May when, in collaboration with Cardiff City AFC, I organised a match in tribute to the memory of Wales rugby international Sid Judd. Sid, who had played for Cardiff and Wales, had been struck down by illness at a young age. For such a good cause it was no trouble finding willing performers to give up their time and probably the most difficult task for me was selecting the actual Show Biz XI. Nearly all the regulars turned up as well but unfortunately, at the last minute, a youthful Sean Connery was unable to appear.

Opposing us were a selection of rugby and football stars drawn from the city's two major clubs. Bleddyn Williams, Jack Matthews, Ken Jones and Rex Willis all changed codes and the Cardiff City connection was made by former players, Stan Richards, George Edwards, Billy Baker and Wilf Grant. The Cardiff Athletic Club put Cardiff Arms Park at our disposal and so for a rare occasion on that hallowed turf, the round ball took precedence over the oval ball.

In less than two years, the Show Biz XI had raised over £10,000 for various charities all over Britain. These charities included the Manchester United Disaster Fund, the Guide Dogs for the Blind, Dr Barnardo's Homes, the Lord Mayor's Polio Fund in Portsmouth and the Boys Clubs. The matches were often shown on television and the standard of play was such that we were frequently given practical assistance from many top sporting personalities.

I have always had a sneaking love for Newport County and it wasn't long before I was able to appear at Somerton Park, though this time I was in the Welsh Sportmen's side against the Show Biz boys. This match was arranged to raise money for the local branch of the Red Cross and I am glad there were plenty of ambulance people around the ground because our side included boxers Dick Richardson, Len 'Luggie' Reece, Eddie Thomas and Darkie Hughes. This time, Sean Connery was able to put in a welcome appearance. I dare say that when interviewed nowadays, Sean would probably say that the finest moment of his career was not playing the part of James Bond but when he ran out at Somerton Park for the Show Biz XI.

Frankie Vaughan was another great star who spent a lot of his spare time raising cash. In his case it was for the Boys Clubs of which he was president. When I was in the *Six Star Show* at the North Pier Pavilion in Blackpool, Frankie was appearing down the road at the Palace Theatre. In no time at all he decided to form a side to play a match to raise funds for the Blackpool Boys Club.

Also in the *Six Star Show* with me was that great singer Michael Holliday and Des O'Connor, at the South Pier was Robert Earl, while my old BAF pal Derek Franklyn from the Hedley Ward Trio was at the Queen's Theatre along with Al Read, Don Arrol, and Coco the Clown. All these agreed to turn up to play against Jock Dodds' team but Jock took a bit of a

Leading out the team at Wigan with Des O'Connor

Dinner for One with Leslie Crowther

Show Biz Xl in Blackpool 1957. Back 2nd left Ernie Wise, me, Tommy Cooper, Jimmy Jewel, Charlie Chester. Front: Eric Morecambe, Kenny Baker, Stan Matthews and Ben Warriss

My Beechcraft Bonanza

Betty and me

With The Minstrel in 1964

Receiving my MBE at Buckingham Palace

On the set of my TV show in 1966

With Roger and Ceri outside Grand Pavilion, Porthcawl 1970

Good Sports World Snooker 1973. Left to right: Bryn Williams, Howard Winstone, Johnny Stewart, Barry John, me and Lynn Davies

Back from Malaya with tan to meet Harold Wilson and Alan Randall 1974

New Theatre Cardiff, 1975. With Reg Dixon and Bryn Williams

With Eric Morecambe at The Roses, Tewkesbury on his final performance, May 1984

Serving Stan Ogden in Coronation Street

Golfing charity day with Andy Gray on left

Albert and Les Ward on Stan at Ease

Where the 'Ell have you been Lavinia with Ruth Madoc (right) at Pebble Mill Studios 1976

This is Your Life, 1982, with Sam our grandson

The cast of Crossroads—but how many can you name?

Handing over another Variety Club bus

Robinson Crusoe, 2000 with Johnny Tudor

History of Mr Polly with Lee Evans

Sooty and Sweep's first panto 1997 aided and abetted by me and Ceri

Betty and me with Prince Charles, 1985

With my old pal Wyn Calvin

Robinson Crusoe 2000. Back left to right: June Campbell, Eddie Hollis, Johnny Tudor, Karen Ashley, Front left to right: William Thomas, me and Ceri

Me as Fagin

Betty and me with Clive Thomas (High Sheriff of Mid Glamorgan) and his wife Beryl

Golfing Charity day with my mate Eric Sykes and two pals

With Norman Wisdom at Water Rats meeting in Grosvenor House, London

Our beautiful home after the 1999 fire

From left to right: Sam, his fiancée Joanna Paul, Ceri's wife Judith Gay, Ceri, Roger and partner Sheila Yeger

The fridge door must be open!

liberty by including Stan Mortensen, Billy Liddell and a couple of other former professionals. The nearest we came to seeing the ball was when it was kicked off at the start by none other than Violet Carson, better known as Ena Sharples from *Coronation Street*.

I was really looking forward to the start of the 1960–61 football season. After months of spending my spare time flying I wanted to come down fair and square and land on the rounded studs of my polished football boots. If you wanted to exaggerate, you could now class me as a sort of unofficial Welsh international player because after all, I did have the boots and jersey of a great one.

While appearing at the Futurist in Scarborough during the summer run of the *Black and White Minstrels Show*, a few of us would go up on to the roof and kick a plastic ball around. Once again however I was in trouble as I blasted the ball through an open window and into the theatre and there was an enquiry into the whole business. Of course I denied being responsible.

And where better to start the new season off than back in Cardiff at Maindy Stadium playing for the TV All Stars against the Handy Angle Ladies XI? Organised by Empire News, all proceeds were going to British Leprosy Relief Association, SOS and the Cory Youth Club. We had a star-studded line-up that included Mike and Bernie Winters, Pete Murray, Alfie Bass from the Army Game, Anthony Newley, Roy Castle and Ronnie Corbett who, at that time, was a popular figure on Eamonn Andrews' television show, *Crackerjack*. I can't remember where the young ladies came from, only that a month previously they had raised a lot of money in a match at the Caemawr stadium in Porth. Tommy Docherty was referee and they were far better than we expected so we only just managed a 3–2 victory.

When I was working in the South Wales area I would join in training with the Cardiff City lads at Ninian Park and so got to know the manager Bill Jones quite well. So well in fact that I tipped him off about a good player I had seen playing for Motherwell while I was doing the rounds up in Scotland. After one match I went up to him and told him I would put in a good word for him at Cardiff City. A fortnight later the lad joined Liverpool. His name was Ian St John.

I will always remember playing for the All Stars team against Stan Mortensen's team at Stanley Park. Over 5,000 came to watch the match which was started by the lovely Yana. Blackpool and England full back Jimmy Armfield was referee and we gave him a hard time. Morty's side shot into a three-goal lead but with Des O'Connor and the Dallas Boys leading attack after attack we soon equalised and it was left to our star striker, Lonnie Donegan to score the winner right at the end. The real winner though was the charity who benefited by over £1,000.

Long before Dave Whelan bought Wigan and relocated them to the impressive DW Stadium, the football club played at Springfield Park. In September 1961 an All Star Soccer side dared to challenge the Blackpool Show Biz team. Organised by the Wigan Round Table, it was the first charity match of its kind in Wigan's history. Didn't they ever play on the Pier?

All our stars were appearing at theatres in the resort with one exception. I persuaded my old mate Trevor Ford to play on the understanding that he couldn't wear the number nine shirt. That was reserved for me. Running down the wings were Des O'Connor and Lonnie Donegan, who was putting on the style at every opportunity. We were all feeling sure of ourselves until we saw the line-up against us. Jack Rowley was leading the line with Wilf Mannion, Henry Cockburn, who played in the 1948 FA Cup Final for Manchester United, Roy Clarke and a number of other ex-internationals were up against us.

The referee was Mr Jack Kelly who had been in the middle for the Wolves-Blackburn Cup Final the previous year but our trump cards were the two linesmen, Michael Holliday and Richard 'Mr Pastry' Hearn. We desperately needed some help from them to keep the score down. The kick-off that day was done by none other than the lovely Pat Phoenix, better known as Elsie Tanner from *Coronation Street*. Once again that was the nearest we got to the ball all afternoon but it was another good day and a number of charities benefited from the game.

Wherever we had the time, we arranged a football match to help a charity. You would be surprised at the requests I received from fellow artists to be picked to play in these matches. Our side had various guises. It might be known as the Show Biz XI, or perhaps the Television Entertainers XI—no matter. What did matter was that team members from the entertainment profession gave their time freely to help those less fortunate and I am proud of the contribution I made in starting the ball rolling.

When I was back home appearing at the New Theatre with Kenneth Earle and Malcolm Vaughan in May 1962, we had another date at Maindy Stadium when the TV Entertainers met the Good Sports. Naturally, I was in the TV Entertainers side which this time had a regal look about it, and I don't mean Dave King. In our side was singer Tim Connor who was a cousin of Grace Kelly, known also as Princess Grace of Monaco. We had songwriter Jerry Lordan who had penned Anthony Newley's hit, 'I've Waited So Long', and Welshman Ricky Vallance who had just topped the charts with 'Tell Laura I Love her'. Trevor Ford was one of the Good Sports but he was at a slight disadvantage because I still wouldn't give him his boots back. Also in their side was another good friend of mine, Johnny Stewart who was a star of TWW's *Land Of Song*.

Another of our May matches saw the Lord's Taverners play their first ever game of football against Tommy Trinder's team of Famous Comedians. The game was played at Craven Cottage, home of Fulham FC where Tommy was chairman.

The Taverners were formed in 1950 and consisted mainly of cricketers, although a number of famous footballers such as Billy Wright and Stanley Matthews were also members. I became great friends with Billy who was married to Joy, one of the Beverley Sisters. When I was appearing in *Crossroads*, I would meet up with him in the canteen at Central TV as by then he was Head of Sport.

Fortunately for us, neither Billy nor Stan were playing for them but they did have double international Willie Watson in their line-up along with Denis Compton. We fancied our chances to start with but when you have someone like Cardew Robinson playing at centre half it doesn't fill the rest of the side with confidence. No matter, another good crowd turned up and we raised a lot of money for the Taverners.

I always thought that if you wanted to play football, why not play with the best, and in August 1962 I did just that when my Show Biz boys took on a *Lancashire Evening Post* side at Christie Park in Morecambe. My team consisted of stars appearing at theatres in Morecambe and Blackpool and included Roy Castle and some lads from the Minstrel Show but in the *Lancashire Evening Post* line-up was none other than the great Tom Finney himself. What a gentleman, both on and off the field. If only today's football stars could behave as Tom did during his career.

In August 1963 a Stan Stennett team took on Joe Brown's team at the Wellesley, the home of Yarmouth Town. At the last moment, Joe couldn't make it so Ronnie Corbett captained his side for the match started by 16-year-old Helen Shapiro, who forgot about her bouffant hairstyle as she braved the wind and rain to kick-off.

The attendance for our charity game was the biggest of the season at the ground. Not many football clubs could boast a fan base including the Bruvvers, Rory Storm and the Hurricanes, the Jaywalkers and the other entertainment artists who turned up that day. And what official match could boast referees, linesmen and trainers of the calibre of Rosemary Squires, Harry Worth, Ted Hockridge, Billy Dainty and Eddie Calvert. Ronnie's side won 6–4 thanks to Rory who scored a hat-trick.

Towards the end of 1963 I had an accident that could have proved very embarrassing for me. I was playing football at Ashton-under-Lyne when I went down heavily and fractured my wrist. I was playing for the Show Biz side against the Central Nomads FC of Stalybridge at Hurst Cross when it happened. I had to have my wrist plastered at Ashton General Hospital and my arm was put in a sling, but I still managed to fly home from the game without letting anyone know of the injury. The injury could have had serious consequences however as I was only a few weeks away from going into pantomime and it would have proved costly if I had been forced to pull out. Jimmy Tarbuck was in our side for that game and the following weekend he made his own break when taking over as compère for *Sunday Night at the London Palladium*.

There were always opportunities to find the time to arrange a game here and there in support of various charities but after breaking my wrist, I became more conscious of the fact that an injury to my hands could prove to be serious. I then began limiting my appearances while still doing a lot of the arranging and sorting the lads out.

A game I did play in was at Macclesfield's Moss Rose ground when the Northern Television Stars, me included, played the Show Biz boys. Jimmy Tarbuck, Glen Mason,

Andrew Ray and Jess Conrad were all part of the Show Biz line-up while we had heavyweight boxing champ Brian London, impressionist Mike Yarwood, pop singer Emile Ford, and Diddy David Hamilton in the Northern Stars team. All proceeds were in aid of cancer research and there was a grand turnout to watch the antics.

The Show Biz side won 6–2 and Jimmy Tarbuck scored a hat-trick. Also on the score sheet was Ziggy Jackson who was a recording manager but used to play professionally for Dunfermline up in Scotland, former Spurs player Len Duquemin, and Des O'Connor. I managed to score one of the goals for the TV Stars. It wasn't our goalkeeper Colin McDonald's fault that we lost. The ex-Burnley and England keeper made many fine saves and even kept out a penalty, although he did cause a few problems for us when he wandered upfield to have a go at goal himself.

In January 1965 I was lucky enough to attend a special night to celebrate the 50th birthday of the great Stanley Matthews. The evening was put on by the Grand Order of Water Rats and it was a superb occasion. I had known Stanley for a number of years and he was a lovely and humble man as well as being the first footballer to receive a knighthood.

No one will ever forget the tragic Aberfan disaster and I was delighted to be able to make the TV All Stars available for a match at Ninian Park on 20 November 1966 in aid of the Distress Fund. This was the first time a match was played on a Sunday at Ninian Park and permission had to be obtained from the Football Association of Wales before the event could go ahead.

We had a gymnastic display first by the Cardiff Olympic Club and then the teams took the field led by the St Patrick's Pipe Band. What a line-up was on show for the thousands who went to Ninian Park that Sunday. In opposition to us was a Welsh International XI that included John and Mel Charles, Derek Tapscott, who lived less than a mile away from me, and Graham Moore. In opposition we didn't do too badly as we had Alex Stepney of Manchester Utd in goal, Jimmy Tarbuck was alongside the immaculate Bobby Moore and Cardiff manager Jimmy Scoular, while I was up front with George Eastham and the great Johnny Haynes. Such was the interest that special buses were put on to take spectators from the General Station to Ninian Park. It was a superb turn-out and more than 15,000 were in the ground to watch the match. As only 5,910 had watched the Cardiff City team play Bury the day before, you can imagine how pleased and delighted we all were that such a good sum would be going into the Fund. It was an extra-special pleasure to run out onto the Ninian Park turf after being a spectator at so many league matches.

Before playing at Ninian Park however, we had added to the Disaster Fund with another game, this time at Bargoed Park where Dave King, Craig Douglas and Brian Poole among others, had given their time for the worthy cause. The organisers were glad of the £500 raised that afternoon.

There were countless evenings and concerts organised to swell the Disaster Fund but I am pleased that in my own small way I helped bring a little order to a terrible and unforgettable event that should never have been allowed to happen.

I hung the boots up over the Christmas holidays, anyway most of the lads were either in pantomime or Christmas specials so it would have been difficult to put out the sort of team that the spectators wanted to see. Therefore the next time we all got together was in February 1967, this time in Swansea, where a Show Biz team played an All Star Managers side at Ashleigh Road. I was chuffed that Tommy Steele was able to put in an appearance for us. Heavy filming commitments caused the plane flying Tommy from Gatwick to Swansea to take off nearly an hour late as he was delayed at Shepperton Studios filming *Half A Sixpence*. We were due to kick-off at 2.30pm but eventually started almost 45 minutes late.

Almost 6,000 waited patiently and braved some icy winds and squally showers to support the match which ended in an 8–8 draw. Also appearing with me in the Show Biz side were Tony Dalli, who had recently returned to this country after finishing filming *The Life of Mario Lanza* in America, and Jess Conrad. The Managers team included John Charles, Jimmy Scoular and Harry Griffiths. Tommy's journey from London to Swansea for a game of football showed just how much the artists were prepared to give of their time to help charities. And don't forget, no one ever took any money out of the pot for expenses.

Tommy was missing when we took on a Welsh International XI at Edgar Street, Hereford in April 1968. This time he was in Ireland filming with Stanley Baker but fortunately we were able to call on Des O'Connor to take his place. Jimmy Henney did all the organising for this match as I had only just returned from South Africa. The Internationals were once again a star-studded line-up with John and Mel Charles, Harry Griffiths, Colin Baker and many others putting in an appearance. Hereford United Supporters club set up a stall outside the Market Hall in the High Street to sell programmes for the match but Des didn't make it because of a little knee trouble he had been suffering.

It was never difficult to raise a side in St Helier, Jersey where for several years we had a Bank Holiday Monday game, usually at the Springfield Stadium. We played against the local Saturday Football league and in 1970 we had Jess Conrad in goals assisted by Ed 'Stewpot' Stewart, Diddy David Hamilton, Brian Cant from TV's *Play School*, and none other than

Anthony Booth, star of *Till Death Us Do Part* and also of course, future father-in-law of former prime minister, Tony Blair.

The following year it was much the same format, the main difference being that in 1970 the programmes were one shilling (1s), whereas in 1971 they became 5 pence thanks to decimalisation. This time Gerry Marsden, of Pacemakers fame, and Richard O'Sullivan were added to the list of celebrities who willingly gave their time. By now, Show Biz football had raised more than £300,000 for charity. As well as Show Biz matches, other games were arranged involving the Good Sports, the John Charles XI and other groups all put together for the sole purpose of raising money.

Football wasn't the only charity sport I took part in. In February 1973 I played in the Good Sports World Snooker Finals at the Gower Hotel in Cardiff. I played against Lynn 'The Leap' Davies in one semi while Howard Winstone met Barry John in the other. All proceeds for that show went to the Salvation Army Hostel Appeal Fund.

It was becoming increasingly difficult to arrange a football match for a number of reasons. First of all, the issue of insurance started to enter the equation and you can't blame any artist wanting to safeguard his livelihood. Some of the Show Biz players commanded huge fees to perform on stage and so insurance began to be a major stumbling block. Another factor was travelling, as it took time to get to a venue. It was easy for me as I could fly my plane to wherever we were playing but for those who needed to catch a train to the nearest station, then it began to take up long hours. And don't forget that the traffic on the roads was starting to increase so even driving wasn't much of an option. Everyone still managed to turn out on occasions but the big boom that saw us play in front of 25,000 at Upton Park in the early days had now gone.

It never dampened my love of the game, my pal Trevor Ford saw to that, but I gradually found myself watching rather than playing. As I lived in Cardiff, I became a frequent spectator at Ninian Park when I was performing in the South Wales area. I never dreamt for one moment that I would ever become an executive director of the club but when chairman Stefan Terleszki approached me I jumped at the chance. After all, my old pal Eric Morecambe was a director of Luton Town and Tommy Trinder had been on the board at Fulham so what did I have to lose?

It wasn't a question of pumping money into the club, more of using my contacts in the game and in show business to promote Cardiff City. I also looked after the visiting chairmen when they came to Ninian Park to make sure they enjoyed the experience. I was friendly with Louis Edwards, chairman of Manchester United and knew he enjoyed a glass of champagne any time of day. So when United came to play Cardiff in a testimonial match I made sure that there was plenty of his favourite bubbly in the fridge for Louis.

I still see a lot of the older football lads when I go off to play in charity golf matches. Ron Atkinson and Andy Gray were regulars, and few remember that Jasper Carrott was once on the board at Birmingham City. That great actor Robert Powell was another who gave his time between acting jobs. In May 1975 I played at centre forward for the Entertainers against a Bristol side in aid of the Avon & Bristol Federation of Boys Clubs. Barry John, Derek Tapscott, Dave King, who I found out was a good friend of Tappy from his days in London with Arsenal, and the excellent actor Tony Selby were also in the line-up at the Eastville Stadium in Bristol that day. In opposition were an assortment of former City and Rovers players while Don Rogers was referee.

Not long afterwards, and while I was still a director at

Cardiff City, I was able to see that justice was done after a particularly nasty event occurred at Ninian Park. I was sitting in the Grandstand with Ceri for the Wales v Yugoslavia qualifier in the UEFA Cup. There were some distasteful scenes at the end of the game and I happened to witness the worst one. A steel-tipped corner flag was thrown into a cordon of police officers, wounding a police sergeant. A youth was arrested and I thought nothing of it until after the trial. A photograph of an 18-year-old named Kevin Frieze, held responsible for the act, was published after he received three years for grievous bodily harm.

As soon as I saw the photo I knew that justice had not been done because the lad I saw throw the corner flag was certainly nothing like Kevin. First I wrote to the *South Wales Echo* to tell my version of events and then the police contacted me and after a few weeks a re-trial was ordered. I was in the courtroom when the jury took just 18 minutes to find Kevin not guilty. Mind you, by then the poor lad had already been inside for a month so he didn't get away lightly, although the real culprit was never found. I was pleased that justice was finally done in his case, yet I remained determined to do all I could to help stamp out hooliganism not only in football grounds but also on the streets. Kevin and his mother were grateful for the role I played in getting the guilty verdict quashed but anyone would have done the same knowing that an innocent young man was in prison.

Normal cabaret work took a back seat when I appeared in Manchester in November 1975. I had been invited to the executive suite of Manchester United as guest speaker at a luncheon for both Manchester clubs. It was quite an honour for me and I am sure the invite came via my friendship with Louis Edwards.

Both teams were invited to the luncheon, together with such football dignitaries as Sir Stanley Rous, Sir Matt Busby, Tommy Docherty the United manager, and Tony Book the City boss. I often had butterflies before going on stage but it was quite an awe-inspiring experience standing up and talking to such an important assembly of soccer VIPs.

My interest in football has been passed on to Ceri and he is heavily involved with the Football Association of Wales as their press secretary. The job carries him all over Europe making sure of arrangements for the players and officials and he is kept busy. Nowadays I rarely get down to Ninian Park to watch a game but I do try not to miss any of the action if the Bluebirds are appearing on television. They seem to have eradicated a lot of the hooliganism that was once found at most football grounds and now the new stadium has been built in Leckwith I am sure it will be family-friendly and well worth a visit.

My last real involvement in football came when I was delighted to take on the role of director at Bridgend Town. Manager of the club at the time was Lyn Jones who was very successful at non-league level. He was manager of Inter Cardiff when they were in the 1994 UEFA Cup. They played crack Polish side Katowice in the preliminary round and Lyn's son Lee played in both legs of the tie for Inter. I enjoyed my spell working alongside the other directors at Coychurch Road but work commitments finally caught up with me and I had to call it a day. My only involvement with football now comes from watching on television or chatting to Ceri who has a much broader view on the game with his work for the FA of Wales.

13

GOING IT ALONE

'. . . Once again I tried to revitalise the entertainment set-up in Wales with homespun spectaculars as good as those in English resorts. By homespun, I didn't mean Welsh choirs, harp players and traditional costume, but good Welsh talent.'

* * * * *

After appearing in the very successful pantomime *Robinson Crusoe* at the Grand Theatre in Swansea I was back on my travels. In March, 1970 I appeared in cabaret up in Yorkshire then went further north to perform in East Kilbride before coming back down to Birmingham.

But there was an idea nagging away inside me that I desperately wanted to bring to fruition, especially as the big managements who made the bookings for the summer season that year had seemed to pass me by. I had now been travelling the country for over 20 years with very few breaks and I felt it was time to work closer to home so that I could enjoy family life a little more.

I had always wanted to present my own shows in South Wales and when the opportunity arose for me to do just that at the 1,000 seater Grand Pavilion in Porthcawl, I decided to make the most of it. I was surprised that a busy resort like Porthcawl, and don't forget it was home to about 7,000 caravans, had never had its own summer show and so I decided to make my dream come true and take up the challenge.

I went to see Ron Harris who was manager of the Grand at the time, told him what I wanted to do and he took my ideas to the council. Ron was actually a commercial artist who had his workshop underneath what became the administrative offices of the Grand Pavilion. He used to design all the posters for the events at the theatre and was a great help to me.

The problem with most councils however is that very few of the members know anything about show business. If only we had been given a little more help at the time I am sure we could have built up Porthcawl to become the shining light of seaside entertainment in South Wales. It beggars belief that a few years later they allowed it all to drift away.

Nevertheless, we were finally given the go-ahead for that first summer but it reinforced my belief that unless you have knowledge of how theatre works, you shouldn't put yourself in a position to pass judgement on it one way or the other. I much preferred dealing with people who at least had a love of the theatre in all its forms.

In fairness, I was eventually granted use of the Pavilion. Almost immediately I set about producing a show that I believed would bring the crowds flocking to Porthcawl. I knew there could be no skimping so to cover the finances I sold my Cessna six-seater airplane and Jaguar car to add to £20,000 of my own money. That gave me the security to go for the best of everything because if I was going to produce a show there was no room for failure.

I arranged for first class scenery, lovely costumes for the girls and some production scenes that stood comparison with any other summer show in Great Britain. We called it *Summer Stars* and it was booked to run for 10 weeks from the end of June until the beginning of September, twice nightly except on Mondays. I was able to sign up some of the cast from the Swansea Grand's hugely successful *Robinson Crusoe* pantomime. I knew that if we could be as successful in the summer as we were the previous Christmas, then the whole project would prove to be a hit.

Betty was with me all the way in this venture, even agreeing to work in the box office, while Roger, now a 20-year-old Cambridge undergraduate, would be front-of-house manager. Even Ceri got into the act as the cast's tea boy.

There was a lot of negotiating with the Porthcawl Entertainments Committee but they gave me their support and within three weeks of suggesting the show, preparations were well under way. It meant a lot of travelling for me initially as the groundwork was done while I was still appearing in cabaret in Solihull, up in Birmingham, but I knew it was all going to be worth it.

I wrote the show, booked the acts, produced and directed it. I arranged the printing of tickets, sold advertising space in the programmes and distributed handbills to everywhere and anywhere from fish and chip shops to supermarkets and coal mines. When booking the performers I contacted agencies, and most of the artists I signed up were well known to me. After all I had been in the business long enough to know exactly what was going on in the entertainment world. If the show was a success then I would be back up in the air flying my own plane once again. I had always worked for other people in the past and usually made money for them but now it was different as I was working for myself.

As every day went by I realised that I had gone too far to turn back, even if I wanted to. But then I would remember all the encouraging words from so many people who wanted me to succeed and make a success of the show. I calculated that I would draw even financially if just over half the seats were sold for the entire 10 weeks.

In all honesty there was far more to putting on a show than

I had first realised with scores of administrative jobs needing doing, but as the opening date drew near I could feel that we were polishing up a fast-moving, colourful show, and not just a series of variety acts. I was delighted when Johnny Tudor agreed to take part. Johnny was a winner on the television programme *Opportunity Knocks* but he started out while still a schoolboy singing in various clubs in South Wales. He had appeared at the Pigalle, the famous top cabaret venue, and had been in a number of West End musicals and plays including *A Funny Thing Happened On The Way To The Forum*. Johnny has been a good friend of mine for many years and still finds time, even now, to appear in the variety shows we take around the country.

Lesley King was from Grangetown in Cardiff, while Roy Lester provided the gags. Perhaps my best idea was to sign up Currie's Dancing Waters. They made a real splash, just as they had done at the Grand in Swansea. By shooting jets of water into the air to music at different strengths and angles, they made a fabulous series of patterns and grand designs in changing colours that thrilled the audience whatever the age group.

Jimmy Currie devised everything in a back-street workshop in Morecambe. He earned himself the nickname 'The Water Wizard' and allegedly could supply anything from a bursting dam to a boat-filled canal to amaze audiences. His made-to-measure water effects were seen in theatres all over the world and I was delighted he was part of the show. We used over 100 gallons of water during the spectacular but not a drop strayed on to the audience.

The show got under way on 30 June with a gala performance in aid of the Sunshine Home for Blind Babies and one of my special guests that evening was Sir Leslie Joseph. He was the owner of Coney Beach and had been helpful during the negotiations. On opening day I had a number of goodwill telegrams from show-biz pals such as Ken Dodd, Harry Secombe, and Morecambe and Wise.

I was pleased with the audience's response after the first night. We had a 10-minute standing ovation and that doesn't happen often but I knew that if I booked the right acts and provided the best of everything to make the show a spectacle, then my financial outlay would be safe. Mind you, it took a few weeks for the numbers to creep up over the half-full mark but by the end of the season we all knew that *Summer Stars* had been a resounding success.

So I was now a comedian and impresario, but at the same time I also became a country and western singer and album maker. While I was putting the finishing touches to the show, I somehow found time to record my first long playing record. It was called *With a Touch of Country and Western* and released on the Cambrian record label. I sang 12 songs including 'Send Me No More Roses', 'When Your Hair Has Turned to Silver', 'Lonesome Me', 'Ugly Bug Ball' and 'Your Cheatin' Heart'.

They were many of the songs I had featured in my act all over the world, particularly during my eight years with the Minstrels, and the record was made in two short sessions. Luckily the musical director was Peter Day, while Ron Huxford was on the drums and I played guitar with Frank Evans. Peter and Ron also provided the music for the Porthcawl show which turned out to be far more successful than my first attempt at becoming a recording star.

When I used to go to Porthcawl as a kid on a Sunday School treat at Whitsun, I never thought that I would one day put on a big summer spectacular in the town. Usually you would have to visit Bournemouth or Blackpool to see a show like that and although there was nothing previously at the venue to compare costs and takings, I had always been confident in the ability of the cast to provide a wonderfully entertaining show for South Wales audiences. What a great way to spend my 45th birthday!

It was back to the BBC in August when I started a six-week series of five minute programmes entitled *Just You, Just Me* for television. It was my first break on TV since the *Stan at Ease* programmes. I sang, talked and told some gags in just about the right mixture for what was a short late-night slot. You may think that five minutes is not very long but after all, why should everything in light entertainment have to be 30 or 60 minutes long? It was always far better to leave your audience wanting more.

At the end of the month I was booked to appear in Bournemouth alongside those boyos from the Emerald Isle known as The Bachelors. We had a great time together especially back stage when I reminded the lads that Con and Dec were still youngsters when their parents brought them back stage to meet me after a show in Dublin.

The summer show had been hard work and a financial worry but I knew in my heart I could do it all over again, and what better time to try than at Christmas. So it was out of the frying pan and into the fire, and I signed a contract to put on a pantomime in Porthcawl. My first thought was what panto to stage, but then I decided that I would follow an idea used at the Glasgow Alhambra which never relied on the usual hackneyed stories but came up with original ideas. I decided to present *The Adventures of Billy and Bonzo* under the umbrella of Stan Stennett Productions.

Of course I was able to weave lots of the usual characters into the story such as Robin Hood, Aladdin and Dick Whittington, but my main concern was that it would contain no goo, no mush, and most important of all—no smut. In the end I came up with *Billy and Bonzo Meet Robin Hood*.

Before the panto began however I delivered some Christmas cheer to three men. In itself that doesn't sound very interesting, but when I tell you that they were on a remote Pembrokeshire lighthouse called South Bishop Rock it takes a whole new meaning. Dressed as Santa Claus with a Mae West strapped to the outside of my outfit I braved a 40-knot wind and heavy rain to be winched down onto the rock from a Naval helicopter. In my sack I had a Christmas cake, pudding and other goodies for the lighthousemen who would be spending their Christmas on the rock.

Back to Billy and Bonzo—I took the part of Billy, Bonzo was played by Bonzo of course, and Bryn Williams had the part of Robin Hood off to perfection. He had a warm, vibrant personality that proved popular with the audience and his baritone voice was heard to best advantage when singing 'Some Enchanted Evening'. He had also spent time with the Black and White Minstrels and had his own show on BBC TV.

Roy Lester was Aunt Maggie and he drew on all his vast variety experience to provide a modern panto dame. He had an enormous range of dresses, wigs and accessories but there was nothing camp about Roy, it was all just good wholehearted fun. The whole crew worked well together from the first rehearsal and I was confident we had another success on our hands after the first few shows. We had a seven-week run and it was indeed a tremendous success with over 900 attending the final performance. The response was fantastic and beyond all my expectations. Billy and Bonzo were now firmly established characters.

Over 32,000 people visited the show during its run and I knew then that the Grand Pavilion had the potential to become a mecca of entertainment in South Wales. Business had rocketed to an all-time high during the closing weeks and we could easily have run another month but for individual commitments. Even before the rehearsals had started however I finally made a return to network television after an absence of seven years.

I had appeared on local shows in Wales and in the north but had never been offered anything on television that was to be networked throughout the country. I was even told by one television producer that they never used club comics, while another said that I had finished my ration of TV appearances. Once again I had the feeling that some TV producers were too young to remember me. I never minded being turned down if they saw my act and didn't like it, but the trouble was they used to say no without even bothering to find out what I could do. It used to send my press agent George Bartram up the wall.

So the only way I could break into the guest star circuit was as a folk singer making an appearance on George Hamilton IV's show which was called *George IV—A King in the Country* which went out on BBC 2 in November. Other guests included John D. Loudermilk and Slim Whitman of 'Rosemarie' fame, while there was a country music group called Matthews Southern Comfort who at the time had a huge hit single entitled 'Woodstock'. Seeing my name included in a roll call of the best of country singers seemed rather ridiculous but that was really the only way I could get on to the television circuit.

I sang 'Life Gets Tedious', which was an apt title under the circumstances. But I was still a comic and to audiences all over the country that is what I would remain. The powers-that-be at Porthcawl were delighted with our two shows and wanted us to put on another *Summer Stars*, not just for 1971 but for the next four years. They also asked us to produce another pantomime for Christmas.

But I was already contracted to do a summer show in Southport in 1971 after a deputation had come down from the Lancashire resort to watch the show in Porthcawl. They enjoyed it so much that we were booked to play at the Floral Hall on the Promenade commencing on 3 July for a 10-week season. The venue had not enjoyed good support and the local council were hoping that a summer show would revitalise the under-used building.

So I decided to take the 1970 Porthcawl show up to Southport while producing a completely new spectacle for the Grand Pavilion which was to open on 26 June. This just about gave me enough time to watch over rehearsals in Porthcawl before leaving for Southport.

I was lucky enough to book Terry Hall with Lenny the Lion as the star in South Wales, while a new West Country group called Shag Connors and the Carrot Crunchers provided the musical interlude. The lads were from Gloucestershire and turned professional especially for the summer season.

After the success of the first summer show I knew that once again I had to present the best possible cast and with Cwmbwrla's very own Julie de Marco, Ronnie Collis and Bill Gore in the line-up, I was confident we had everything necessary for another rip-roaring success. After all, Julie had won *Opportunity Knocks* and earned a five-year association with TV's successful quiz programme *Double Your Money*, while Ronnie Collis's impression of Charlie Chaplin was a real showstopper.

So 1971 was shaping up as a busy year for me, and it was to get even busier when I had a call to go up to the Granada Studios in Birmingham. If you are a registered agent you receive lists of castings available for shows and programmes in the entertainment world. George Bartram, my press agent, received his and spotted that there was a part coming up in a highly popular television soap.

He contacted the studios and in no time at all I was on my way to the Midlands. When I arrived at Granada I was asked if

I minded doing a little reading from the script. Something like that never bothered me and I was quite happy to read the part in front of producer Reg Watson and two or three other interested people from behind the scenes who were present at the time. I felt the reading went well but as there were probably five or six others also going for the part I was told that I would be informed in a few days whether I was successful or not.

Fortunately for me I was given the job and so won a small role in the ATV favourite *Crossroads* which was about to celebrate its 1,500th performance. I played an ex-GI with a chip on his shoulder called Harry Silver who sheltered in Mrs Hope's house. Harry held her and Mr Booth hostage at gunpoint and while my appearances lasted only seven episodes before being caught and sent down for a long stretch, it was an enjoyable few weeks being part of such a famous cast.

I got on particularly well with Noele Gordon, or Meg to all the viewers, as I had known her for many years after appearing on her lunchtime television programmes at Aston Cross. She had been a big musical comedy star in her time and one of her best remembered roles was as Gypsy Rose Lee.

It was a huge change from anything I had ever done, but I had achieved most things in show business except play a straight part so there was nothing like going in at the deep end. In my line of business you had to turn your hand to whatever came up. In any case, I was far more scared putting on my own show at Porthcawl than I was of playing a straight part in front of millions of viewers.

In the beginning I felt I wasn't as good at acting as the real professionals but then I realised that they couldn't do what I could do, so I soon felt better. I quickly learned that you mustn't play to the camera—that was the secret. It was totally different to being on stage where you wanted reaction from the audience. I was surprised at seeing myself on television in the part of Harry. It was like hearing yourself on tape for the first time. The power of television hit me when people I had never met before stopped to tell me they had seen me on *Crossroads*. One old lady even told me that she never thought I was that sort of villain. But it was only a small part and after just a few episodes I was written out and could concentrate on my summer activities.

The Porthcawl show started well to nearly-full houses and good reviews so I was quite happy leaving for Southport to finalise rehearsals at the Floral Hall. My aim was to bring back good wholesome summer entertainment to the Lancashire resort. I had always been an admirer of the old-time music hall stars. Their songs were ageless and could be heard in every pub bar from Wigan to the West End of London. Modern music was fine but a song heard today was often forgotten tomorrow.

Many of the artists of the Seventies were also a different breed—top of the charts one week and fresh out of material the next. They couldn't compare with the old maestros like Al Jolson or Flanagan and Allen. After all, their immortal signature tune, 'Underneath the Arches' is as popular today as when first recorded during the great depression of 1926, and it was in Southport that Flanagan and Allen first included the song in their act. Such was the impact that not only was it successful in this country, it also made the American hit parade. Southport must have had many more nostalgic ties and that was what I wanted the theatre audiences to re-discover.

But all my efforts looked like failing when we lost £1,200 in the first fortnight. Despite having a fast well-run show, the audiences just weren't there and in a hall with a capacity for 1,000 patrons, we were only selling between 300–400 tickets. I went on record saying that we were the biggest family production to visit Southport in years and that probably other companies would obviously think twice before they took the gamble of coming to the resort. There was no danger that we would take the show off before the end of the run, but it left little incentive to return another year.

One reason mooted for the poor attendance was the cost of tickets—some reckoned that they may have been a little too expensive. Even allowing for cost of living rises, I don't think 25p was too much in those days to see an entertaining summer show. Fortunately, the townsfolk and holidaymakers woke up in time and by the end of the run we had recovered financially, but it was a difficult summer up there on the Lancashire coast.

Betty and I had just enough time to enjoy a holiday in Majorca with the boys before it was back to work producing one pantomime in Porthcawl, and appearing in another in Wolverhampton. The Porthcawl panto was *Cinderella* with Johnny Stewart playing the part of Buttons, while I was in the Black Country in *Red Riding Hood* playing opposite the lovely Susan Maughan.

By September we already had over 7,000 bookings for *Cinderella* while the *Red Riding Hood* season had been extended to 11 March due to the huge interest. Two months before the Wolverhampton show opened, over £3,000 had been taken in advance bookings.

When I was looking to cast Baron Hardup for *Cinderella* I had the idea of offering Richard Burton the part, thinking he would jump at the chance of returning to the seaside resort he used to visit as a child. Unfortunately he turned down my offer in a letter explaining that the tax boys had told him he couldn't work in Britain—and that included Wales—until at least another year had passed. Still, we managed a few pages of publicity out of it and I still have his letter.

Dear Mr Stennett,

Thank you very much for your offer of the Baron in Cinders. I would love to do it—especially in front of a Welsh audience and particularly with you, as Eliz and I like your work very much. And that is not meant chauvinistically (Christ what a word!) I assure you. But lamentably I am heavily committed for the next hundred years or so. Also, the tax boys say that I must not work in Britain—which unfortunately includes Wales—until next summer—if then.

Give my love to Rest Bay. I cannot tell you how many times I was lost in Porthcawl on Sunday-school 'outings' crying for my sister.

Good luck for the Pantomime and thank you again.

Sincerely,
Richard B.

Both pantomimes were great successes and on a personal basis, my production company was able to make money in Porthcawl while I also earned my salary in Wolverhampton. This went a long way to softening the small financial blow left over from the summer season in Southport.

Mike Bailey, captain of the Wolves football team, made a surprise appearance in the Wolf's Lair during *Red Hiding Hood* on Christmas Eve and other Wolves players turned up during the run. The theme of using the local football stars caught on well and each night there was a buzz in the audience as the latest player to appear was revealed.

After *Cinderella* completed its record-breaking run in Porthcawl, I invited the entire cast to the Grand to see Red Riding Hood as that also broke all records for the theatre.

Stennett, the impresario, was now beginning to make his mark.

The council in Porthcawl gave me a contract to continue to produce shows at the Grand Pavilion while I was also contracted to stage a 10 week *Summer Revue* commencing in July 1972 at the Prince of Wales Theatre in Colwyn Bay. It would be the first major variety season staged there since the end of the war.

The programme would consist of nightly shows with two on Wednesdays and Saturdays. It would not be just variety, but a first class revue programme with top class artists. I felt that there was a need for good holiday entertainment up in North Wales and set out to present programmes that were as good as those to be seen at the principal English holiday resorts.

One thing my shows would not be resorting to was 'blue' jokes. Frankly, if I had to turn to filth to keep on working I would have much preferred going back on the lorries. This was about the time that Bernard Manning rose to fame in a TV programme called *The Comedians*, and most viewers and listeners knew what to expect when he was on stage. I never thought much of that programme anyway and I doubt whether any of the comics on the show claimed they were telling original gags. In any case, a number of years previously, Morecambe and Wise, Billy Dainty, Derek Roy and myself used to do a radio programme from Manchester called *Make 'Em Laugh* which was much better as it was completely unscripted.

As far as Stan Stennett Productions were concerned, it was all systems go. In order to overcome transport problems in the moving of scenery, props and all the other show paraphernalia between Porthcawl and Colwyn Bay, I renewed my heavy goods vehicle licence and purchased a suitable wagon well equipped for the job. It seemed that my life had turned a full circle and I was back behind the wheel but you know the old saying—the show must go on.

The summer of 1972 was meticulously planned as I needed to be in two places at the same time. I was starring in the Prince of Wales Theatre in North Wales while *Summer Stars 72* was on a 10-week run in Porthcawl. Once again I tried to revitalise the entertainment set-up in Wales with homespun spectaculars as good as those in English resorts. By homespun, I didn't mean Welsh choirs, harp players and traditional costume, but good Welsh talent.

The formula had proved to be a hit in Porthcawl in a setting once believed to be a white elephant, and I believed that a venture in Colwyn Bay would be much less of a gamble even though it was only a 430 seat theatre. The Welsh Tourist Board was going all out to attract visitors and it was up to us to provide good entertainment for them.

Summer Stars 72 opened at the Grand Pavilion in a heatwave. It was a good start and there were large audiences for the show. A new comedian called Del Derrick topped the bill for the first time and he had a light style and engaging personality that soon endeared him to the audience. He also proved to be a bit of a wizard on the xylophone. Lesley King, Karl Rainer and the Lyntones delivered their songs in their own contrasting styles as did a young singer called Peter Lewis. Peter had won a talent contest at the Ideal Homes Exhibition in Cardiff and as well as a £25 prize, he also scooped a recording test with Cambrian Records, a three day holiday in Jersey staying at the Merton Hotel and, best of all, a chance to appear in *Summer Stars*.

The 29-year-old bass-baritone was a principal singer with the Penarth Operatic Society and had never entered a talent contest before, but his rendition of 'If I Were A Rich Man' from *Fiddler on the Roof* won him the contest. Peter has worked with me many times over the years since that first stage appearance. Up at Colwyn Bay we were playing to full houses in *Summer Stars* from the first performance and as we changed the programme twice a week, there was enough for everyone to enjoy.

Our eldest son Roger was with us after gaining his BA degree in history at Christ College, Cambridge. A member of the Cardiff AAC he was the only Welsh schoolboy to win the British high jump title and he wanted to get back into training while still helping us run the show. Roger's ambition was to represent Wales at the Commonwealth Games in New Zealand and he cleared six feet in his first practice jump at Colwyn High School.

In all, I had 16 artists with me at Colwyn Bay including Roy Lester. For him it was a return to the area after an absence of 18 years. It was back then that he decided to get married in Colwyn Bay but at the time they had no registry office. Roy and his bride-to-be travelled to Abergele and then returned to the Metropole Hotel for their reception. He used to claim that at least he had two wedding cakes. As soon as he arrived in North Wales, Roy began looking for a suitable caravan site where he could spend the summer while the show was on. Unfortunately, I was busy commuting between Colwyn Bay and Porthcawl at least twice a week so there was no caravan for me.

Both shows drew to a successful close although I made very little money from the productions. In fact I would have earned more doing my act on stage for a couple weeks, and it wouldn't have been so stressful. So what did I have up my sleeve for the next few years? More shows of course, starting with Christmas 1972 at the Grand Pavilion in Porthcawl.

14

PRODUCING
THE GOODS

'We had a fair dinkum time in Australia and had the opportunity to see many of the usual tourist attractions. While there I met this bloke playing Abba's "Dancing Queen" on his didgeridoo. I thought that's aboriginal.'

* * * * *

Christmas 1972 we were back in Porthcawl at the Grand Pavilion in a new production of *Billy and Bonzo meet Mother Goose*. Once again it had been a strenuous time putting everything together as after all, I produced the pantomime, directed it, starred in it, and even wrote the script. Somehow I still couldn't get used to being called an impresario. When all was said and done, I had a mortgage, not delusions of grandeur. But with the production company now up and running, I could understand why people thought of me in that way.

As usual the accent in the show was on good clean comedy, popular tunes and plenty of audience participation, which is the stuff of any good panto. On the opening night, Wally Dunn was still suffering from the after-effects of an operation, yet his Mother Goose couldn't have been better. Peter Lewis was appearing in his first pantomime as the cunning Count Vermin, while Bryn Williams as Francis and Sian Hopkins as the Princess were both in fine voice. Actress Mari Claire played the

Queen of Hearts who helped Billy and Bonzo rid the village of a plague of rats.

In all there were 16 scenes, all with excellent sets and first class lighting, and I was delighted with the overall effect. We were lucky to have Alex Winter working with us backstage. He had always been fascinated by all things electrical and became our main electrician and sound man. He could always be relied on to produce superb lighting and sound systems and I am glad to say the good work is continuing as he is still working with us even now.

Wally and I did the 'Busy Bee' scene in *Mother Goose* where we tried to spray each other with mouthfuls of water. That probably helped Wally a lot because he was suffering from a sore throat for the first few weeks of the panto. This was the first time that Bonzo was played by a real dog.

The audience came in droves from as far afield as Gloucester and Haverfordwest and the bookings were so good that we had to extend the run for a week until 10 February. Roger was a valuable member of the crew at Porthcawl but we were soon to lose him for after graduating from Cambridge he was about to start a new life as assistant director of the South-Western Arts Association based in Exeter. Ceri was still at school but he was a big help to us behind the scenes during the holidays. As usual, Betty busied herself in the front box office selling tickets or programmes so it was a family affair, I can't take all the credit.

Unfortunately for us, what we gained on the pantomime we tended to lose on the Summer Show. With the weather being such a variable factor we could never guarantee regular audiences in summer as we could in winter for pantomimes. People are always complaining about the weather, but no one ever seems to do anything about it. I began saving for a rainy day and I already had a sou'wester, two macintoshes and a canoe. Without any sort of subsidy from the council, the Summer Show was a luxury I was seriously considering dropping. It was something I needed time to think about carefully.

Two weeks after the successful end to the pantomime I took part in the World Snooker Championship again—well the Good Sports version. Held at The Gower Hotel in Cathays, Cardiff it was in aid of the Salvation Army and we raised an impressive amount of money. Defending champion Howard Winstone went out to Barry John in the first round, much to the dismay of his supporters who had travelled down from Merthyr. Howard called for the white ball to be changed as he reckoned it was playing tricks but it didn't matter, he couldn't catch Barry.

Referee Johnny Stewart inspected the studs in my size 37 boots before allowing me to select a number nine cue from my golf bag when it was my turn to play Lynn 'The Leap' Davies. Despite one rather unorthodox shot when I potted a ball off three cushions while sporting kingsize sunglasses, I failed miserably to unnerve the Olympic gold medallist and he went through to the final where he beat Barry to win the trophy—an inscribed chamber pot.

Continuing the sporting theme I was then invited in March to join the *TV Times* Tournament of the Stars which was a new kind of event in the international golf calendar. It was to take place at the spectacular Nueva Andalucia course in Marbella, Spain and taking part were 14 famous show business golfers who would be partnered by 14 *TV Times* readers, each playing as champion of their own TV region.

We flew out on 18 March to the Costa del Sol and on the plane with me were Stanley Baker, Charlie Drake, Adam Faith, Michael Medwin, Norman Wisdom, William Roache (Ken Barlow of *Coronation Street*) and Jimmy Hill. It was well organised and the forerunner of many other charity golfing events that would raise huge amounts of money for charity.

Usually of course, at some stage or other, the performing artists would be asked to put on a show and at that first event Norman Wisdom and I played the leading comic parts in an impromptu all-star cabaret at the Andalucia Plaza Hotel.

After a great deal of soul-searching when I was back home I decided that I would give Colwyn Bay another chance despite having suffered a big financial loss the previous year. Everyone had been delighted with the standard of that show but it only attracted a total audience of 15,000 compared with a full house potential of 35,000. Box office receipts had been just enough to cover expenses but I worked for nothing so for the new show I decided to do something different in the 10 week run.

There would be three changes of programme each week, while each Monday night would be known as the 'Johnny Stewart Special' night where there were competitions for the audience and prizes to be won. It was a good family spectacular and I really believed it to be the best show in Wales.

Never one to shirk work, I now found myself producing and appearing in the show in Colwyn Bay while also recording a series for BBC Wales called *Pass the Buck*. Every Monday I would take the day off, hence the Johnny Stewart Special in Colwyn Bay, speed down to Cardiff and record the show, get home for the night, and then drive back up to North Wales on the Tuesday. *Pass the Buck* was a general knowledge knockout quiz contest between social clubs in Wales and it ran for a total of 31 weeks. Mari Claire, who was my panto Queen of Hearts and came from Barry, was the hostess.

At the same time as this I also appeared in a six-week run in *Jokers Wild* for Yorkshire Television, had a guest appearance on *Golden Shot* and made a celebrity appearance talking snooker on *Pot Black* so I was exceptionally busy. It was good to be back on television after such a long absence but strange how things work out. In all, by September, I had made 39 appearances on television in 1973, a big turnaround after having so little TV work prior to that.

The highlight for me at Colwyn Bay was a second house during August. There was a familiar face in the audience that particular night as Eric Morecambe had driven his wife Jean and son Gary up from his Hertfordshire home in his Rolls just to watch the show. He wanted to recall a little of the old days when we trod the same boards in variety. Poor Eric had to drive himself because his chauffeur was on holiday. We had a long chat after the show and it was good to see him as we had been pals for a long time. Eric very kindly said that the show was far better suited to Blackpool than Colwyn Bay which was praise indeed and much appreciated.

I still felt however that although we had our fair share of visitors through the doors, the support was lacking from local people. Perhaps the answer was that admission charges of 60p and 70p were too high, but we had to set a budget for ourselves. If that was the case, fair enough, I would rather play to 15 full rows at 50p than 10 full rows at 70p. I was generally satisfied with the response but had hoped it would have been even more financially successful. We had 20% more people than turned out the previous year but then overheads had increased by 30%. An average cost of £600 a week then had now risen to £800.

After two seasons at the Prince of Wales I decided that I would only return if it could be a paying proposition. If the council wanted me back then I would have to look long and hard before making up my mind.

But then I was presented with an interesting opportunity. My press agent George noticed that there were castings coming up for a drama in the BBC series *Play for Today*. He remembered that my old mate Bill Maynard had recently been seen in a dramatic part and so sent my brochure, a kind of artist's CV, up to Yorkshire where they would be producing the play. In no time at all I was asked to go to London to read for a part in a drama by Colin Welland called *Leeds United*.

When anybody offers you work you go and have a chat with them, but I never knew it was going to be such a serious play. All the same I read a few lines for drama producer Roy Battersby and he said I'd do. Then he gave me a script weighing about a ton and told me to go away and learn it all. It was the toughest job I've ever had and I am still not quite sure why he picked me.

In case you think *Leeds United* was a forerunner to *Footballers Wives* I can assure you it was nothing to do with football, despite the title. The word 'United' described how workers all came together as this was a story about the 1970 women rag trade workers who went on strike for better conditions and pay.

Colin Welland made his name as an actor in *Z Cars* but then turned his hand to writing. The subject matter appealed to him as his mother-in-law was one of the original strikers. This was to be a massive production with a budget of over £150,000, the price of three normal plays, and the biggest ever for a single play for the BBC.

I was delighted when offered the part of a disillusioned militant strike organiser called Joe Pike who worked on behalf of the Leeds clothing workers. So off I went to Yorkshire to begin filming. The BBC producer Kenith Trodd realised that despite the huge budget for the play, the story essentially involved 30,000 women going on strike. Obviously the cost of paying so many extras would be prohibitive. So he and Roy came up with a cunning plan. Everyone who turned up at the appointed time was given a raffle ticket and every evening there was a draw with the prizes ranging from colour television sets to package holidays. It would have been impossible to pay the extras in the normal way but with the raffle creating so much interest there was never a shortage of willing bodies to appear in the crowd scenes. There was also a bonus for everyone on the last night of filming as members of the cast put on a free show at the Leeds Town Hall where a number of scenes took place.

Duggie Brown also took part in the play. He was famous at the time for appearing regularly in *The Comedians* on network television. Duggie took the part of a happy-go-lucky bus conductor who was well known by those workers who bussed it to the factories. Duggie's real life sister Lyn Perrie was also a member of the cast. Now Lyn, who sadly passed away a few years ago, was better known as Ivy Tinsley of *Coronation Street*.

Towards the end of the play she had to give me a slap on the face and she didn't hold back. I had a red cheek for a week afterwards. Adding weight to the proceedings were Royal Shakespeare Company actress Elizabeth Spriggs who played the part of my wife, and Terence Frisby, a playwright who wrote *There's A Girl In My Soup*.

It was daunting being in such esteemed company but I had one great advantage and that was my ability to be able to talk to, and control, an audience. In this case of course it was a crowd but it was the same principle. While fellow comic Duggie's part allowed him almost to be himself, my role was different as I played the part of a bolshy, militant shop steward intent on bringing the factory bosses down.

You see the women went on strike against a wage settlement which their union had concluded. My role was to use the situation to cause problems for management. In the end I conspired with the union representatives against the strikers and helped bring about a return to work. Hence the slap on the face from Lyn Perrie.

There was one other novelty about the play. It was filmed in black and white to stress the drab background, not we were assured, to save the BBC some money. I was excited about appearing in a dramatic role and would certainly have thought seriously about doing any others that came my way, but I still wanted to maintain my interest in comedy and entertaining. We finished filming in late 1973 but the drama never reached the television screens until almost a year later, in November 1974.

I finished filming on location in Leeds on the Monday, and the following morning Betty, Ceri and I flew off to Sydney, Australia. It was all very hectic but that was because of the timing of *Leeds United*. I had planned a leisurely week looking around Sydney before opening in cabaret at St George's Rugby League Club where I had been booked for a four-week season until 8 December. Because of taking on the work in Leeds, I had to open in cabaret just a few hours after arriving in the country. Incidentally, appearing with me at the club was the popular singing star, Olivia Newton-John.

We had a fair dinkum time in Australia and had the opportunity to see many of the usual tourist attractions. While there I met this bloke playing Abba's 'Dancing Queen' on his didgeridoo. I thought that's aboriginal.

No sooner had we arrived back home than I was off in the opposite direction to Belfast to entertain the troops. I also took part in a television programme called *Late Call* which was recorded before an audience of Welsh Guards serving in Belfast. I arrived back from there in the middle of December and went straight into rehearsals for the 1973 pantomime at the Grand Pavilion, Porthcawl.

That year was notable for probably the longest title of any pantomime ever staged in Great Britain. It was called *Billy, Bonzo and Their Butty Meet Jack and the Beanstalk*. I played my usual role of Billy and my Butty was none other than Johnny Stewart. Johnny had appeared in many of my productions but this was the first time we had ever been on stage together in the same pantomime.

Also appearing with us were Lesley King as Principal Boy, Mari Claire as the Princess and Les Ward as King Crackpot. It was his first pantomime away from his brother Albert. Peter Lewis had all the children, and grown-ups too, hissing and booing whenever he came on stage as The Demon. It was another tremendously successful season even if the programmes were a strange shape due to the long title of the pantomime.

After a few days' break when the curtain came down at Porthcawl I made a fleeting visit to Malta to entertain troops. Then I was back on the road playing the clubs before getting down to organising another summer show for Porthcawl.

Because I was contracted to the Grand Pavilion, I was forced to turn down an acting part most straight men would have given a year's dole money to be offered. I was invited to appear with Keith Michel's new Chichester Theatre company in *Oedipus Tyrannus*, by Sophocles, playing the part of a shepherd. On top of that, Diana Dors was in one of the starring roles.

I made a few appearances on television in *Golden Shot* and I joined up with the Grumbleweeds and old pal Billy Dainty for Yorkshire Television's *Junior Showtime*. That was a programme showcasing young talent and one of the children appearing was a tiny little girl called Lena Zavaroni.

Then it was straight into rehearsals for our fourth summer show in Porthcawl which was scheduled for an eight-week season. Advance bookings were great which put us, and the Ogwr District Council, in good humour and that is always a good sign just before a show starts its run. A last minute addition to the cast was a semi-professional group from Porthcawl called Driftwood. They joined old favourites Johnny Tudor, Lesley King, The Falcons, Linda Good and other supporting artists in a well-balanced show.

At last it seemed as though councils were starting to realise the value of live entertainment at seaside resorts as for this season they backed us to the tune of £800 per week. Mind you, that £800 was only enough to cover the cast's wages and some of the production costs. There was nothing in it for me. We had a rousing start playing to a near-capacity audience who were still clapping and cheering for more after a performance that lasted a solid three hours. Public demand was so great that we extended the run for a further fortnight. We had to step up to two performances nightly, except Fridays, to cope with the demand and as the show was changed every Thursday, it gave holidaymakers the chance of doubling up during a week's stay in the resort.

Once again we had produced the type of show the public wanted but we had to close in mid-September because so many of the artists had been booked to appear elsewhere. I was heading for a reunion with the company I had spent so many wonderful years with as in November I joined the *Black and White Minstrel Show* in Derby. It was for a five-day engagement taking over briefly from Don Maclean who was having time off to rehearse his part in the BBC Christmas pantomime.

I was flattered that impresario Robert Luff had thought of me after being away from the show for so long. But I did make one proviso—no blacking up. My complexion had only just returned to normal after those earlier years with the Minstrels.

In November *Leeds United* was finally shown on television to critical acclaim. I never realised how grim and gaunt it would look being filmed in black and white.

On to happier events and Christmas 1974 for the Stennett family was yet another when I needed to be in two places at the same time. The Grand Pavilion in Porthcawl was staging a Stennett production entitled *Butty Meets Red Riding Hood*, while I was appearing as Billy in *Aladdin* at the New Theatre in

Cardiff. It was my first pantomime in my home town and my first major appearance at the New since my Minstrel days almost 10 years previously.

It was always one of my ambitions to play panto in Cardiff and very appropriate in a way because if I hadn't stepped in to help by financing my own show back in 1960 then there may not have been a New Theatre. Ceri, now 14 years-old, was my dresser for the show. He was following in Roger's footsteps as he had been house manager, dresser and most of the other jobs in the theatre before becoming assistant director to the South West Arts Association.

Ronnie Coyles had played the Dame alongside me in many a pantomime and his Widow Twankey was always a firm favourite with young and old alike. It was a good cast including Gillian Humphries as Aladdin and Mari Claire who I had worked with many times.

Meanwhile Johnny Stewart was going it alone in Porthcawl and doing a splendid job getting on friendly terms with the children as soon as the curtain opened. Appearing with Johnny was my old Minstrel pal Glyn Dawson who played the part of Mangy the Wolf.

Both pantos played to near capacity audiences throughout the season but it was hard work for everyone involved and a relief when both runs came to a close. Proof of success came when I was asked to return to the New Theatre the following year for *Mother Goose*.

In February 1975 I received an offer to rejoin the long-running ITV series *Crossroads* as the character I played in my earlier visit. Apparently, the scriptwriters had decided it was about time Harry Silver was released from prison and were discussing ways of re-introducing him into the programme. I would have been happy to go back into the show provided it was at the right time. It wasn't the only offer to come in the post around Christmas. I had to turn down the part of a councillor in *Coronation Street* because it clashed with *Aladdin* at the New Theatre, and the same thing happened to me when I was offered the lead in a new stage play called *The Comedians*. That part was eventually taken by Jimmy Jewell and he made a great success of it. You can't dwell on what might have been in this business, just thank your lucky stars that you are still wanted.

Fortunately, I was wanted because I had another summer show to organise in Porthcawl and I was delighted to obtain the services of Penny Nicholls, my old partner from the Minstrels. While she was still a teenager, Penny had done films, been on radio and had her own series called *Penny Serenade*. Then her big break came when Henry Hall asked her to be his resident singer and she replaced Betty Driver, now playing the part of Betty Turpin in *Coronation Street*. It was after her time with Henry Hall that she joined me working with the Minstrels and of course we got on well together for a number of years.

Penny had later given up the business after getting married but following the sad loss of husband Derek she decided to make a come-back despite being off the boards for eight years. And everywhere she went she took her pet budgie with her. Biffy the budgie came to rehearsals every day and at the drop of a hat would sing her old signature tune, 'Pennies from Heaven'.

On the bill for us in Porthcawl was an unusual artist called Bill Gore. He had received an overwhelming vote earlier in the year in TV's *Opportunity Knocks* when he appeared with his magic boots. The yodelling cobbler had also just won the World Championship Yodelling Competition. You don't get them like that nowadays.

A few days before the show started its run I was informed by the Borough Council that they had awarded the contract for the Christmas pantomime to another production company who were going to stage *Aladdin* starring Freddie (Parrotface) Davies and Yana. I was disappointed at first but at least I knew that I would once again be heading for the New Theatre and *Mother Goose*.

We all wanted to make the summer show a big success and, with Penny performing as though she had never been away, the audiences loved it. It was still during the time of the Miners Fortnight at Porthcawl when the resort, and caravan park, would be filled with the lads who went digging for the black gold, and of course their families.

I used to tell a story about a friend who worked in the deepest mine in the world and how the dust which caused the dreaded pneumoconiosis was so bad that when he came home he used to spit on the fire to bank it up. Do you know it got the biggest laugh from miners and victims of the dust disease? And to think people reckon we can't laugh at ourselves. At the end of the season we said our goodbyes and I had a few days off before travelling round the country in cabaret.

That Christmas, *Mother Goose* was a riot from start to finish. We played to packed audiences from day one and broke all the records for the New Theatre for the second year running. At one performance I persuaded an old friend of mine, Dan O'Neill to make an appearance on stage. Dan still writes a column in the *South Wales Echo*. We dressed him up in a very loud check suit and he came on stage to sing 'Little Bit of Heaven'. As he was singing objects began falling on his head but when a stuffed cow came down he thought it was time to go and so beat a hasty retreat.

In 1976 I received some repeat fee royalties from the BBC for my part in *Leeds United*. The show had been sold to Yugoslavia and I received a cheque for £1.54. I was a little worried about that because if the play ever reached Taiwan I would probably have had to send them money. That didn't stop me from taking more straight acting parts.

I was in a half hour play rather quaintly entitled *Where The 'Ell Have You Been Lavinia?* for BBC Wales. My co-star was the lovely Ruth Madoc and it was recorded at the Pebble Mill studios. I also appeared in a St David's Day BBC TV presentation of *The Welsh Not*. This was a fairly serious play about the decline of the Welsh language and was previously shown as a series on schools programmes. The play told of how children who persisted in speaking Welsh in school had a label saying 'Welsh Not' hung round their shoulders.

Music never took a back seat either as I recorded a new LP entitled *Stan Stennett Sings Country and All That Jazz* for Line Records. Making the album was like a bolt from the blue. I received a telephone call from Ken Jones, an old army mate of mine from my days in Italy. He told me that he was now a director of Line Records and that he would like to make an album using the type of numbers he knew suited my style. Songs on the record included 'Snowbird', 'Careless Love', 'September Song', 'Old Shep', and a specially written number by Denny Wright titled 'It's Tough Being a Cowboy in Wales'.

All that fitted in quite well because in August I hosted my own radio record show on BBC Radio Wales called *Stand By For Stan*. In it I played records with a set theme and also talked to listeners on the telephone.

I took a gamble that summer because I refused all offers of a summer season just so I could stay at home, put my feet up, and wait for the offer of a good acting role. It cost me about £10,000 in lost fees but against that in the past I had already been obliged to turn down offers because of prior commitments. Now I decided I would be ready and waiting. I thought about it long and hard and felt that I wanted to become an actor more than anything else. I knew acting wouldn't pay as much as light entertainment but I was willing to take a cut in salary to satisfy the urge to become an actor.

I was still available for concert bookings and one I was delighted to attend was a special concert and dinner at Sophia Gardens held in honour of the Prime Minister, Mr Jim Callaghan. I had no particular political leanings and in the past had appeared at functions for the Tory Party but I was asked to organise an hour-long cabaret and as I had a great deal of experience doing that I was pleased to accept the offer.

We were very proud when Roger had his first book of poems published. He had also written work which the BBC were considering staging. Ceri was still in school but he wanted to go into the production side of the business and was already clever at creating special effects. It looked as though second generation Stennetts were going to make their mark in entertainment.

It was around this time that my gamble of waiting for acting work paid off when I was invited to join the cast of *Coronation Street*. I was to play Hilda Ogden's brother in four episodes of the soap and as he was a fish and chip shop proprietor I needed a spot of practice for my new role. So off I went behind the counter of a chippie in Caerphilly Road, Cardiff, quite close to a Coronation Road funnily enough. I worked behind the counter there for three or four days just to get the hang of frying so as to make my role look authentic.

I am pretty sure it was my part in *Leeds United* that put the Corrie people on to me. They liked the role I took and also the northern accent I used. They had been trying to get me to join the cast before but I was always booked up at the crucial times. There was also the possibility that I could be asked to do a few more episodes than the four on the table.

It was 8 November 1976 when I first appeared on screen as Norman Crabtree and I was nervous. My chip shop wasn't in Wetherfield, it was in Eccles, perhaps that is why Stan Ogden found it so inviting as it was a quiet haven away from the Street and of course, from Hilda. Apart from making sizeable inroads into my deep-fry goods, Stan also became a close companion of my screen girlfriend, Edie Blundell. The line in the story was that I was trying to rid myself of my bone-idle brother-in-law and send him packing back to Hilda.

> *'He comes in here skint and helpless, and ends up not only stealing my chips but my bird as well.'*

Stan, or Bernard Youens as he was really known, was a lovely man who was totally opposite to the character he played on screen. He had been troubled by ill-health for many years having suffered from arthritis and heart attacks yet always recovered to appear as the lovable layabout. Jean Alexander, or Hilda Ogden, played Stan's wife for over 20 years and it was a sad day when Bernard passed away in March 2007.

Jean is still going strong and can been seen regularly on television in one of my favourite programmes, *Last of the Summer Wine*. When I first arrived at the studios it meant a reunion with my old friend Betty Driver. We used to meet up occasionally when we were on the same bill when we both did variety, though of course we were much younger back then. Betty was a singer with a number of big bands but most notably for Henry Hall on his *Guest Night* programme.

I was booked into a hotel in Manchester and started rehearsals in the afternoon, on the same day I arrived. We would rehearse Monday and Tuesday, part rehearse and part record on Wednesday, and record Thursday and Friday. This meant canteen food for the week as we spent a lot of time in the Granada Studios. Fortunately it was good grub.

The studios were huge and all the sets were laid out ready for the filming to take place. There was the cobbled street of course, the inside of the Rovers, various characters houses, and over in one corner was the inside of a chippie where I would spend most of my time on set. *Coronation Street* went out four nights a week then so it was an extremely hectic schedule and we had to make sure we kept ahead. This meant being word-perfect and knowing exactly where to be at the right time. I was given a script a week before going up north so I was able to read it on the train.

As well as knowing Betty Driver, I also knew Geoffrey Hughes, the bin man in Corrie but also well known for playing the part of Onslow in *Keeping Up Appearances*, Johnny Briggs, alias Mike Baldwin and William Roache, aka Ken Barlow, as they were all acquaintances I had met up with several times at charity golf days. All in all they were a kind and welcoming bunch and made my short stay in the Street a very happy one.

I believe my appearance in *Coronation Street* made me one of the first actors to have played in both major soaps, *Corrie* and *Crossroads*. When I left the series I received a letter from Granada saying how pleased they were with the character of Norman and expressing the hope that they could use him again in future episodes. When they did finally get in touch I had to turn them down as I was already committed to another popular soap.

15

FROM PANTO TO PALACE

'Betty and I stayed the night in a lovely hotel in London. Nothing was too much trouble and it was a joy to be looked after for a short while. Mind you room service was terrible. I ordered a hot chocolate and they sent up a Cadbury's Flake and a box of matches.'

* * * * *

The Christmas 1976 pantomime was *Cinderella*, and once again I was booked for the New Theatre in Cardiff playing the part of Billy. Also on the bill were singing stars Tammy Jones and Craig Douglas and it turned out to be the most successful panto ever organised by Cardiff's New Theatre Trust.

The Ugly Sisters, Val Derma and Germolena, were played by husband and wife team, Howell Evans and Patricia Kane, and my old friend Peter Lewis was Baron Hardup. Olive Guppy's charming Olivettes entertained the audience with slick dance routines and the two Shetland ponies used to pull the magic coach always had the children wide-eyed.

Originally scheduled for a seven-week run starting on 20 December, box office figures were so good that we were signed up for a further week. Almost 100,000 people saw a total of 92 performances and the show made a staggering £133,000 during its run. Bearing in mind that the theatre only had seating for 1,100 people you can see what a tremendous pantomime we put on and takings were up 60% on the previous year.

Perhaps it was the crazy Baron's Barmy Bathroom sequence we did that kept the crowds flocking in to the New. I originally used it in Dick Whittington in Dudley back in 1957 only then it was a ship's cabin that rocked up and down. For Cinderella I sat on a toilet seat that shot five feet up in the air. There was water everywhere as we incorporated special effects that wouldn't have been possible if the water shortage earlier in the year had persisted.

It was hard work but very rewarding to see the audience enjoy the whole spectacle. On Saturdays we did three shows and for me that meant nine hours on stage either flying through the air on a harness, running through the audience, or just doing my routine on stage. Running through the auditorium almost led to a serious accident during one performance as a little lad accidentally tripped me up as I was racing down the aisle. I caught my wedding ring on the edge of the seat and turned a couple of somersaults on the floor before jumping up and carrying on with the show. My finger was badly bruised for a week or so after that incident.

I had to tell the other characters not to do or say anything nasty to Billy because the children would be down on them like a ton of bricks. It wouldn't have mattered if it was the Fairy Princess. The kids all identified with Billy and they didn't like it if anyone was unkind to him.

I used to receive letters asking me how Bonzo was getting on and many times I received little rubber bones in the post for him. And when any children came up on stage they usually asked me if Bonzo would bite. It was a stuffed dog for goodness sake, you can't buy that sort of attachment. That is the magic of pantomime.

In January, 1977 when the FA Cup came round, I organised my own telephone hot line to keep in touch with events at Ninian Park where Cardiff City were playing Wrexham in the third round. With three performances on a Saturday there was no way I could get to the game so I asked officials at the club to telephone the theatre's stage door every time there was some news from the match. If I wasn't there to take the score myself, one of the stage hands took the message for me. Don't forget that it was around this time that I was an executive director of the Bluebirds.

Never one to rest on my laurels, I decided to take over the concessions on a couple of cinemas in Porthcawl. Caesar's Palace had 800 seats and Cinema Two could hold 160. Both were in Trecco Bay in the middle of the largest caravan park in Europe. I planned to show films for a year but then wanted to present live shows at one of the venues. In May I presented the first British showing of *Gulliver's Travels* at Caesar's Palace. The first night's takings were donated to charity. I had always dreamed of attending a film premiere and now I had been given the opportunity of staging my own. Unfortunately, Richard Harris, the star of the film, was not able to attend the premiere because of tax reasons as he was a tax exile and could only enter the country on a certain amount of days in each year.

After an appearance on *Celebrity Squares* I was off to Germany for a television show. The visit came as a result of the comedy bathroom spot in the pantomime. Martin Williams of the New Theatre had received many requests for the sequence from various European TV stations and the first to book it, and me, was Bremen.

After that it was Elstree Studios where I filmed a play called *What a Performance*. It was part of the Comedy Playhouse series and I played Arnold Bingham, the caretaker of a village hall who becomes an unwilling member of the cast of the village dramatic society's latest play. My power mad character eventually takes over and makes a complete mess of things.

Also appearing were Robin Bailey, Rosemary Martin, Andrew Sachs, who was Manuel in *Fawlty Towers*, and Anna Quayle. The play was written by Kenneth Cope, a well-known actor on television who had appeared in *Coronation Street* and in *Randall and Hopkirk Deceased*. As I had already just completed work on another TV play, this one for BBC called *How's Business*, I could honestly say—very brisk, thank you.

In July I was very disappointed to hear that Cardiff City had decided to dispense with my services as an executive director. I knew I had friends on the board at the club but it also appeared I had a few enemies as well and I was surprised at the rather casual way I had been dropped. I felt that I was a good ambassador for the club without ever costing them a penny as I always paid my own way whenever I went away to support them or was on City business. Nevertheless, I remained a City fan and continued to follow their results with interest.

The German trip proved so popular that I was asked back later in the year. This time the show was similar to our own *Generation Game* and I was able to throw in a little of the army German I remembered from the war, but it wasn't much help. I sang 'Old MacDonald had a Farm' in German, which made me one of the few British comics to become a Common Market entertainer. It was on that show that I first met Roger Moore.

Although I continued to do cabaret all over the country, the acting bug had really bitten me and I was thrilled to be asked to take part in another Play for Today for the BBC. This one was filmed at their Birmingham studios and was called *Scully's New Year's Eve*, so naturally it wasn't shown on the box until the end of the year. When the BBC said they wanted me to play Scully, and no one else but me, how could I possibly refuse?

It was the strangest and shortest part I had ever played. I was talked about all the way through, then I had to create a character in just four pages of script. Jane Freeman, who can be seen in *Last of The Summer Wine*, John Junkin and Janine Duvitski were also in the play about families getting together over the holiday period.

> *'Yer all invited to our house for this party of me Mam's. She doesn't know yer coming yet but it should be good for a few laughs—if yer stuck like. 'Meself, I'd rather be at this other rave-up in the next street, but me Mam's insisting so . . . see yers, and don't bring a bottle, bring a crate.'*

You can gather from that what the play was all about, but it was good fun playing the part of a drunken scouser. When it was eventually shown on television I was putting the finishing touches to *Billy and Bonzo Meet the Babes in the Wood* at the New Theatre in Cardiff. Once again for me, and most other entertainers, Christmas was a one-day wonder although I usually tried to stretch it a little by not working during Christmas Eve.

The pantomime opened on Boxing Day and we went straight into working 14 hours a day with two performances daily and three on Saturdays. The late Ivor Emmanuel played the part of Robin. He flew in from the Costa del Sol where he lived at the time, and went straight back when the curtain came down at the end of February.

Wyn Calvin was playing in his 25th pantomime so for him it was a Jubilee presentation. Just to confuse the audience we also had double trouble in the shape of the Cox twins and their wives, the Miles twins. Fred and Frank Cox were from Cardiff and the versatile duo sang, played guitars, saxophones, pianos, and also tap-danced. Pauline and Estelle Miles played the parts of their sweethearts and sang the pop songs of the day.

It was my fourth straight pantomime at the New—a record that we thought would never be broken—until I was booked for a fifth year in succession. I was then offered a six-part series of *What a Performance*, the play I had done in the Comedy Playhouse series. Luckily enough I had just purchased a four-seater Comanche 250 similar to the one Sheila Scott broke the world record in.

I flew to the airstrip at Elstree Studios where the producer was waiting, we discussed the scripts, and then I flew back to Cardiff. I was needed back in south Wales because I was busy preparing to turn one of the cinemas in Porthcawl into a theatre so that I could present my own Minstrels Show in the summer.

I liked the thought of being my own man putting on my own shows, and it was working for me because I had as much work as I could handle. Of course, preparing the theatre in Porthcawl was no five-minute job. A summer season for any entertainer in a popular seaside resort usually conjures up visions of lolling in a deck chair by day, and doing an act for about 30 minutes in the evening. But a 10-week stint for me at Caesar's Palace in Porthcawl meant a 16-hour day as box office salesman, cinema projectionist and star of my own variety show. All of which was for less money than I could have earned from a week in a night club anywhere in the country.

The first decision in the morning would be to show a film to divert the energies of Trecco Bay's juvenile holidaymakers who were bored by the rain. A quick cup of coffee between changing reels of film and then it was into the box office selling advance tickets for the variety show, stocking up with cold drinks, and planning a lunchtime showing of a film such as the *Pink Panther* if it continued raining. Then I would be around the campsite sticking up bill posters for the show.

It was hard graft but I loved doing it. After years of working with councils and encountering repeated problems, I really fancied running my own theatre. I would wake up in Cardiff, look at an overcast sky, and dash down to Porthcawl to put on a film. By the time the film was shown, sometimes it was baking outside and there was nobody in the theatre except me, but there was still the satisfaction of working for myself.

My Minstrels Show had a first class cast including Glyn Dawson, Sian Hopkins and Olive Guppy along with her excellent dancers, The Olivettes. They were worthy of a special mention because their slick routines and gorgeous costumes were one of the highlights of the show.

During 1978 I had to turn down a part in a John Schlesinger film because of my involvement at Trecco Bay. You should have heard the language from George, my press agent, when he found out. It was at this time that the six-part comedy series for ATV was cancelled but I received a reasonable financial settlement which just about paid for my summer in Porthcawl that year.

Instead I was offered the job of hosting a new ITV series in September called *Star Games*. Each of the four programmes featured teams of celebrities competing in a variety of sports— a sort of a poor man's *Superstars*. Making it to the final programme were stars such as Kenny Lynch, Dave Dee, Rula Lenska, Robin Sarstedt, Colin Baker and Julian Holloway. They competed at swimming, rowing, golf, running, five-a-side football, an obstacle race and other energetic pursuits.

All money raised for charities was trebled for the final show so plenty was raked in for good causes. Later that month I travelled west to Llanelli where I put on my *Stars from the Black and White Minstrels Show* at the Llanelli Entertainments Centre. It was the first professional production sponsored by the borough council at the centre which the local authority had bought for around £300,000. As a publicity stunt to publicise the three day show, I went down to the booking office and started selling tickets. They went quite briskly and there was a good support for the final performance on 23 September.

In no time at all it was pantomime season again and on Boxing Day I walked on to the stage of the New Theatre for the fifth year in succession, a proud record that has probably not been surpassed in modern theatrical history. Once again I played Billy along with my dog Bonzo in *Jack and the Beanstalk*. During the season I was on stage for nearly 100 shows. On Saturdays, for example, we did three performances meaning 14 hours in the theatre. I certainly needed plenty of throat spray to get me through as on Sunday mornings my voice had been reduced to a whisper. Giving a nod instead of a shake of the head could have landed me with a hefty bill for new clothes for the wife.

There were new faces and old friends in the show and I was joined by the lovely Julie Rogers who played Jack, singer Bryn Williams, comedians Dailey and Wayne, Ken Wilson as a dotty dame, the Wayne Warlow orchestra and the Olivettes. Before the panto opened however I had an invite to join Michael Parkinson at the Shepherds Bush studios for a look at pantoland. In it I demonstrated the antics in the barmy bathroom scene I had used so successfully in a number of shows.

Expense was no object for the Beeb as they transferred the heavy prop from Cardiff to London just for the show. Once there it was filled with hundreds of gallons of water ready for the act, and then afterwards it was dismantled and taken to Oxford where it was being used in pantomime. I did try and get Parky to come into the bathroom with me but he wouldn't budge. The programme was billed as including some of the greatest performers in pantomime at the time and I was proud to be on the show along with people such as Charlie Cairoli and Company, Les Dawson, Lauri Lupino Lane, Little and Large, and the Prince of Principal Boys, Pat Kirkwood.

Jack and the Beanstalk opened to great reviews thanks in no small part to Julie Rogers who sang her songs to perfection while displaying a great command of the stage. One of the highlights of the show for me was the space age dance theme to the *Star Wars* music which ended with me and Bonzo fired up in a rocket to join Jack at the top of the beanstalk.

We also had a giant in the show played by Paul Kidd who doubled up as the front end, or was it the back end, of the cow. He wandered around the stage in a 12ft tall contraption to amaze the audience. And there were always great cheers from the children when Jack fought the monster in mortal combat. There would always be groans when Jack lost his sword but they quickly turned to cheers when I came to the rescue with an outsize syringe to put an end to the bad guy.

Once again, in spite of the atrocious weather and strikes, the pantomime took substantially more than the previous year so I knew that I had proved to the city council that they had been wrong to ignore me for so long. Five straight years of success was unheard of yet there was a time when Martin Williams and the powers-that-be preferred to ignore local talent. How wrong they were.

But I had something else to feel proud of although, for a week or so, I was unable to let anyone know anything about it. In the 1979 New Year's Honours List I was awarded the MBE for services to entertainment and to charities. It was a wonderful surprise and one that made me feel very humble. A number of stars from the entertainment business were also honoured at the same time. They included Gracie Fields who became a Dame, Tommy Steele, Olivia Newton-John, Bernard Miles and Gordon Jackson of *Upstairs Downstairs* fame.

It wasn't until March that we all gathered at Buckingham Palace for the investiture ceremony. The Queen presented us with our medals and it was one of the most marvellous days of my life. Betty, Roger and Ceri all went up to London with me for a special day that I will never forget.

'Mr Stennett, I wish to congratulate you on all your theatre and charity work,' said Her Majesty.

I could only reply rather quietly and humbly, 'Thank you, Ma'am'.

Betty and I stayed the night in a lovely hotel in London. Nothing was too much trouble and it was a joy to be looked after for a short while. Mind you room service was terrible. I ordered a hot chocolate and they sent up a Cadbury's Flake and a box of matches.

It was back to a bit of straight acting next as I played the part of a self-made tycoon called Arthur Evans in a BBC Wales play called *How's Business?* Evans owned a Wellington boot factory and when he came into contact with a couple of visiting sheiks, he enlisted the help of the wily Myer Clapham, played by a wonderful actor called John Bluthal.

The summer of 1979 was a little different as my production at the Caesar's Palace didn't feature any household names, but it did give budding Welsh stars the opportunity to prove how good they were. And prove it they did as more than two hours of entertainment became a great hit with the holidaymakers. While this was going on of course, I was also putting on films in the other theatre. There's nothing like having fingers in a number of pies.

And that was evident later in the year when I appeared in another Play for Today on BBC called *Cries From The Watchtower*. I played the part of a market stallholder called Big Ben whose arrival at a Nottingham market with a load of fast-selling digital watches spelt disaster for my neighbouring stallholder Andy who repaired conventional watches. He was played by a young actor named Paul Copley. Andy's wife was expecting a baby and the loss of his craft caused his withdrawal from her and their child. Desperate for a job he eventually goes to a seminar for digital watch salesmen. It seemed very heady stuff but like most plays of its kind, there was a message in there somewhere.

The part came easily to me as after all, market men have to be entertainers. Ben had a few gags to attract attention to his stock. The theory of the play was that jobs would get scarcer as new innovations took hold. Maybe that has turned out to be true, I don't really profess to know. All I do know was that at the time it was a powerful story.

As a complete contrast to that I also appeared on Terry Wogan's quiz show *Blankety Blank*. One of the celebrities on the programme with me was Jack Douglas. Now Jack won fame by being a northern clown with a flat cap and a sort of recurring St Vitus Dance but he was joining me, Max Wall, Duggie Brown and Jimmy Jewell in also branching out into straight acting. Jack told me that he reckoned it took six months to shed the role of flat cap Alf. He also admitted that straight acting was a relief after the pressures of being funny.

As far as my acting was concerned, I really felt that I had to make a move into it because of the show-biz Mafia. If you were outside the Mafia's close-knit circle you had no chance on television. It was made up of a clique of stars with their own mutual admiration society, each scratching the other's back. When they were appearing in a show they made quite sure through their agents, that their pals got on as guests.

The number of star permutations was nobody's business. I was very much against this sort of set-up so I suffered because of it. On the other hand of course, one has to take whatever opportunity comes along. After my record-breaking run in panto at the New in Cardiff it was time to break new ground.

Billy and Bonzo were to meet Red Riding at a completely new venue, the Club Double Diamond in Caerphilly. Not only was it a new venue, but also the first time that a full pantomime production would be presented in a cabaret club as a daytime and evening attraction. While I produced it, I was delighted with the involvement of my sons Roger and Ceri who adapted the scripts. It was a panto with a difference because there was no Principal Boy and the part of Red Riding Hood was shared by two local youngsters Alice Brown and Genevieve Davies. Only in the wonderland of pantomime can Red Riding Hood meet Robin Hood who can, in turn, meet the sinister Count Vermin or of course, the Wolf.

Only in shows like that can a character such as Billy, dressed in a crumpled hat, knee-length multi-coloured jumper, long shorts, scruffy socks and the regulation big boots earn so many laughs and get such great support from an audience. After all, everyone in the theatre were 'Billy's Butties', and part of his gang. That is what pantomime is all about and at the Double Diamond that year we had a truly Welsh show that the audience took to their hearts. Mind you, with afternoon and evening performances it was hard work.

Christmas week, just before opening day, I appeared on HTV with my old pal Eric Morecambe in a programme discussing pantomimes. Eric recalled early pantos including the time in Sheffield at the Lyceum when he and Ernie played a pair of robbers in my panto, *Babes in the Wood*.

While I was busy completing a successful season in Caerphilly, Roger was also setting up a good 1980 for himself. He had been writing poetry for many years but during that year he had no less than six plays staged within two months of each other, quite a remarkable feat for someone not really established as a playwright. In 1978 his debut stage play *Taxi* went on in London's East End Half Moon Theatre and before that he had written a full length documentary about the Welsh Prince Madoc. Now in 1980 he had two new short plays produced by the Playwrights Company in Bath, and then running from July to August, four one-act plays in a full evening show. It was all exciting stuff and it made Betty and me feel very proud.

It became even better later on in the year when HTV West agreed to show three of Roger's shorts on television in a single programme, and I took a part in each of them. The first one was about a man who dreams of becoming a football star, the second was about a Welsh miner who tries to negotiate a productivity deal with the Prime Minister after a nuclear bomb has gone off, and the third dealt with three soldiers in occupied France during the Second World War. All three had previously been performed at Le Metro Theatre in Bath by the Playwrights Company and they were filmed by Harlech in front of a live audience.

On top of that, I then branched into films. Well almost. I was given a part in a supernatural thriller called *Possessions*. I was cast as a retired Welshman who helps a new neighbour, played by Caroline Langrishe, move into her house. The house is then haunted by the furniture she had bought from an antique shop. It was only a B movie lasting 30 minutes but at least I had now made it onto the big screen.

I had appeared in big production pantomimes, broken many attendance and financial records at a number of venues and taken a panto out to a night club for a season, so you would probably think that there was little else I could do with the country's favourite Christmas pastime. How wrong you are. For Christmas 1980 I took a complete pantomime *Billy and Bonzo meet Cinderella* on tour for the very first time. We began a four-week season at the Memorial Hall in Barry on 22 December, and then moved to the Community Theatre in Bedwas for two weeks from 19 January. After that it was pastures anew at Treorchy and Ferndale.

Starring as *Cinderella* and making her stage debut was Porth-born Ann Martin who won a talent contest in Porthcawl earlier in the year. Another newcomer to show business was DDT, which was short for Dobbin from Dowlais Top. He was a redundant pit pony who starred as the panto horse. I played the part of Billy Buttons while Howell Evans and Patricia Kane were the Ugly Sisters. It was a pantomime in the true tradition with loads of action, plenty of audience participation and a good hard-working cast.

I was pleased to be going on to Bedwas as yet again, here was another hall that had fallen on lean times. Originally the Bedwas Workmen's Hall, it had been bought for local use by the Bedwas Community Council and was completely renovated by volunteers. It was something close to my heart because at about the same time, I took over the running of Tewkesbury's council-run Roses Theatre which I proposed to run as a theatre as well as a cinema.

The local council had opened the 350-seat Roses about four years previously and had lost money every year so now they had decided to give an outside body the opportunity rather than closing it down altogether. I knew it would need a lot of time and organisation but Betty wanted to help, so together I knew we could come up with ideas to fill the theatre on a regular basis.

Once all the pantomime paraphernalia had been stored away for another year I received a call to take over from Joe Loss at the Royal Spa Centre, Leamington. Joe had fallen down a flight of marble steps in an art gallery in Haifa—one of the QE2's port of calls—and injured his ribs. It meant that he couldn't do the concert so I stepped in as a special guest. After all, I knew Joe well and was a huge fan of big band music. In fact, it was quite an occasion and I loved every minute of it.

The first eight or nine months of 1981 were mainly spent either at Porthcawl where I was running the two cinema/theatres, in Hereford where I took over the lease of a theatre, or in Tewkesbury where we had the Roses up and running. On top of that I also took over the Castle Cinema in Caerphilly where I hoped to establish live theatre on a regular basis. The cinema had two separate screens and I wanted to stage live shows in the larger ground floor theatre.

Caerphilly was central for the valley area and I believed live entertainment would prove popular there. First of all though it required complete redecoration. This was where Ceri came to the fore as together we worked long hours putting in new seating, painting the walls and fitting a new carpet. We also put in new spotlights and drapes. The two of us did most of the work on our own, without any sort of a grant, and the total cost of the renovations came to around £25,000.

The work had to be done because how could you expect people to go to any theatre that was so rundown? We had to try and fight the new threat from videos and to do that we had to make theatres and cinemas more comfortable so that people would want to leave their home to be entertained. The replacement seats were bought from the Stoneleigh Club, Porthcawl and the drapes came from the Capitol Cinema in Cardiff.

But Christmas wouldn't be the same without a pantomime so after the success of touring in 1980, we decided to write a new show entitled *Billy and Bonzo go Christmas Crackers* to stage at the Bedwas Community Theatre. We packed just about every pantomime character in this show and the story began when Captain Hook stole the fairy's wand. None of the pantos could go ahead until the wand was rescued by the heroes and heroines and that was how Robin Hood, Cinderella, Jack and many more characters came to be involved.

We were pleased with the response from the Bedwas people and those from the Rhymney Valley who supported our efforts, particularly as there was no tradition of pantomime in the area. However, I had to interrupt the pantomime's run, and so afternoon and evening performances were cancelled throughout January 1982. I was giving up my role as Billy to become a garage mechanic.

16

AT THE CROSSROADS MOTEL

'. . . And our week in the sun wasn't much good either. It only rained twice but once was for three days and the other was for four.'

* * * * *

Nowadays it is hard to imagine that *Crossroads* was at one time as big as *Coronation Street*, regularly drawing a viewing audience of around 15 million for each show. Beginning in 1964 it was on our television screens for 24 years, finally calling it a day in 1988. It was already well established in 1982 when I once again became involved. But the time had come for a big change in the programme.

Meg Richardson, owner of the motel and played so beautifully by Noele Gordon, was to be written out of the script. The trouble started because she was such a well-loved character that no one knew quite how to write her out of the storyline. She had been a part of *Crossroads* since its beginning in November 1964 and in the 17 years she had played Meg Richardson, she had made more television appearances than any other actress in the world. She was also the first actress ever to be seen on colour television, long before most of us had colour sets at home.

In 1938 when John Logie Baird was carrying out

experiments at Crystal Palace, he would send a Rolls Royce round for Noele who would then sit in front of his camera wearing brightly coloured scarves and hats while he tested his equipment.

Lots of fans sent in their suggestions for her leaving the programme. They ranged from heart attacks to abduction by aliens or to just walking out into the sunset, so you can see that it became a huge problem for the scriptwriters. Eventually it was decided that Meg would leave the country on the QE2, never to come back but, in true soap style, it was only after she had survived the fire that burned the Crossroads Motel down to the ground.

During a quiet moment between performances at the panto in Bedwas I decided to ring my old friend Jack Barton, one of the producers of *Crossroads*, to offer my suggestion. I told him that Harry Silver, the character I played in the soap some seven years earlier, should be due for release from prison. Why not have Harry return to the motel to exact revenge upon Meg by shooting her?

There was silence at the other end of the line as Jack thought about my idea. He told me I must be stupid for coming up with a crazy idea like that. He said that if Harry Silver came back and murdered Meg it would probably be the end of my career in show business as I would always be known as the man who killed her off. But you never know what can happen in show business and that call eventually led me back to Birmingham and the Motel.

Jack let it be known to me that there was a small part coming up for a garage mechanic, and if I was interested he would be pleased to see me up in the studios in Birmingham to discuss a return to the soap. I travelled up to meet Jack and other members of the backroom staff, read the part for them, and luckily enough was given the role of car mechanic Sid Hooper along with a six-to-eight-week contract.

Straight away I had to make arrangements for the pantomime in Bedwas to continue on a reduced scale. It was agreed that as I would be in Birmingham during the week, the panto could continue for the duration on Saturdays. This meant that I travelled back down the motorway on a Friday evening to spend the night at home with Betty and the boys, and then off to Bedwas to do three shows on the Saturday. It was a hectic period for me but I owed it to the people of Bedwas who had been supporting the pantomime to see it through as best I could.

Back up in the Carlton Television studios in Broad Street, Birmingham, I was welcomed by all the cast members. There were only a few left from when I played gun-toting GI, Harry Silver. Before I was due to start I was sent scripts for four episodes so that I had a good grounding when I arrived for my first rehearsals.

It was a rigorous routine. On Mondays, Tuesdays and Wednesdays we started at 10.00am and rehearsed through to 6.00pm. On Thursday mornings we would record one programme in the morning, have lunch, and then record another in the afternoon. The same thing happened on Fridays so by the end of the week we had four episodes in the can.

On Friday evenings I was free to travel back home, bringing another four scripts with me to read over the weekend. Sunday night and I was back on the motorway driving up to Birmingham. Sometimes the schedule changed and I had to stay in the Midlands for an outside broadcast on the Saturday, or perhaps delays had happened during the week and we had to catch up, but that was not very often.

I would run through my part while I was lying in bed. It was also important to know what was happening in my scenes, rather than just learning my own dialogue. The character of Sid Hooper evolved over a period of time but I was given a broad outline as soon as I turned up for rehearsals. Sid had been living in London but wanted to get back to the Midlands to try to make another go of it with his wife Mavis who ran the local boarding house. Mind you, she didn't want Sid back home and it never got any better throughout the storyline although it was made to look as though I was trying my best to rekindle the relationship.

Mavis was played by Charmian Eyre and she captured the spirit of the part so very well. We had many scenes together, as you would expect from a married couple, but Betty was never jealous of my 'other woman'. She reckoned that the time to worry would be when I got involved with a big busty blonde in some future episode of the show. One weekend I was late getting back to Cardiff from the studios in Birmingham. Betty had gone to bed and left a note for me on the table. 'Dear Sid, waited till 10.30pm. Have gone to bed, love Mavis.'

The other side of my character showed me as a bit of a lad, always on the lookout for a deal. Sid was a wideboy, but loveable nevertheless. He was brought into the soap as a temporary replacement for Benny who had been written out of the programme for five or six weeks. Benny's absence was put down to his father being ill but Paul Henry, who played the part so wonderfully, had really been booked to appear in pantomime so needed the time out of the programme.

As soon as I read the script I looked forward to developing the character as Sid was a mean person, a bit of a gambler, and something of a womaniser, giving me plenty to work on. The scriptwriters did such a good job for me that Sid Hooper quickly became a favourite in the soap but after the initial seven or eight weeks that I was originally contracted for, Sid had to make his exit from the show.

In an earlier episode he had been offered a bribe of a thousand pounds to leave the garage—and accepted it. That was how Sid was written out. He was going to pay off the bookies and blow the rest on a holiday in Spain.

A week later I was really flying off from Luton Airport with Betty on a short break and I couldn't believe what happened. From all sides people were asking me whether I still had all the money and if I was going to spend it all. It was amazing. I couldn't believe the reaction. After all I had only been in the soap for a matter of a few weeks and my first thought was that it must be a gag. But to the travellers at the airport, my sudden appearance there was merely an extension of the television series.

Even when I was in Spain I had people coming up to me and asking if I was Sid. And our week in the sun wasn't much good either. It only rained twice but once was for three days and the other was for four.

As it happened, my departure from the motel garage was only temporary. Sid had proved to be so popular that I was only away for two weeks before being written back in once again. It was frustrating to have spent 40 years in show business trying to make a name for myself as Stan Stennett, and then being recognised everywhere as Sid Hooper after only six weeks on television.

But don't get me wrong, I couldn't have been more pleased. After touring the world, having my own radio and television series, and appearing at world-famous venues like the London Palladium, nothing gave me so much recognition as *Crossroads*. I was delighted and privileged to be part of the cast. Some people tended to put the programme down, but then certain people often try to put down a commercial success.

'I failed the audition for *Crossroads*,' Arthur Askey used to joke. 'I remembered my lines.'

A lot of other comedians took up the gag and over the years knocking *Crossroads* became a national sport. If you believed what they wrote you would have expected actors to fluff their lines and scenery to fall down during every episode.

Everybody from the most highbrow critic to the humblest armchair pundit had a bad word to say about it, yet despite all that poor press it became a legend in its own lifetime and went from strength to strength. How else could it have been loved and watched regularly throughout that lifetime by up to 15 million viewers each programme? Everything about the show that the critics hated, the viewers loved. In fact the professionalism of the programme never ceased to amaze me. We did three shows a week and the way it was produced—the application, rehearsal and so on—was very professional.

The only difference between *Dallas*, *Dynasty* and *Coronation Street* was the time it went out. Because it was the early evening slot the writers and producers were careful not to embarrass anyone. The programme dealt with romance rather than sex, there was no bad language and surprisingly enough, no one ever smoked during the programme.

Mind you, there was plenty of everything else. By the time the 20th anniversary and 4,000th episode of the programme was being celebrated in November 1984 there had been 25 deaths, assorted kidnappings, manslaughters, heart attacks, suicides, rapes, abductions, blackmail, motor accidents and embezzlements. No shortage of storylines there.

I loved being involved in it but it is strange when you stop to think that you can be more famous after a few weeks on television than after 40 years in the business. As far as being recognised in the street, that never bothered me. Very often when I was outside the television studios, people would shout out, 'Hello Sid' and I was always ready for a quick chat. Usually I replied as Sid, because that is who the people were talking to, not Stan Stennett, and I never refused to sign an autograph when someone asked for it.

It was what it was all about, and you are a long time forgotten in this business. After all, we were entertainers working to please the public. I would go out of my way to help make someone's day. It never cost me anything and I believed that anyone who didn't like getting a reaction from the public should be working at something else. You have to take time out to put a bit of sparkle in people's lives, even if they did forget my real name and call me Sid.

Because he was a bit of a gambler and con-man, I was usually asked for racing tips, or told to keep my hands off Benny's money. Once, later on in the programme, when Sid was supposed to be going on holiday with the young girl he was knocking around with, somebody saw me at Birmingham airport in real life and asked me where my bird was. I pointed to Betty.

I hadn't realised the true pulling power of television. People would come up to me in the street and really believe that I was Sid, it was quite amazing. I could have played a provincial theatre twice a night for 25 years and still not have been seen by the same number of people who watched just one episode of *Crossroads*. It was no wonder I was delighted to play the motel's rogue mechanic.

When I started in the soap, Noele Gordon had just left. That was a shame because I knew her from way back when I appeared on her television programme, *Lunch Box*. She had been a stalwart throughout the first 18 years of the soap but reckoned that leaving was a blessing in disguise as it gave her the opportunity to change her life. When she left, the scriptwriters had to think of new storylines and introducing Sid Hooper as an incorrigible rogue was just one of them. The programme's viewing figures dipped slightly with Meg's leaving but soon recovered to regularly hit 15.5 million every episode and Sid was the one most viewers loved to hate.

In my minstrel days there was a certain amount of stardust, but nothing like being part of *Crossroads*. I found it strange when going into a pub for a packet of crisps only for the woman behind the bar to warn me quite seriously, that if I didn't give Benny his money back my car tyres would be slashed. A young lad once pleaded with me not to take any more money from Benny. To them, Sid was a real person not just a television character. Although I basically played myself in the role, I don't drink and have never bet on horses.

The over-riding theme was that I was somehow taking money from Benny, who as you remember, was a little on the slow side. But there was much more to their relationship than money. He was a little slow and needed protection so I took him under my wing. There were a lot of people just like Sid and Benny—both ends of the spectrum. Sid was a bit of a shark but not really a villain and the scriptwriters were to be congratulated for coming up with characters like those two, and all the others in and around the motel.

Even though I had this new-found recognition I was too long-in-the-tooth to have all my eggs in one 'motel' basket. I had a guitar in my dressing room and regularly played to keep my hand in. Being in Birmingham during the week made it easier to dash over to Tewkesbury or Hereford to supervise the theatres I ran under lease. The others, two in Caerphilly and one in Porthcawl, were managed successfully by our youngest son Ceri. I was no business tycoon, I just loved every aspect of showbiz.

Our eldest, Roger, had a play called *Philby Comes Home* accepted by the Royal Shakespeare Company and he was busy writing another play about Buffalo Bill for Channel Four. When I asked him about the possibility of playing Buffalo Bill he told me I was too old. There is nothing like hearing the truth from your own family.

I had been in *Crossroads* for a couple of months when I received a letter from the BBC. Imagine my surprise when it turned out to be a cheque for royalties for my performance in *Cries from a Watchtower*. The fee was my percentage following the play's sale to Saudi Arabia of all places. But I couldn't retire on the proceeds as the cheque was made out for the princely sum of £6.00.

When I started work in the motel garage I wasn't the foreman. That job belonged to Joe MacDonald, or Mac as he was known to everyone. Life hadn't been too easy for poor old Mac as his wife Trina had left him, taking their baby son Ben with her. Mac was played by Carl Andrews and he eventually joined Benny by lodging with me and Mavis at the boarding house.

There was also another mechanic, a little slip of a girl called Carol Sands. For young Joanne Good who had come straight from repertory theatre in Sussex it was a real culture shock. She actually blazed a trail for Kylie Minogue who became a tomboy mechanic in *Neighbours*. The manageress of the garage was a woman, Sharon Metcalfe. The place was run far more efficiently after she arrived to do all the admin work, though no one would ever tell her that. The lovely actress Carolyn Jones was Sharon and she attracted all sorts of men but had the nerve and skill to cope with each and every one of them.

Carolyn had played both ends of the acting spectrum. She had worked for Lord Olivier at the National Theatre and yet also had a role in the infamous revue *Oh Calcutta!* She had also appeared in the London Weekend television series *Within These Walls* alongside Googie Withers. And then of course there was Benny.

Thousands of characters appeared in *Crossroads* but few made such an impact as the slow-thinking Brummie who was so anxious to please everyone. He was a warm loveable, harmless person yet his strange way of speaking, his size, and his awkwardness made him almost a menacing figure. In real life, Paul Henry was married to Sheila and they had two children,

Justine and Anthony. Sadly, while still a teenager, Justine was killed in a motor accident.

Paul was born and educated in Birmingham and he joined the Birmingham Rep, spending eight happy years appearing in plays such as *Romeo and Juliet*, *Othello*, and *The Merchant of Venice*. He also had parts in favourite television series such as *Roads to Freedom* and *The Sweeney* and featured for a while as a regular character in The Archers on BBC Radio. Despite all that experience, it was as the hapless Benny that he gained national popularity.

At first 'Miss Diane' looked out for him, then Mac, and finally I arrived in the guise of Sid Hooper to take him under my wing after Benny was found a job working in the garage. I was the only 'real' mechanic in the garage. Sid made out that he was a top engineer but straightaway he was turned into a shifty fellow always looking for an easy way out of any problem. It took a while to work on the character but eventually we ended up with a loveable rogue—and that was how I played him. I knew quite a few people who earned a quid or two through their wits, just like Sid, and that was him down to a tee.

As soon as Jack Barton told me they wanted Sid back in the show after those first eight weeks I knew I would be in for a long spell playing the part of the garage mechanic and things would never be the same. At one time it looked as though Sid was trying to con Benny out of his £25,000 inheritance. I received hundreds of letters threatening dire consequences if I didn't leave Benny alone. And Paul had even more mail warning him to have nothing to do with Sid.

I owed much of my success in *Crossroads* to Benny. He was the outstanding attraction and some of that did rub off on an actor like me as I was closely associated with him in the scripts. There was no way I would have wanted Sid to do anything nasty to Benny, it could literally have been more than my life was worth. There was no telling what some enraged *Crossroads* fans might have done to me.

In one storyline Benny was suspected of killing a girl. Fans rang or wrote in saying Benny was innocent. Some were even willing to go to court and give evidence on his behalf. If viewers can do that, then they can do anything. When a viewer stopped me in the street it was to talk to Sid Hooper and not Stan Stennett, and I would always be wearing Sid's clothes. In fact they were my clothes because we all wore our own for the show and were given a monthly allowance.

Paul and I got on famously and I introduced him to the game of golf. He became such a keen golfer that we used to play a round about three times a week. He became so good that he used to take money off me. Now there's a twist—I was the one getting conned.

Every week the show had a different director and we would have a word with him if we were worried about any characterisation. Every member of the cast took their roles seriously and most of them were in early for rehearsals. After all, we had to cram a week's work into three days learning our lines, rehearsing, and then shooting the episode. It was hard work and we had no time to waste.

Many stars wanted cameo parts in the soap and I had many a long chat with the great Max Wall who played a car park attendant at the motel. I still worked on the cabaret circuit as much as possible when circumstances on *Crossroads* permitted. Sometimes a cabaret spot would seem like an albatross around my neck as there would often be a clever so-and-so in the audience who wanted to make cracks about the soap. I usually tried to get it over with right at the beginning and then continued to do my act. Usually by the time I had finished they had all forgotten who Sid Hooper was, and that was fine by me.

Around November 1982 I began having a little trouble with

a kidney stone. It meant I never wanted to be too far away from the 'conveniences'. It was about that time that I was occasionally working at Clearwell Castle in the Wye Valley near Monmouth. Bryn Williams joined me and we did the cabaret at their medieval evenings. As I used to get a little pain during those shows I worked out a routine where I wore a kilt. Nothing like being prepared.

Jack Barton was aware of my problem and that it had to take its course and come out naturally. In the end, I needed an X-ray in a Birmingham hospital because of the back pain it was causing me and I eventually had two weeks out of the soap when I had an operation in the Royal Gwent to remove the stone.

That brought the memories back because it was when I won the Royal Gwent Talent Contest soon after I was demobbed that my career in show business started to take off. After the operation I had to use a caffeta, as did the chap in the next bed. He was lucky because he covered his in a Harrods carrier bag while I had to make do with one from Tesco.

I owe the Royal Gwent a debt of gratitude for the way they and Professor Peeling looked after me. Even now, when I am working at the Dolman Theatre in Newport I always find time to pop across to the Royal Gwent to meet up with the nursing staff and I help by raising money whenever I can.

Anyway, back to *Crossroads* and a bright November day. Jack and I met up on the set and he asked me if I would go down to HTV Studios in Bristol to help him with an outside broadcast, suggesting it may take my mind off my medical problem. I thought to myself how caring the people at the top were in making sure I was comfortable. Little did I know what was in store for me.

We jumped into his chauffeur-driven car and made the journey down to Bristol with a stop on the way for Jack to make a couple of calls. Just before we arrived at the studios he told me he was a little cold so I let him have my top coat, as I was also wearing a casual jacket underneath. Well, it was winter.

We pulled up outside the studios in Bath Road and Jack told me to wait there while he went looking to see if his appointment had arrived. A few minutes later he came back, called me in, and we both walked through the main doors into the foyer. As we went in I noticed Carolyn Jones, Jack Haig and a few of the other *Crossroads* actors disappearing through a side door. I never had time to wonder what they were doing in Bristol because the next person to come into view was none other than Eamonn Andrews. He walked right up to me and said, 'You thought you were here for an outside broadcast but tonight Stan Stennett, comedian, actor, *Crossroads'* very own Sid Hooper . . . This Is Your Life'.

I was flabbergasted. True to the show I had no idea at all. Mind you, I should have guessed when my brother rang from Australia totally out of the blue and reversed the charges. The sight of dear Eamonn with his lop-sided smile and red book tucked under his arm is one I will never forget. When he ushered me into the studio almost all the cast of *Crossroads* were sitting down on one side of the stage waiting for my entrance. On the other side Betty, Roger and Ceri sat together with smug looks on their faces.

I later found out that as soon as Jack had spirited me away on the bogus outside broadcast pretence, everyone downed tools in the *Crossroads* studios, climbed into a couple of coaches and motored down to Bristol. Jack's phone calls had been to make sure everyone was keeping to time. His other neat little trick was to ask for my top coat so that I would go into the studio wearing just the jacket. Mind you, I would have chosen something else to wear rather than that awful casual jacket had I known what was going to happen.

It was a superb evening though a bit traumatic and probably one of my most anxious moments in show business. Eamonn asked Benny what it was like to work with Sid Hooper. 'Very expensive,' said Benny. Visitors came and went including Leslie Crowther who I had known for many years, my old pal George Chisholm and some of the biggest names in entertainment.

Ivy Benson came in to recall when we first met soon after the finish of the Second World War when I transported her and the girls all round Italy. Well someone had to do the hard work. Another making the trip to Bristol for the show was the master of mirth himself, Ken Dodd. I also had a kind tribute from Mr George Thomas who was Speaker of the House of Commons.

From the sporting world came John Charles who I had known from his Cardiff City days and through playing for the Show Biz XI, and also Trevor Ford. He reminded me that I once went to Sunderland with West Brom's manager Ronnie Allen to watch him play alongside the great Len Shackleton.

One of my most cherished moments was meeting up with my brother Peter again after 12 years. He had flown from Australia just to be on the show.

The final guest was relayed in by film from America. It was none other than my old friend Billy Daniels who said some nice things about me from a hotel in Salt Lake City where he was performing. By now I was starting to squirm on my seat at all the plaudits that were coming my way, but Eamonn seemed quite happy at the way the programme had gone.

To end the programme our dear little two-year old grandson Sam, Roger's boy, toddled on to the stage. The only problem was that he went straight to George Chisholm who did look a little like me. Fortunately, we soon sorted that out and my very own night came to an end, as far as the cameras were concerned.

As soon as the programme finished, all the guests were

ushered into another room where a large buffet was laid out and the drink began to flow. Unfortunately for me, with my kidney stone forever in mind, I had to refrain from any refreshments and most of the *Crossroads* bunch decided to return to Birmingham after a couple of hours as it was an early start the following day.

There had been changes to the television franchises earlier in 1981. ATV lost theirs and Central Independent Television grudgingly continued with the production of *Crossroads*. CIT and Head of Programmes Charles Denton decided to get rid of Meg Richardson as they thought that would kill off the programme for good. This didn't happen of course but in 1985 they carried out another splurge of changes with a new motel owner Nicola Freeman, played by the lovely Gabrielle Drake. Many other characters were written out including David and Barbara Hunter. The theme tune was updated and the opening titles replaced with a longer version. Finally the show was renamed *Crossroads Motel*.

A year later a new producer, William Smethurst , who had worked on the radio programme *The Archers*, took over the series after his predecessor was sacked. Smethurst was known by the cast as Butcher Bill because of the ruthless way he dropped actors from the soap. Even Diane Hunter and Benny were pushed out. For those of us left, it was not a happy time as Butcher Bill had cut out the very people that made the show so popular.

I still had some good storylines including a few heartbreaking episodes following the death of Mavis. I received a number of first class reviews for the way I portrayed a sad Sid Hooper. Further changes were planned and the series name was altered once again. This time it would be called *Crossroads King's Oak*, with the idea being that the powers-that-be could drop the *Crossroads* part of the title and completely revamp the whole thing. In June 1987 the series was axed completely.

I finished my time in the soap by marrying Ivy, played by Stella Moray, and driving off into the sunset in an open top car to start a new life running a small hotel on the south coast. The final episode was broadcast on 4 April, a bank holiday, with the Crossroads hotel finally becoming the King's Oak Country Hotel. So those in charge had won the day after all, never mind what Joe Public wanted.

The last words were said rather appropriately by Jill, played by Jane Rossington, as she left the building for the last time. Asked what name she would give the hotel she would be running in her new life, she replied a little sadly 'I always thought Crossroads was an awfully good name.'

It was revived in March 2001 as a Carlton television production but the only characters brought back were Doris Luke played by Kathy Staff, Jill Richardson and her ex-husband Adam Chance, played by Tony Adams. Kathy later left in dismay, disgusted by the amount of sexual innuendo in the new production.

It went off the air in August 2002 only to return in January 2003, produced by Yvon Grace, with people more associated with light entertainment such as Lionel Blair, Les Dennis and Tim Brooke-Taylor. Ratings understandably declined and the show went off the air once more five months later. It was a sad way for the programme to finally end but at least I am proud to say that I had almost eight years being part of a wonderful cast and programme that brought great joy to millions of viewers.

17

FULL CIRCLE

'. . . At the same time, youths broke into the Hereford Theatre and smashed up the kiosk, stole money and ripped out the telephones. We called the local constabulary but they couldn't help, although they did tell me about a successful case the previous day. They arrested two youngsters, one for drinking battery acid and the other for eating fireworks. They charged one and let the other off.'

* * * * *

My life as Sid Hooper never kept me away from appearing on stage in cabaret, although I was becoming much more of an administrator with my involvement particularly in the Roses Theatre in Tewkesbury and the two cinemas back in Porthcawl.

To add to that list we now had the Castle Cinema in Caerphilly which Ceri and I had worked so hard at renovating. By now, Ceri was becoming good at all things backstage and he could be relied upon to tackle problems at any of the theatres we were now leasing. He never had any inclination to follow me on stage but really enjoyed the challenge of working behind the scenes.

The Castle Cinema was split into two with the downstairs studio seating 375, while the upper floor seated 112. New spotlights were fitted and the downstairs studio doubled as a theatre. It had never really recovered from being the venue for a performance by the notorious Sex Pistols but I believed the people of Caerphilly and the surrounding area needed a cinema/theatre where they could enjoy the best of both worlds.

My role in *Crossroads* still gave me the opportunity to do shows for a number of charities and also the occasional cabaret appearance. One show I was proud to be part of was the Val Terry award show staged at the Theatre Royal in Nottingham.

The show itself was in aid of the South Atlantic Fund and it was hosted by Bill Maynard who was in a television series called *The Gaffer* at the time. Also appearing was an old pal of mine, Billy Dainty, who was a brilliant comic and dancer. His Nureyev contortions brought tears to the audience's eyes as well as his own. I still have two stage suits belonging to Billy that he left for me to look after.

Sue Pollard, who later found fame on television as the chalet maid in *Hi-De-Hi*, was another to go down well that evening. Bill Maynard came from Leicester and after his partnership with Terry Scott ended he forged a successful career as a comedian and actor with memorable creations such as *Selwyn Froggatt*, followed by *The Gaffer*. Somehow, he always appeared on television looking like an unmade bed. I met up with him much later when I appeared in *Heartbeat* for ITV while he was still playing the part of that loveable rogue, Greengrass.

We had turned a big loss at the Roses into a break-even figure but I thought we needed to show the locals what could be possible at their theatre. As far as I was concerned, the two most important things were to establish continuity at the Roses and bring live theatre back within reach of the people in the area.

I decided that I would make full use of my connections in *Crossroads* and put on a full professional pantomime in

Tewkesbury, and so *Little Red Riding Hood* was booked for four weeks starting Christmas Eve, 1983.

Carolyn Jones, Carl Andrews and Jack Haig all became involved and I was fortunate to be able to book my three friends from *Crossroads*. To have Sharon Metcalfe, Mac and Archie Gibbs in the same panto was a bit of a coup but I didn't cast the role of Little Red Riding Hood herself as I wanted a local youngster or two to take it on. That way I received even more publicity and increased the likelihood of filling more seats every evening.

It was a real family show because the script was written by our boys, Roger and Ceri. I played a comic character known as Billy the woodcutter's son who had a pet dog. I was excited at being in pantomime once again as the previous year when we had *Crossroads* commitments was the first time in almost 34 years that I hadn't been involved in panto and I had really missed it.

Being in *Crossroads* enabled me to have sufficient money to plough my own cash from TV and cabaret appearances into the Roses theatre. With no grants or subsidies it was all down to me. I was back out on the cabaret circuit during the summer and it was amazing how being on *Crossroads* helped me in so many ways. When I appeared on stage the audiences were ready for me and I didn't have to remind them who I was. That was the power of television. Appearing three times a week on the box meant I was being seen by millions of viewers. It didn't matter that in many cases the cabaret audience wanted to see Sid Hooper clowning about rather than Stan Stennett. The public saw me as Sid and often asked me to do their MOT, mend their car and so on.

On Christmas Eve we opened *Red Riding Hood* and the early takings were promising. Betty worked in the box office, Ceri was stage manager and Roger was the playwright. If my grandson Sam had been a little older I am sure he would have pitched in as well. Unfortunately, prior commitments meant that Jack Haig couldn't take part but I enlisted the help of another *Crossroads* actor, Denis Gilmore who was the villainous Count Vermin. Denis played the part of Diane Hunter's brother in the soap.

Carolyn was a marvellously leggy Robin Hood, Carl played the part of Wizz the Wizard to perfection, while my old friend Glyn Dawson played a baddie known as Mangy the Wolf. In the lead role were two young local school girls who alternated the part of Red Riding Hood each evening. They had come out on top in the auditions I held earlier in the year.

I have always known that it's the kids who ultimately determine whether a pantomime is a success or not. Get them on your side and you're home and dry, otherwise you might as well pack it in. After all, it was the time of year when you could really let your hair down and as usual, the cast enjoyed the pantomime just as much as the audience.

Seeing 'House Full' notices outside the theatre showed that we did get the kids on our side and that year's pantomime was a marvellous success with a 97% capacity rate. In a bold plan, I decided to dispense with some seats in the theatre to make room for 25 wheelchairs in the auditorium. This meant that the Roses had a higher ratio of seats for the disabled than any other theatre in the country.

In three years at the Roses, I turned a £100,000 loss into a £20,000 profit which showed what could be done with a little bit of hard work. It's no use just talking about it. If you really believe in a project you've got to do something about it as well. I have always been suspicious of some members of the entertainment industry who publicly moan about the closing down of theatres and cinemas. But when approached to give a charity performance which might help one, they demand a fee and expenses, or perhaps say they are unable to help because of prior commitments.

In March 1984 I attended a public enquiry in Birmingham's Council House concerning the future of the King's Norton Cinema. It appeared that Kwik Save wanted to turn the elegant 1938 building into a supermarket and car park. Once a cinema has closed that is usually the end of it. If it keeps open, even as a bingo hall, then there is still hope. Actually at that time, Ceri had been working on the Stennett family tree and by a strange coincidence had discovered that my grandfather came from King's Norton before moving to South Wales to work on the railways. So you could say that I had a family interest in the outcome as well.

Back at the Roses I had plans for a different kind of entertainment. In May I began *An Evening With . . .* series with Eric Morecambe first up, to be followed by John Hanson and Ernie Wise. Our first night would turn out to be one of the saddest evenings I have ever experienced in the business.

Having been given the go-ahead by the council to increase the number of disabled places I persuaded Eric, my friend for over 30 years, to do the first *An Evening With . . .* show to help raise some of the finance needed for the alterations. Eric was at the top of his form that night. It was sheer brilliance, magical, and bordering on genius. He conjured laughter out of nothing. Most of the show's second half was taken up by an unscripted session I shared on stage with him. We exchanged jokes and reminiscences going back to our first meeting in pantomime back in 1953 before answering questions from the audience.

Eric spoke with honesty and humour about his health problems but told everyone that he felt very well and even pulled out his waistband to demonstrate how much weight he had lost. He mentioned Tommy Cooper who had died so tragically on stage and remarked on the strain of a comedian's role. Eric's wife Joan was in the front row sat next to Betty and he kept calling to her and cracking jokes with her. They had travelled up together from their home in Harpenden, Hertfordshire.

People in the audience asked him about his heart attacks and Eric told them that he was proud of undergoing surgery. He tried to encourage others to take the risk and said he was so grateful for the extra years he had been given. He finished his routine by frantically playing a number of musical instruments and I could tell that he was really enjoying himself.

But within seconds of going off into the wings doing his 'Bring Me Sunshine' walk, Eric complained of feeling ill and slumped backwards against a wall, hitting his head as he fell down. A stagehand ran out and called Dr Andrew Crowther, Tewkesbury's mayor, who was seated in the front row. Still wearing his badge of office he climbed on to the stage and ran to help.

Dr Crowther stayed with Eric giving cardiac resuscitation on the 12-mile ambulance ride to Cheltenham General Hospital. There, soon after 4am and with his wife at his side, the great Eric Morecambe, my dear friend, died without regaining consciousness. To have put on a true professional performance, then just walk off stage and collapse out of sight of the audience, I don't think you could have written anything more dramatic in fiction.

After realising that something was wrong, the audience left the theatre dumbstruck. They had been laughing so much only a few minutes earlier but somehow they knew that they had shared in a national tragedy. We decided to cancel the following week's film shows as a mark of respect but it took far longer than a week to get over such a terrible tragedy.

For a reason I will never know I was left out of the Thames Television £2m Christmas show *Bring Me Sunshine—A Tribute to Eric Morecambe*. It was only natural I should be disappointed at being snubbed because after all, he had been my friend for more than 30 years and I knew him far better than quite a few of the acts who were booked to appear. The excuse from Thames was that there were so many people they had to disappoint and I was just one of them.

I decided straightaway that when possible we would have our own show at the Roses in memory of Eric, and that helped me overcome my disappointment at missing out with Thames. As it happened, I was later invited to appear on the tribute but by then I had agreed to open Gloucester ambulance station's new social club.

That was a small way of saying thanks to the ambulance men who had tried to save Eric's life on that black night. I was sure Eric wouldn't have minded the decision I made in saying a personal thank you to those dedicated men. There was no way we could possibly have another *An Evening With . . .* show so we cancelled the visits of John Hanson and Ernie Wise although of course, Ernie would have found it impossible to have appeared in that theatre knowing what happened to his lifelong friend.

But the shows had to go on and by then we were well into rehearsals for our 1984 pantomime at the Roses, *Billy and Bonzo meet Jack and the Beanstalk*. As usual I was the gang leader, clown and continuity man ably abetted by Ricky Rich as Aunt Maggie. The youngsters all rated the jet-propelled skateboard routine with the filmed back-cloth as their favourite part of the show. Once again we pulled it off and drew large audiences for every performance. The secret was to give the public what they wanted whilst achieving it without smut or double meanings.

Early in January 1985 we received the news that the City Council had given us a 10 year lease on the old ill-fated Nell Gwynne Theatre in Hereford. The theatre had closed the previous summer with £250,000 of debts but the council had promised to pay £25,000 towards an immediate facelift and also pay an annual grant of £30,000 for at least the next three years.

When I arrived home and told Betty we were opening another theatre she said, 'Are you having me on?' I told her I would give her an audition but couldn't promise anything. We couldn't wait to get live theatre back into the Hereford community but to make sure the facelift was done to the highest possible standard, I added £15,000 of my own money to the pot.

We purchased 500 seats from Caesar's Palace in Porthcawl and transported them up to Hereford where we replaced rows and rows of old and worn seating. We were quite sure that it would pay because we knew we could make a complete success of it. Roger would look after the accounts while Ceri's job was to plan a lively film programme to suit all tastes from commercial films to offbeat foreign productions.

We opened in April, to a full house, with a four hour marathon of singing, dancing and juggling acts that brought the house down. Mind you, I was still limping around the stage as I was slowly recovering from my knee operation. I used to leave my crutches in the wings before limping on.

With future attractions including the musical *Annie* and films such as *Splash* and *Romancing the Stone*, we were confident of getting off to a good start in Hereford. It was a hectic period for me because after working on *Crossroads* during the day I drove either to Tewkesbury or Hereford for the evenings, and at weekends I drove home to Cardiff to be with Betty. If you thought that was over the top, I also sometimes used the airplane to get to one night shows.

In September I filmed a 30 minute sit-com for HTV Wales called *Very Small Business*. It gave me even more pleasure than usual to take the part of an entrepreneur called Tyrone Evans as the play had been written by Roger. Filming was done entirely on location in the Rhondda Valley and was about Tyrone being inspired to set up his own business after reading Government literature. He came up with the brilliant idea of selling the slag heaps and opencast coal sites of South Wales to the American film industry who may have been looking for moon-surface scenery for their science fiction films. With the profit Tyrone expected to make from this venture, he wanted to re-open his local cinema so there was a little bit of me in there somewhere.

I decided that we would have a pantomime at both Hereford and Tewkesbury for 1985 so we decided on *Aladdin*, beginning in December at the Nell Gwynne Theatre, which I had now renamed the New Hereford Theatre, before transferring to Tewkesbury where it ran until late January. Of course it also included the children's favourites, Billy and Bonzo.

It was a grim start to the New Year though as on New Year's Eve I skidded and twisted the chassis on my car. At the same time, youths broke into the Hereford Theatre and smashed up the kiosk, stole money and ripped out the telephones. We called the local constabulary but they couldn't help, although they did tell me about a successful case the previous day. They arrested two youngsters, one for drinking battery acid and the other for eating fireworks. They charged one and let the other off. Damage in the theatre came to about £5,000 and as the insurance didn't cover criminal damage, the cost of repairs had to come out of my pocket.

The third disaster happened on *Aladdin's* opening night at the Roses when the lighting failed just as we were ready to start the pantomime. We adapted the spots so the show could go on but once again expensive repairs were needed.

Despite the setbacks we were sure of a good response at both theatres and this proved to be the case. Mind you, we never skimped on scenery or costumes as I have always believed you have to put on a good visual show for audiences. Hereford and Tewkesbury could never have happened if it wasn't for all the hard work my A Team put in. That was my name for Betty, Roger and Ceri who worked tremendously hard behind the scenes to make sure those theatres, and the Castle in Caerphilly along with the two in Porthcawl, continued to offer the public the sort of entertainment they deserved.

Betty was usually found in the box office at any of the theatres selling tickets, programmes, ice cream or sweets. Ceri would be backstage making sure everything was in order. Roger's input came in the written word as by now he had several plays being produced on stage, including *Out of the Sun*, first performed at the Spitfire Museum in Southampton.

There was a rather grand reunion in March 1986 held in Wedmore Road, Grangetown. Frank Hennessey had a special Radio Wales show and I was asked to appear with my old pals Steve Gibson and George Hodge. The Harmaniacs were back but only for the one show. It was great to be performing with Steve and George once again and the old magic soon re-surfaced. We had a great time doing our old act and chatting about old times.

It was at Porthcawl that we staged our next successful pantomimes with *Aladdin* in 1986 followed by *Robinson*

Crusoe in 1987. The theme was the same then as it is now, with Billy and Bonzo important members of the cast. If you have a successful theme then why change it. Children of all ages could relate to Billy and would want to be his 'butty', while Bonzo was always on stage sitting down quietly waiting for someone to go too close to him so that all the children in the audience would scream out loudly for Billy.

And so it continued with the Roses, the New Hereford Theatre, Porthcawl, and the Castle in Caerphilly all paying their way with a mixture of films, stage shows and pantomimes. We were producing Dick Whittington in Porthcawl in 1990 when I remembered a letter I had received from a young lady called Ruth Jones. She was desperate to obtain her Equity card so I asked her to take on the assistant stage manager's role working alongside Ceri. There was the added bonus for her of playing the part of a Ninja Turtle in the pantomime. She jumped at the opportunity and was full of life and industry. So much so that I called her Ruth-less because she would really get stuck in to any task needing doing. She was the one who came out and had a sword fight with the rats at the end. Now I see that Ruth has gone on to greater things by co-writing and appearing in the hit show *Gavin and Stacey* that has been such a huge BAFTA-winning success.

That was also the pantomime where Ceri had to deputise for Bryn Williams who was taken ill. Ever since then he has managed to combine his backstage duties by playing various parts in other productions. I enjoyed all the planning and producing but I found that I had become more of a manager than a performer. I was either backstage or in the office directing operations and that was not what I was all about. It was performing that I was interested in and I missed the interaction with a live audience. There was no spontaneity in what I was doing. I wanted to tell gags and see the audience's reaction immediately, instead of which it was almost tell gag—laugh later.

We eventually came to the end of our lease at the Roses. Because we had made such a good job of running the theatre for over 10 years the local council, in their infinite wisdom, decided that they would not renew the lease but put it out to tender. Presumably this was to see if they could get a better deal as it was now a profitable going concern.

After all the hard work we had put into it we should have been given better treatment but unfortunately there were council members who thought they could do better for the local people. The tender went to another company who were unable to make the success of it that we did and the Roses closed down for a couple of years. They then threw a lot of money into the theatre, much more than was ever offered to us, and I believe it is now back in operation.

As far as the Hereford Theatre was concerned, the end of the lease came at a time when they were awarded a large sum of lottery money so they promptly pulled the old theatre down and built a new modern glass-built building called the Courtyard. I wish both venues well as we spent a lot of time, and a great deal of money, in preserving live shows at both theatres for a number of years. I have been back to the Roses a couple of times but I have never been back to Hereford.

A change of policy at Porthcawl meant that they closed both cinemas and turned them into amusement arcades, and while we were prepared to purchase the Castle in Caerphilly the council wouldn't sell. Eventually, some time after we left, it was sold to a snooker company but that didn't last long and so it was pulled down and an office block built on the site.

A huge number of theatres had closed down all over the country as they found they were losing the battle to television.

There were very few left on the Moss circuit for instance so touring became difficult. Night clubs were no substitute as they catered for a totally different type of audience. If you went to the theatre you expected to be entertained with a show, but go to a nightclub and first and foremost you expected something to eat, a lot to drink and the opportunity to chat to your friends.

Top cabaret artists could demand that the bar was shut during their performances but the noise levels from the audience were always a problem. Comedians, for example, would be primed up with ad-libs before going onstage to counter heckling from well-oiled patrons because if you couldn't hold your own, you were sunk.

That wasn't what I wanted. I liked going on stage and entertaining people who wanted to see a show whether it be variety or a pantomime. We came up with a plan whereby I could still do a little cabaret, have a regular touring show, and also maintain my tradition of a good family pantomime.

Bless 'Em All was born and has since blossomed into variations of a well-worked show full of nostalgia that is well supported wherever we perform. We recreate the music, songs, jokes and dancing of the performers of yesteryear. I call it the 'War and Peace' of variety shows as the first half is set in wartime and the second half in peacetime. It's aimed at the over-50s, a group of people who don't seem to get a lot of attention and we are always delighted with their support whether at St David's Hall in Cardiff or outside the area at places such as Stafford, Croydon and High Wycombe.

Of course, none of this would be possible without the help of some dear friends of ours. Alan Davies of Merthyr Motor Auctions helps us set up shows with his valuable sponsorship, Cyril and Margaret Norton keep my vehicles in their depot in Ystradgynlais and sort out MOTs when needed.

Ken Rattenbury, owner of the cold store down Cardiff Bay, lets me store all the scenery in his warehouse in Cowbridge and last but not least, Eddie and Maureen Whitney of Blazers Caravans regularly help out by sponsoring shows. They even invited Betty and me to their daughter Victoria's wedding—on board a ship. We had 12 days of bliss sailing around the Med. How lucky we are to have close friends like all those who are all so willing to help in any way they can.

Billy and Bonzo were such well-known characters that we decided to come up with new versions of the old well-loved pantos and so we continued to produce pantomimes full of family entertainment to tour round south Wales, making sure that schools were involved and given the opportunity of attending wherever we were performing.

It was after we had just finished a short season of *Cinderella* at the Lyric in Carmarthen when we were devastated by the fire at our home on Rhiwbina Hill. In January 1999 Betty and I watched as our lovely house was turned into a smouldering ruin and it was almost 12 months to the day before we were able to return following extensive rebuilding works. We both missed home like mad and while Betty was in rented accommodation in Lisvane, I stayed on site in a caravan I positioned right outside the front door.

We were able to spend Christmas 1999 and the New Year back home and it was like starting out again in a new house. We had possessions spread around seven or eight garages in all areas of Cardiff so that took us a while to gather up, bring back, and find a permanent place in the house. I now had my own upstairs 'office' where I could put up loads of posters and photographs and where I could file all my scrapbooks, progammes and videos.

As soon as we were settled, thoughts turned back to show

business and I did a little cabaret and 'after dinner' performances while also receiving some offers of straight acting roles. I appeared in *Casualty*, and that was a bit of type-casting as I played a grumpy old man, kept up the medical theme in *Doctors*, and also played alongside my old mate Bill Maynard in an episode of *Heartbeat*. Bill played the part of scruffy old Greengrass so well that I felt that the programme lost a little when he was eventually written out of the series.

But my favourite role came at the Sherman Theatre in Cardiff when I took on the part of Fagin in *Oliver Twist*. It was a superb role to play although I don't suppose many people recognised me underneath the make-up, wig and beard. Out of all my straight acting roles I think that particular one gave me the most satisfaction.

In 1999 I was proud to be awarded a Fellowship by the Welsh College of Music and Drama. For someone who left school when only 14 years of age it was a moving experience particularly being dressed up in all the regalia.

Bless 'Em All and spin-offs along the same lines kept us all busy during the next few years. Don't forget that we had a number of different back-drops for the various shows together with all the special lighting effects that needed to be transported to the theatres whether it was local or at places such as Crawley, Felixstowe or even up to Theatre Clwyd. Of course, the same thing applied to the pantomimes each year only there is far more equipment to be transported for them.

Our pantomimes travel around south Wales. We regularly visit Blaenavon, the Dolman Theatre in Newport, the Paget Rooms in Penarth and for the first time we went to Monmouth. Here we varied the show a little to make use of local performers who fitted in well with the regular cast and it was a rewarding week.

One other change was Ceri adding to his many duties

backstage by continuing to perform onstage in the pantomimes. Very often it may have only been the front or back end of a cow, but it was still good to see him getting involved.

That level of travelling is about as much as I want around Christmastime these days. I don't want to work in places such as Hartlepool or Middlesbrough when I can appear in my own shows locally. I no longer want to be away from home living in a hotel costing about £60 a night. You have to be earning a lot of money to cover that sort of expense and you can't take a caravan with you anymore, not like in the old days.

I paid a nostalgic visit to Leeds and the City of Varieties Theatre in 2006 and met up with my very dear friend, Joan Regan. We did a little show together full of nostalgia which went down well with the audience.

I really enjoyed playing a part in a film called *Plots with a View* which should have gone on general release. It was shot in south Wales and the comedy revolved around a funeral director played by Alfred Molina who loses a lot of business to a flashy American rival played by Christopher Walken. I had the part of Mr Edwards who goes to see Walken about having his wife buried. All sorts of mishaps arise as the two funeral parlours try to outdo each other. It was re-titled *Undertaking Betty* but only released in America.

Another part I played was that of Grandad in a Frank Vickery play called *A Night on the Tiles*. We started off in November 2007 at the Grand in Swansea and then toured the Valleys. Also in it was Ian 'H' Watkins of Steps fame, but I spent most of the time in the outside toilet permanently confused as I was a bit of a drunkard. It is a funny play as you would expect from Frank Vickery.

More recently I worked for HTV on a re-make of *The History of Mr Polly*. It starred Lee Evans and I played the part of his uncle. It was shown nationwide towards the end of 2007 and had good reviews. I have worked on several productions with Lee, including *Plots with a View*, but while he is a nice young man I am not a great lover of his type of 'alternative' comedy. I still cannot make out what is meant by alternative comedy. Alternative to what? As a comedian you are either visual or verbal—where does swearing come into that?

Towards the end of 2009 I was delighted to be asked to play a part in a film written by Ruth Jones. I played a character sat in a railway carriage. It was called *The Tracks* and I only had a small cameo role but I received a fee and get a percentage for repeats.

In March 2008 Betty and I celebrated 60 years of married life. I can honestly say that without the help and support of Betty and our two boys, Roger and Ceri, I doubt whether I would have achieved so much in my life. Betty and I are proud of our two sons who have backed us all the way in the entertainment business while also carving out their own important niches in the world.

Roger is coming up with loads of new ideas for plays and he is getting a lot of interest from television for his scripts, while he recently opened premises in Bristol where he carries out hypnotherapy. Ceri continues to work as the media officer for the Football Association of Wales but has also added another string to his bow by working closely for UEFA, football's governing body.

We are also proud of Sam, our grandson, who has come a long way since he toddled out on stage in front of millions of viewers during my *This is Your Life* programme. Sam began piano lessons when he was nine and then I taught him to play guitar and he has become quite an accomplished guitarist. He presently works as an acupuncturist in Bristol.

As for me Red Riding Hood will once again come up

against the wolf in my panto this year and I am still producing *Bless Em All, Flying Solo, Slice of Welsh Rarebit, Hooray for Hollywood, We'll Keep a Welcome* and the *Golden Days of Hollywood*. So if any of these shows appear in your locality, pop in and say hello.

As I get older it would be wrong to say it doesn't get any harder, because it does. But I can still do everything I need to do on a stage. In show business these days if you are over the age of 30 then you are past it, which means I am over 55 years out of date in some people's eyes. Yet I know I can still turn an audience and make them laugh.

You just have to keep using the old grey matter because it's when you don't use it that you lose it. If you give people what they want they will support you. The smell of the greasepaint just will not leave me and we are already booked up for shows throughout next year.

I am often asked why I carry on after such a long time in the business as a full-time professional artist. The answer is easy. I do it because I love it. I love the stage, I love performing and most of all, I love making people happy.

Anyway, when I go into the kitchen, open the fridge door and the light comes on, I still want to do a 10-minute turn.